T0206691

Chicks Dig Gaming

Edited by Jennifer Brozek, Robert Smith? and Lars Pearson

Published by Mad Norwegian Press (www.madnorwegian.com).
Edited by Jennifer Brozek, Robert Smith? and Lars Pearson.
Cover art by Katy Shuttleworth.
Design: Christa Dickson and Adam Holt.

ISBN: 978-1935234180. Printed in Illinois. First Printing: September 2014.

Also available from Mad Norwegian Press...

Jennifer: To Richard Taylor, one of the best GMs I've ever had. He showed me what a feminist man was like in both words and deeds.

Robert: To Kate Orman, my feminist mentor.

Lars: To Christa, who makes me a better person.

Table of Contents

Table of Contents

Editors' Foreword

Jennifer

There comes that moment in every person's life when they first pick up a handful of polyhedral dice, a deck of cards, a game controller, a board game, or even something as simple as a chess piece, and their lives are transformed: they become a gamer. For me, it was learning to play *Canasta* at eight and *Monopoly* at nine. From there, the game play grew into a love of gaming that has spanned several decades, multiple gaming platforms, and many different types of games. I started playing *D&D* on a weekly basis in college and I was hooked. There was no going back. I became an RPG junkie. This eventually led to my award-winning professional career writing and editing games.

When I approached Lars about this editing this book, I had an idea of what I thought *Chicks Dig Gaming* could be. With his attention and guidance, this collection has become so much more. It is an editor's greatest love to find the right pieces for an anthology. My greatest love, as an editor, is to learn something new in the process. *Chicks Dig Gaming* did that for me.

Despite the progress made in gender equality in various gaming arenas conventions, online gaming organizations, gaming podcasts and shows, and with professional authors, game designers, and artists – there is still an element that believes "girls don't game" and that "women don't belong in gaming." With this collection of non-fiction essays from both game lovers and industry professionals, I wanted to show the diversity of the women in gaming and the women who love all kinds of games.

I hope you love these essays as much as I do and that you learn something new as you read them. We are here. We love games. We create games. We're not going away.

Lars

The dirty-yet-open secret about Mad Norwegian Press has been that, for all the success we've enjoyed with our *Chicks Dig...* series, I don't actually think very highly of essay books as a breed. Quality control becomes even more complicated when you're working with dozens of writers as opposed to just one or two, and – worse by far – too many essays have no more ambition than telling you what you already know. Some fun was had by the people writing the text, but it's an exercise in futility for the people reading it. (The example that always springs to mind is a *Star Wars* essay I read years ago entitled something like "Boba Fett: Rogue Bounty Hunter," which detailed at length how Boba Fett was, in fact, a rogue bounty hunter. Well, who would have thought it?)

With the *Chicks Dig...* books, our goal has always been to shine a lantern into the overlooked corners of fandom and the relevant industry, to have the reader walk away with many new perspectives to consider, or to have answered questions they never would have thought to ask. It's deliberate that we don't lump the essays into like-minded (read: overly homogenized) sections; it's more like we're turning a crystal so you can see as many facets as possible in the time allotted. Or, if you prefer, imagine that we're throwing a variety show; each act is intended to be *very* different from the ones before it. Obviously, it's impossible for any given reader to connect with every single essay, but I hope that – like me – at least *some* of the essays in this collection knock your socks off (and I say this as someone with a low boredom threshold; funny how much of my life had been predicated on that).

The story of women who game and work in gaming is still being written, but it's already far more intricate, changing and *interesting* than so many people might suspect. With the essays here included, I hope you find that to be the case.

Thank You, Mario, but Our Princess is in Another Castle

Catherynne M. Valente is the author of over a dozen works of fiction and poetry, including *Palimpsest*, the Orphan's Tales series, *The Habitation of the Blessed*, *Deathless* and *Six Gun Snow White*. *Time* magazine named her fantasy novel *The Girl Who Circumnavigated Fairyland in a Ship of Own Making*, the first in Valente's Fantasyland series, as among the Top 10 fiction books of 2012. She is the winner of the Tiptree Award, the Andre Norton Award, the Mythopoeic Award, the Lambda Award, the Rhysling Award and the Million Writers Award. She was a finalist for the World Fantasy Award in 2007 and 2009, and the Locus and Hugo Awards in 2010. *Indistinguishable from Magic*, a collection of more than 60 of her essays, was published in 2014. She lives on an island off the coast of Maine with her partner, two dogs and an enormous cat.

It is dark.

We are in the Pre-Incarnation Universe.

A body appears, the image of the illusory, temporary, yet carnal self, along with minimal information about our physical location in the Cosmos, and a number, revealing to us the duration of our stay in the current shape.

We are about to enter Samsara, the Wheel of Birth and Rebirth.

We are also about to play *Super Mario Bros.* on our dilapidated grey-and-black eight-bit console, the one we still blow into and jimmy the cartridge an even number of times in vain superstition that we can somehow convince the box to work *one more time*. For most folk of my age-group and particular intellectual persuasion, Mario is already an icon, one of our first bright, electronic avatars (remember that word, kiddies), teaching us how to project ourselves into that small grey box and become, well, a fat Italian plumber. Without waxing poetic about how much better things were when I was a kid, the simplicity of graphics, gameplay and story in those early Nintendo games allow for the kind of player-insertion and mythography that today's perfectly rendered RPGs and FPSs cannot deliver. Is it nostalgia? Undoubtedly, yes. But anyone will tell you: God doesn't live at St. Peter's or at Nara or even floating down the Ganges, but in the cracks and crannies of pop culture.

And, since folklore is my stock in trade, I'm gonna wrangle that cartridge into cultural resonance for you, my fellow plumbers, and fill that console with Divine Breath.

With his portly belly and puffy cheeks, the resemblance of Mario to the Buddha is almost too obvious to mention. As Buddha was an avatar of Vishnu, Mario is an avatar of Buddha, but also of ourselves, the player, whose own journey through Samsara is reflected through the deceptively simple game. That we use the word "avatar," a loaded religious term, speaks to the subconscious understanding of the possibilities inherent in gameplay-as-meditation.

Mario's shadow-self, Luigi, is tall and slender, the Buddha-as-Siddartha, ascetic, the Buddha of the Lesser Wheel, where Mario is the more worldly image of Buddha, the one most familiar to the West, embraced by popular thought, and therefore ascendant in the West-marketed game. His three physical states (small, big, and fireball) align to the Three States of Conditioned Existence: anatta – the undisguisable, baseline essence of self unchanged by the vagaries of incarnation (small Mario); anicca – the state of change, vulnerability to constant mutability (big Mario); and dukkha – suffering, with which fireball Mario is consumed, and which he deals to others from his own hand. Of course, Mario also has a fourth state – the number four is constantly repeated within the construct of the game – a state reached either through injury (Suffering) or through a Star (revelatory Enlightenment), and this is his non-physical satori-self, a state of temporary and invisible nirvana in which the Mario-avatar cannot be harmed at all.

This Mario-Buddha ascends through eight worlds, corresponding roughly to the Eight-Fold Path, each divided into four levels, symbolizing the Four Noble Truths.

For example, in World 1 [Right Understanding], Mario beings to comprehend the world around him, the souls of the kingdom having been turned into mushrooms, representations of death and decay, just as the divine spark (*atman*) in humans is disguised and buried within a flawed, corporeal shell. In level 1-1 [Life is Suffering], Mario has his first experiences with pain, striving and the illusions of the Mushroom Kingdom. In level 1-2 [All Suffering stems from Desire], he plunges into the Underworld, the subterranean source of earthly desire, full of darkness and opportunities for descent and ascent. Importantly, it is on this level, should Mario understand that he is capable of "walking above" Desire even at this early stage, he can achieve a Warp Zone, and ascend furthest when he is in the furthest depths. In fact, in virtually all of the worlds, the second level is an Underworld level, either represented by water or sewers. In level 1-3 [Suffering can be overcome], he walks on high platforms, beset by the flying fish of earthly cares, tenuously threading through the fish in order to find the Middle Path. In level 1-4 [The way to overcome Suffering is through the Eightfold Path], Mario encounters for the first time the fortress which, repeated in increasing complexity, becomes his primary proving ground.

At the successful completion of each fortress-level, Mario encounters a False Princess. These may be seen as the daughters of Mara, the demon-king who tempted Siddartha to abandon his quest for Enlightenment under the fabled Bo Tree (not so coincidental, I think, is it that the symbol of Mara's defeat is the sudden blooming of red flowers all around the Buddha – no player of *Super Mario Bros.* could miss the connection to the flowers which grant Mario his most powerful state). So too do these False Princesses tempt Mario to end his quest and seek succor with them, even though "our" Princess, the Real Princess, is perpetually "in another castle." It is not enough that Mario rescue a princess, or defeat a fortress, he must rescue the correct princess, conquer the correct fortress, just as it is not enough to practice Thought, Action, Speech, but *Right* Thought, Action or Speech – the final fold of Mario's path is not only Right Concentration, but Right Princess.

When Mario has achieved Right Fortress and is prepared to gain Right Princess, he must face Mara in the demon's truest form – and indeed, most Buddhist art portrays Mara as a huge dragon or lizard, whose final attack against Siddartha is to throw flaming discs at his unprotected head. As a tableau invented in a Buddhist country, the resemblance cannot be coincidental.

If we construe Right Princess as Mario's ultimate Unification with the World-Soul, of his plumber's *atman* achieving nirvana, we are left with two possible interpretations of the game's conclusion.

One: that Mario, as are we poor, flawed players, is ultimately unready to achieve this union, and must return, inevitably, to Samsara, to begin again his quest for self-awareness and Enlightenment. This return is encompassed by the Second Quest, in which the mushrooms are largely replaced by beetles, further symbols of death, rebirth and suffering, but also symbolic of the similarity of all cycles of incarnation: only the scenery changes.

Two: that Mario *does* achieve nirvana, and unifies with Princess Toadstool, the representation of the Source of Atman to which all incar-

13

nated beings long to return. If this is the case, Mario *chooses* to return to Samsara as a Bodhisattva, to show others (players) how to walk in his footsteps.

Either way, the wise and canny player may retain the knowledge from one incarnation to another by pressing start + A, just like the Dalai Lama does.

'Round the World with Nellie Bly: Inspiring Generations of Chicks

Rosemary Jones writes and collects. Sometimes the two passions collide, as in the recently released *John Carter, Tarzan & Friends: A Reader's Checklist* or the earlier *Encyclopedia of Collectible Children's Books*. She's also written a number of stories for gaming companies large and small, including two novels and an e-serial set in the Forgotten Realms (*Dungeons & Dragons*). Currently, she's expanding her collection of Photoplay novels illustrated with stills from silent movies as well as working on new steampunk stories. She rattles dice in a variety of RPG games and regularly smacks down her iPad in Scrabble. You can find more information about all her varied activities at: www.rosemaryjones.com.

If there was ever a chick who gamed and won, it was Elizabeth Jane Cochran, better known as Nellie Bly. Her exploits inspired a board game that thousands of American children played from the 1890s to the 1920s.

From where I sit, typing away at this article, I can see my battered-but-obviously-beloved board. It is propped open on the top of a bookcase, gracing the end of my hallway. On the back, the faded lettering still faintly reads "Round the World with Nellie Bly."

Saved from oblivion and stowed away until I happened upon it in the twenty-first century market of marvels known as eBay, this relic of someone's childhood is a century old or more. But, glancing at it, you might take it for an illustration for a recently released steampunk adventure.

There's Nellie in the top corner of the board, her nom-de-plume emblazoned above her faintly Sherlockian hat. She's clad in a practical checked coat and clutching a small satchel. Beneath her feet runs the legend: "The World's Globe Circler."

In opposite corner is the profile of Jules Verne, godfather of science fiction. Here the creator of Phineas Fogg, the author who posited that technology would allow someone to travel around the world in 80 days, gazes at the gal who gambled she could beat that fictional record.

The lower left corner is illustrated with a steamship plowing through stormy waves above a script that proclaims: "Speeding Across the Atlantic."

Opposite that, a coal-fueled train whistles through the countryside, black smoke streaming from its stack, pulling one single passenger car with Nellie's name etched on its side. Below the tracks, you can still read: "Over a Mile a Minute."

It's a simple game, designed originally to be played with single, six-sided dice and pennies or checkers. Roll the dice, move forward as many squares as the numbers rolled, and follow the directions on the square. Children have been playing games like this since printed boards began to appear in American toy stores around the 1840s.

In this game, a multi-colored track begins in wide circle around the board. The path starts at Nellie's feet, curves past Jules, the train, the steamship, and then curves inward. Each square is numbered consecutively "1st Day, 2nd Day, 3rd Day..." and so on. Each brightly colored square bears a small picture in the center. Some show a ship becalmed, others a storm, and others are labeled with the names of far and – for girls of the nineteenth and early twentieth century – exotic foreign ports.

Below certain squares, instructions are given for those who land there. Hit "9th Day, Amiens" and you see Nellie shaking hands with Jules. The instruction below reads "One More Throw." By "43rd Day," the player has reached Canton, and an exploding firecracker costs a turn.

The spiral turns inward. Each throw of the dice and hop of the piece brings the center closer and closer. Here's a ship with full sail augmenting the steam crossing the Pacific; here's "68th Day" proclaiming "Golden Gate" and a return to American shores; and then the player skids around the final curl of the every tightening circle.

Avoid being snowbound in the Sierra Mountains and losing five turns, drop into Omaha and then leap ahead to the final golden curl of the train track. At the very center of the board, a trumpet blares out in giant script: "All Records Broken."

The player has reached the center of Nellie's universe, the island of Manhattan, marked by ships gathered in its harbor and Lady Liberty holding her torch.

This game first appeared as a black-and-white newspaper page in the *World* on January 26, 1890. Players were told to supply their own pennies and dice.

McLoughlin printed the colored version, which came boxed with spinner and tokens, later that same year. As mentioned earlier, the game stayed in print and sold steadily into the 1920s, with very little change. At various points, the game company would update the box, eventually adding airplanes (non-existent when it was first printed) and updating Nellie's outfits on the box lid.

But the board itself remained the same. Nellie in her checked coat, marching into her spiraling adventure, never changed. How could she? It was all true.

For nearly 30 years after the fact, little girls hopped their pieces around a board that told them a woman could beat all the records.

On November 14, 1889, at age 25, Elizabeth Jane Cochran sailed from Hoboken, New Jersey, to begin her global encirclement. She returned to where she began, in a blaze of media frenzy accompanied by cheers of a crowd and the boom of cannons, on January 25, 1890, exactly 72 days, six hours, 11 minutes and 14 seconds later.

The trip was a stunt, meant to sell newspapers, and it worked. Nellie Bly's newspaper, the *World*, chronicled her every move, printing her dispatches as she went from port to port, city to city, catching steamers, trains, horse-drawn carriages and all the other modes of transportation available to this most American of chicks in the nineteenth century.

It was not Cochran's first "stunt reporting," as it was known in those days. Writing as "Nellie Bly," the young journalist already had tricked a judge into incarcerating her in an insane asylum to expose its mistreatment of women, posed as a maid to show how employment agencies cheated women seeking work, passed herself off as an unwed mother to people who bought babies for adoption and tried to flush out a kidnapper operating in Central Park by walking there alone.

But those exploits were largely confined to the New York audience, although her articles about her time in the lunatic asylum were syndicated and eventually published as a book.

Her biggest stunt, that one that kept her name on a game for 30 years, almost didn't get started. For one thing, her editors fretted that a woman would need too much luggage to travel quickly. For another, she would want a chaperone.

Nellie told her editors that neither were needed or wanted. She went alone and packed light. She took only the heavy plaid overcoat that would become her signature garment, a lighter raincoat, two dresses, various sundries and her jaunty cap. All of her gear, including pens, an inkstand, pencils and paper, was stuffed into two small satchels, the largest measuring ten inches long and seven inches wide.

The 1889 photograph that would inform almost all drawings and renditions of her on later merchandise shows a slight, smiling young woman dressed in the ankle-length plaid coat waving her cap goodbye before she boarded her first boat.

She returned a hero, lauded and congratulated. The merchandise bearing her image appeared throughout the United States. In my collection, I have a glass plate commemorating her trip, a set of trading cards with highly whimsical images of Nellie shooting among the stars and belting the world, and that nineteenth century colorful board acquired in the twenty-first century.

My fascination with the Nellie Bly game, and Elizabeth Cochran herself, began at an early age. In my teens, I came across a picture of 'Round the World With Nellie Bly in a history of board games compiled by Brian Love (*Great Board Games*).

The children's books, toys and games of the Victorian era already fascinated me. There, on a double-page spread, were Nellie Bly's jaw-dropping adventures laid out in color and a far too brief explanation of the exploits that inspired them.

Books about Nellie were scarce then. Most were brief chapter books written for schoolchildren. I remember a writing assignment in college, where I was supposed to propose a book for a publisher. I outlined what I believed would be a better and more complete treatment for a biography of Nellie Bly, still aimed at young girls. As a student struggling to find out how my writing skills would fit into newspaper world at the end of the twentieth century, Nellie's own battle for acceptance in the nineteenth meant a great deal to me.

Although I received some encouraging words from my professor, I abandoned the book. I was stymied by the lack of original material available in the Pacific Northwest and couldn't journey to New York to examine archives of Nellie's original articles. The easy availability of her most famous works as e-books was many years away.

Nellie, and her brightly illustrated game board, faded into memory. I discovered *Dungeons & Dragons*, cheerfully playing adventurous gnomes and wicked witches. Even in those days, my dice only rolled well for nonstandard characters!

My favorite campaign started late on Thursdays. By my senior year in college, I was on the staff of the student newspaper, holding one of the few paid positions, and I laid out the paper on Thursday nights. We were supposed to finish by 9 p.m. so the paper could be sent off to the printer. Instead, it was usually 10 p.m. or later by the time I could leave. A fellow gamer would swing by, pick me up, and we'd drive to another friend's house, playing *D&D* until 3 a.m. or later. Then it was back to the dorm and sleeping until noon. The sleep-deprived giddiness of those games inspired my first novel for Wizards of the Coast many years later.

But, after college, Nellie snuck back into my life.

Shortly after graduation, a friend proposed traveling around the world. She was heading to Taiwan for a nine-month language study there. After that, she wanted to head home the long way 'round, traveling through China and then to Europe, before coming back to Seattle. Her older sister was also interested in the trip.

If I'd meet them in Hong Kong, we could travel together, she said.

Since we were both huge fans of Jules Verne, we certainly had the "80 days" idea stuck in our head. Because we were traveling in summer, rather than winter like Nellie, we didn't need to worry about snow stopping us in our tracks. I can't remember which of us proposed trying to get tickets on the Trans-Siberian Express, but that became our loose game plan. Head into China, see if we could make it to Beijing, buy the tickets there and continue on.

The idea was never to beat any records. We'd stop and start where we could, taking time to see the sights (something neither Phineas or Nellie could do), and eventually land in Europe. When the money ran out, we'd go home.

So, at the age of 25, basically a century after Nellie made her trip, I was looking at maps and thinking about my chance to circle the globe. After a mad scramble to find a job and save up as much as I could in nine months, I boarded a plane from Seattle to Hong Kong.

Like Nellie, I traveled light, one backpack only, that I stuffed into the overhead bin. I arrived in Hong Kong in June, and returned, without any fanfare, to Seattle in late August. By traveling ever westward, I permanently lost a day that I will never regain unless I circle the globe going east.

The trip, like all trips of discovery at that age, was wonderful and well worth it. Over the course of the next three months, and slightly more than 80 days, I traveled on every mode of transportation available in twentieth-century China, Russia and Europe: planes, trains, taxicabs, boats and, yes, one overloaded and rather unsteady pedal-powered rickshaw.

I still remember one overnight ferry ride to Suzhou. Our below-deck cabin was stuffy and reeked of mosquito repellent. I escaped to doze away the dawn up top. The boat sailed past green rice fields where the only human in sight was a lone man bicycling along the canal's edge through the morning's mist. It was quiet, timeless moment, so like something that Nellie might have witnessed.

We did manage to secure Trans-Siberian tickets. The route we took left China by following the Great Wall for miles, eventually swinging into Mongolia, a green land of rolling hills and horsemen galloping down to the station to greet family members getting off the train.

Then the train continued west across the vast territories once united as the Soviet Union. Siberia in late August was full of sunshine and sunflowers, nodding seed-laden heads for mile after mile as we clicked-clacked past. I crossed so many time zones that I lost all track of days and locations. Because money was beginning to run low, and there had been issues with visas when we were in Beijing, we ate and slept on the train, only getting off to take brief walks up and down the station platforms before moving on.

A cold train-station floor served as a bed in Moscow, because it was the height of the summer tourist season and no hotel rooms were to be had. So we stopped for only 24 hours, but did enjoy a mad tour of the city by public transportation, led by a Chinese wheeler-dealer whom we met on the journey. We never knew exactly what he did, but he spent the previous week on the train disappearing into the back car to play poker with the train staff when he wasn't trying to buy Western currency off the passengers.

Then we headed out, crossing multiple borders in the middle of the night by train again.

I still have the fondest feelings for the Polish customs officer who shook me awake at 2 a.m., asked me what nationality I was and, seeing my sleepily waved passport, said, "Ah, American, go back to sleep."

Which I did until we reached Germany. There I stumbled through more customs officers asking questions and passport stamping, before eventually landing in a hotel with the most marvelous bathtub ever to welcome a woman who had spent almost nine days in continuous motion from Beijing to Berlin.

From there, the journey finished in Amsterdam, where a taxi snafu led to a mad dash across the airport in a full sprint. As I recall, I was the very last person to make that flight bound for New York, and they practically slammed the door shut as soon as I scrambled aboard. To this day, I remain permanently paranoid about missing planes, although unaccountably happy once the wheels leave the tarmac.

A few months later, I happened to be at an estate auction with my mother, who was a dealer in antiques at the time. A pressed glass bread-plate was hoisted aloft by the auctioneer. He began to rattle off a list of city names circling its rim. At its center was embossed the figure of a young woman dressed in a plaid coat, clutching a satchel, staring serenely at the world as she gets ready to set off on her own journey.

Nellie and I had met again. I spent money that I certainly couldn't afford at the time with a bank account drained by three months of travel. That glass version of Nellie still sits on my desk, holding a few odd notepads, pens, and a utility bill that I must mail after writing this.

Other images of Nellie, and books about her, fill the corners of my apartment. There are the trading cards propped up on my dresser. I see Nellie belting the world every morning and walking among the stars every night.

At the end of hall, that game board reminds me each time I glance at it that Nellie and I are both world globe circlers.

Games inform us. Games change us.

For 30 years, from 1890 to 1920, in the decades when American women were truly second-class citizens, legally barred from numerous professions, with little or no control over many aspects of their personal lives and unable to vote in national elections, little girls spun a spinner or rolled a dice and hopped their pieces from "1st Day" to "All Records Broken."

How many thought, as I still do, that if Nellie dared and won, why can't I?

Author's Note:

Elizabeth Jane Cochran has become the accepted spelling of Nellie Bly's real name. Some early biographies cite her last name as Cochrane, but others suggest that she added the "e" at some point to sound more sophisticated.

Although arguably the most famous female of her day, Nellie was not the only American woman employed in journalism – nor the first. Women had been writing for newspapers since the colonial days. Several thousand female reporters worked beats of all sorts from coast to coast in the 1890s, although typically paid less than their male counterparts and often disparaged as being unfeminine.

Nellie was not the only woman to circle the globe in 1889 either. Elizabeth Bisland was sent from westward from New York by *Cosmopolitan* magazine in an attempt to beat Nellie. But travel delays made her journey last 76 days (still besting the fictional Phineas Fogg).

Elizabeth never received similar fame or game tie-ins, although she later published an account of her travels.

Both women have, in recent years, become subjects of scholarly, lengthy and fascinating biographies published for adults, as well as even more books for children.

Select Hero or Heroine

Dawn Foran is a maritime systems engineer who spends far too much time running around the world fixing other people's (and her own!) mistakes and keeping a boatload of vessels in working order. She also enjoys bad puns. She has been chronicling her somewhat unusual journey for the past year and a half at dawns-yatb.blogspot.ca. She had the wonderful opportunity to grow up in multiple places around the world, but has finally found her true home in her birth city of Montreal, where she currently lives with her two cats... because three would make her the crazy cat lady.

I started gaming when I was around five years old. This was back in 1983; we had a "State of the Art" Commodore 64 hooked up to our black-and-white TV. And, while it took a year or two until we actually got some commercial games, my dad would read pure machine code out of the back of computer magazines, enter it into the C64, save it on tape (literally, cassette tapes; I wiped out a lot of his old Dylan tapes a couple years after), and we'd take turns playing games in which you were an "@" symbol, wandering around maps fighting monsters which looked like "*" and "!"

Terribly exciting.

At this point in my life, video games were a curiosity. I've always had an affinity for technology (I'm sure being exposed so young helped in that regard), but they weren't the end-all and be-all of entertainment. I still loved running around the neighborhood with my friends, making things, playing pretend, all those usual kiddy activities.

The first time that I recall seeing gender in my video games was a few years later, in 1988, when I was now gaming on the awesomely incredible and uber-powerful Amiga 500!!! The 512kb RAM upgrade was a four-inch square circuit board that you jammed into the underside of the keyboard, and it never fit properly, so the keyboard would wobble. But I digress.

Somehow, I got my hands on a game called *Sword of Sodan*. I remember kicking it up and being presented by a choice I have never seen before in a game. The splash screen had a picture of both a man and a woman, and then, when you hit the action button, you were given a screen which read "Select Hero or Heroine."

A picture of a buff, overly tanned, six-pack-abs guy on the left holding a shield and sword, and on the right, the picture of a just-as-buff, just-as-six-packed, and not overly busty woman wearing a metal bra, holding the exact same shield and sword. I remember being a little confused by this, and thought, "I wonder what the difference is between the two?" (Turns out there was none as far as gameplay was concerned, something else which was a rarity for far too long in this world.) With trepidation, I moved my joystick to the right and hit the button.

I had other friends who loved playing video games as well, all of them being boys of course, as it was a very male-dominated pastime back then (and, in many ways, still is), and, while they occasionally chose a female character to play with, it was always followed with typical comments like "yeah, I just want to look at someone *hot* while I play instead of a dude" or "boobies!" When I chose her over him to play as – and back then the amount of times you even got that choice could be counted on one hand – it was just because it felt correct. I'm selecting an avatar, and of course I'll choose her, why wouldn't I?

In the very late 80s and early 90s, a new type of video game steamrolled into the public eye, bringing along with it untold controversy. The fighting game. I swear, according to the media, *Mortal Kombat* and its fatalities were going to be responsible for the collapse of western civilization.

Sonya from *Mortal Kombat* and Chun-Li from *Streetfighter 2*: those two women cost me a ridiculous amount of quarters. Of course, there was only one female fighter per game (thankfully this changed as the years went by), but, finally, I could move the stick over to the one woman, and *none* of the guys would blink an eye. No more comments, no leers or jeers like "of *course* you're gonna choose her, ugh" (other than "you do realize that Sonya sucks"). The women were actually acceptable. Chun-Li was a monster in the arena and feared by all, and, while Sonya was never regarded as a great character, if you could hold your own with her, it was like a badge of honor, like winning a fight with a handicap.

When I was given the rare opportunity to choose a female character, the boys that I played with noticed. I, of course, didn't make the same comments as they did as I selected the buxom blonde and the teasing started. Random comments; you just wanna be a girrrlll!!! Even my father joined in: you girly boy, you wanna wear a dress to go with your long hair, ha ha ha ha ha. I laughed it off at the time; after all, that wasn't possible, becoming a girl, ha! I even learned how to parrot their childish comments when I felt like I needed to blend in with them, guilt hitting me each time they came out of my mouth. Because for me, when I chose the heroine over the hero, I didn't see the breasts and the skimpy armor, or tiny outfits and Barbie-styled hips and waistlines. I didn't realize that it was pure objectification; I was a little boy, how could I understand that? I simply saw *woman*, and I chose her, every single time.

Sword of Sodan was the first time I had an indication that I was different from the other boys I knew by means of a video game. My transness was peeking its head out of every crack it could find, but I didn't understand what was going on; after all, in those years, there was no internet, so I tried my best to ignore the fact that I kept putting on my mom's clothes and playing with her lipstick (all in secret of course). I figured it would go away at some point. If you weren't lucky enough to live in a larger city, or have extremely liberal and open parents (and I had neither, living in small country towns, with conformist parents), there was a good chance that you had never been exposed to the concept of "gay" or "trans." Hell, I was 13 before I finally learned what the words "gay" and "homosexual" meant. Took even a bit longer to learn the word "lesbian"; my mom was convinced they didn't even exist... Go figure.

Looking back now over those years, which were tough years for any trans kid (puberty and all that, your body growing and changing, but *not* in the direction you were hoping for), I realize that, as I found other outlets in which I could "pretend," my acting out at home went down. I fought less with my parents, I raided my mother's closet less, but my thoughts were always on those avatars, those women, waiting to be assumed by anyone brave enough to select them, to let me fantasize for just a few minutes, until I stuck the next quarter into the machine. I'd spend my school hours learning their combos and even designing new outfits for them. (Yeah, that should have been an indication of what was going on right? Either that, or I was destined to be *fabulous!*) It was the same as the next few years went by as fighting game after fighting game came out – Mileena and Kitana in *Mortal Kombat 2*, Orchid in *Killer Instinct*, Nina in the *Tekken* series, all the ladies in the *Soul Edge/SoulCalibur* series. I mastered them all, except for Sarah in *Virtua Fighter*... that game just sucked.

It was around this time that I started to consciously notice the complete and utter absence of actual girls playing video games. Aside from the couple of boys whom I played games with and got in trouble with, the vast majority of my friends were girls. I would talk to them about gaming, and how much fun it was, and they would roll their eyes at me and proclaim proudly "That's not what girls like" or "That's not for girls, it's for boys" (remember, it was the late 80s, beginning of the 90s at this point). I would tell them that there *are* girl characters to play, they *could* choose someone that was like themselves, and not just big muscular men or monsters, and they just ignored me, kept repeating the party line, "It's not for girls."

Strangely enough, while their response frustrated me a bit – after all, I would have loved to play *Mortal Kombat* with my girlfriends instead of my guyfriends – it did make me feel a bit better, a bit more "normal." If every single girl I knew said they didn't like video games, and I loved video games, I guess maybe, just maybe, I really was a normal little boy.

The internet, thankfully, destroyed those notions, but I'm getting ahead of myself.

The next few years were an exciting time in gaming: the birth of the first-person shooter, *Dune 2* and the original *Warcraft* created the real-time strategy genre, the god game (*Populous, Civilization*) was created, and I loved them all. Finally, a type of game where I wasn't forced to choose. I was a hand in the sky shaping a world, a commander issuing orders, or just the tip of a gun running around a screen shooting monsters and aliens. Gender had suddenly vanished entirely from my PC, and, while I missed my one secret and safe outlet to "pretend" that I was who I had always wanted to be, not having to even think about it while relaxing and saving (or destroying) the world was wonderful.

Of course, this meant that I needed an outlet again, and once again my mother's makeup started to disappear, and my bad dreams would come back, my stress, my guilt. For crying out loud, I developed a bleeding ulcer at the age of 13 and another at 17 due to internalized stress. Who would have thought that just being able to pretend through some pixels on a screen would be able to give that little boy such relief? In fact, before sitting down to take on the challenge of writing this piece, I don't think I quite realized it myself. I've been mulling this piece over in my head the past two days non-stop, and it has been enlightening to say the least.

In 1996, two things happened that rocked my world. The first was that I managed to get onto what passed for the internet back then (no pictures on the screen, no browsers as we know them, pure text, you would navigate between links with the arrow keys and follow a link with the spacebar) and a friend introduced me to MUDs. The second was that I met Lara Croft.

Let's start with Lara. Here was a game, an unbelievably high-budget game, one of the first games to really put 3D accelerators to the test, that didn't allow you to play as anything other than a woman. How is this going to sell, I asked myself? Guys aren't going to want to play this! But, as it turned out, they didn't mind, because the game was amazing. I remember hearing those old comments yet again: "At least she's hot," "It's fun looking at her while playing," "Look at the handstand I can make her do!," and, of course, "Boobies!," although now I was old enough to turn it back on them: "Look dude, you really don't have to make macho bullshit excuses about the fact that you like playing the game, just shut up and play it." But of course in reality I was talking to myself, trying to tell myself that it was okay that I identified with her so much and wanted to be her. Seeing Lara Croft turn into one of the biggest video game franchises ever was almost vindication for me; we're taking over! (Waitaminute, we? I'm not a girl – or am I? Repress repress repress...)

Over to MUDs now. MUD stands for Multi-User Dungeon[1] and was the original MMORPG[2]. It was a purely text-based interface, and you would read your way through the game, like the old text-adventure games from ten years before. You are standing in the middle of a town, there is a castle to the north, fields to the east and the main street stretches out to the west. What do you do? "Go North." You are on a path to the castle and there is an orc here. "Cast Fireball Orc." Get the idea now? And this game could have a hundred other players all doing their own thing and you could actually talk to them!

I spent a good three years of my life playing one specific MUD. I started with a male character. Since I was playing with a couple of guys that I knew in real life, I recall being too scared to make a female one yet. I was going through a bad time with my desires and knew I wouldn't be able to handle the teasing. Six months later though, I had two "secret" characters, both female, and this was the first time in my own personal video game history that I could actively pretend to be her instead of him. Since our characters would form groups to take on the more difficult areas in the game world, we would need to communicate constantly, and, as it was all done by typing, I could be anyone I wanted to. My male character was respected but largely ignored; he was solitary, only grouping when absolutely necessary before going on his own path,

---

1 The term later came to include Multi-User Dimension and Multi-User Domain.
2 *Massively Multiplayer Online Role-Playing Game.*

almost always strong enough to do it himself, something he was proud of. My female characters were loved, sought out, known by everyone, always invited to group or just to chat (not to mention be flirted with). I felt like part of the world when I played Alera or Vanta; I was a lone wolf when I played Telkar.

But here's the thing: *I never consciously did anything different while playing these characters.* I remember telling my mom how much nicer everyone is to my female characters than my male ones. I always chalked it up to my belief that the world is nicer to girls than to boys (and any woman reading this knows what an absurd idea it truly is). That's actually a concept that I brought with me into adult life, and even through transition, until, with the help of my mother and good friends who have known both sides of my own particular coin, I realized that it wasn't the world being nicer to me, it was me being nicer to the world because I finally felt right with myself. I projected a more positive and peaceful energy to the world, be it the real world or a virtual one, and the world tended to react in kind.

I continued to show my femininity (or at least my non-masculinity) through my video games as my transition got closer and closer. I was proud that I had no shame playing games like *Dance Dance Revolution* and other dance games (which the vast majority of guys turn their noses up at, not wanting to be seen as stupid or girly). In fact, I sought out non-stereotypical games, collected them and happily showed off my eclectic collection. They let me be openly proud of being different before I was ready to reveal exactly *how* different I actually was. My avatars online were always femme, my Xbox360 avatar was always female, and it drove my girlfriends (the romantic types) nuts. Why do you always choose a girl? You're the only guy who I know that has never chosen the dude to play as, do you have something you want to tell me?

And, before I knew it – while at the same time at the end of a very long road that took 35 years to get to – I transitioned. I started my hormone treatments, came out to my everyday world (work, not-as-close friends, family), threw out the old clothes and started wearing the nice ones every day, finally got to show off my makeup skills that I've been working on since I was a little boy, and my legal name change was just accepted by our government. I made it.

And you know what? I have no problem choosing the male character now in a video game. After all, it's just a game.

How I Learned to Stop Worrying and Love the Numbers: a Girl, a Rulebook and Arithmetic

Seanan McGuire has been gaming since middle school, when she first discovered the Fighting Fantasy books at a library book sale. She went on to dabble in many systems before embracing *Champions* (because math) and White Wolf (because the Order of Hermes). She can still recite the Code of Hermes, which is occasionally disturbing. Seanan is the author of multiple series, under both her own name and the name Mira Grant, and, while she doesn't game as much as she used to, she is still comforted by the sound of rolling dice. You can find her at www.seananmcguire.com, should you feel so inclined. Seanan likes prime numbers, large cats, Disney Parks and horror movies.

I am a gamer girl. I have run campaigns in at least eight major systems and six minor ones, including a home-brewed live-action/ dice-based system that swelled to involve me, my cousins and all the kids I babysat. I ran a two-year LARP[3] on my own, and spent three years helping run another one. The farthest I have ever traveled for a weekly session is two hours by train. Even when I don't have a regular gaming group, part of my brain is devoted to remembering the Houses of Hermes, the *Cinematic Unisystem* combat rules, and how to set up a variable power pool in *Champions*.

I am, in short, one of *those* people: the ones who can always whip out a funny story about a session, or sit down and explain how a system evolved. I've been like this all my life, but my evolution into the gamer I am today began not with dungeons or dragons or looting tombs.

It began with math.

Here's a secret that isn't really a secret if you've ever spent any time with me: I am an enormous math nerd. I love numbers, the way they fit together and divide and tell us stories about the foundational building blocks of the world. Numbers are the universal language, and I am always delighted and awed by the things that they can do.

---

3 *Live Action Role Playing.*

But, like many little girls, I was discouraged from pursuing my love of math. Teachers told me that I had difficulty showing my work not because the answers were so obvious to me that I couldn't backtrack and explain how I got them, but because I was cheating; because math was too hard for my female brain. By the fifth grade, I had stopped saying that math was my favorite subject, retreating to more socially acceptable answers like "English" and "art." I still loved math. I just felt that we would never be allowed to be together.

Skip forward a few years, and I was your classic high-school geek girl. I read too much, where "too much" means "in the bathtub, during PE when I was supposed to be playing dodge ball, under my covers in the middle of the night." I didn't socialize very well, because I didn't understand why all the other girls didn't want to talk about the X-Men, or *Doctor Who*, or the possibility of life on other planets. I had played my share of *Advanced Dungeons & Dragons* – 2nd Edition, naturally, which everyone I knew believed was perfect and would never be replaced – but I hadn't found a game that could hold my attention for more than a few sessions.

And then, like a strange miracle, everything changed. My boyfriend at the time, whom I had met through our shared love of *The Rocky Horror Picture Show*, asked if I wanted to come to a session of his *Champions* game. It was, he cautioned, very math-centric, but he was willing to help me come up with a character if I wanted to give it a try. I didn't have anything better to do that day. I said sure.

That first game was terrifying. I was coming into a gaming group that had been meeting for years, and that contained players of all ages, from a woman who could have been a contemporary of my grandmother's to my boyfriend and me. There were a few other players near our age, and the four of us wound up sitting together, joining ranks against the fear of looking foolish in front of our elders. My first character was largely created for me by the helpful men in the gaming group, who listened to what I wanted to do, explained why it was or was not possible and handed me a character sheet covered with numbers. These numbers, they told me, were the keys to everything that my new character could do.

After the simple stats of *AD&D* – an 18 is good, a 3 is bad, and everything in-between is some shade of okay – and the straightforward one-to-five stats of White Wolf, the columns of figures and variables that described my *Champions* character were practically indecipherable. I asked a lot of questions, and made a lot of mistakes, generally looking like a fool in front of the people I wanted to impress. At the end of the night, I borrowed a copy of the main rulebook. I took it home, studying it and my densely written character sheet with the sort of passion that I had almost forgotten having for anything involving numbers. My inner math nerd was stirring.

At the next session, I shyly presented a new character sheet, this one filled with numbers and equations that I had worked out for myself. I wanted a variable power pool – that is to say, I wanted my character, who manipulated sound and light, to be capable of using them in many different ways – and I had carefully done the necessary math, balancing my stun and killing attacks with disadvantages and limitations. I remember the gamemaster (GM) smiled. He knew he had me.

Champions is played using the Hero System. It's a dense system, infinitely flexible and infinitely frustrating if you don't have the right group. I was fortunate: I had the right group three times over. On Wednesday nights, I played Golden Age superheroes, where Broadway – my sound and light manipulator – would eventually go on to marry her industrialist playboy boyfriend, get outed as a mutant during the McCarthy era and flee to the lost Kingdom of Atlantis with her family. I later played her granddaughter, who also used the name "Broadway," in a modern-day *Champions* game. She was my first generational character. She was far from my last. On Fridays, I played *Zero Hero*, a game where we had started our characters with literally zero points and acquired all our advancements through disadvantages. And, on every other Sunday, I played *Wild Cards* using the *Champions* system, where my seemingly useless Deuce, Redraw, would eventually bring about the most epic dice roll of my gaming career.

But I'm getting ahead of myself.

Champions quickly became an integral part of my social life. I enjoyed gameplay, and the turn-based nature of combat meant that even playing three nights a week wasn't a problem. Each turn was divided into 12 phases, and whether you had to do anything on a specific phase was determined by your character's speed. I tended to play speedsters – characters that moved more often than not – and even I didn't move on every phase (although I got close once, with the original Broadway, after her final stat upgrade). There was plenty of time during a normal combat round to do my homework, draw storyboards showing where all the characters were at any given point in time, and even take the occasional nap (which usually ended with my GM calling, "Broadway on deck!"). I have dozens of combats lovingly illustrated in my high-school sketchbooks, and I remember every one of them.

For a while, I felt like a superhero myself: ordinary schoolgirl by day, secret math nerd by night. I could "stat" a *Champions* character to do almost anything I wanted, but I was still failing basic algebra, because I had so deeply internalized the idea that girls couldn't be good at math. I was good at gaming. That was something completely different, and even if the two had some aspects in common, you couldn't generalize.

The *Zero Hero* game ended. I joined a more "modern" superhero game, playing the second incarnation of Broadway. This version was intentionally less flexible than the first, because I had learned one of the most important rules of playing in the Hero System: Thou shalt not intentionally break gameplay. I knew how to tweak the numbers that would allow me to get away with virtual murder. I chose not to, preferring to be a fair and balanced part of a team. And that was the epiphany.

If I could manipulate the numbers to make a character that was awesome, but was also slightly less than perfect, that meant I *understood* the numbers. There was no way I could have accomplished that by banging blunt instruments together; I needed a honed comprehension of every moving part of my character. I needed math.

I went back to school the next day and got my first math-related A+ since I'd started high school. A game that focused on understanding and using mathematical concepts couldn't undo years of self-reinforced neglect and refusal to learn, but it still felt like it made all the difference in the world. I was a girl; I was a gamer; I loved math. And all of these things were equally allowed.

My life didn't change overnight. I still had to deal with teachers who thought that girls weren't good at math, their opinions now backed up by my own poor grades. I still had to cope with the normal trials and travails of a teenage gamer. I started dating one of the guys in my primary *Champions* game, and, when we broke up, things got pretty awkward for a while. Another boyfriend wanted me to go out on Friday nights, rather than insisting that it was more important I spend my time pretending to be a superhero. Through it all, gaming was so important to me, so central to my life, that I found a way to continue making it work.

In the end, it was time that did us in. Time is good at that sort of thing. High school ended; I went to college, although I stayed in the same geographical area. The same couldn't be said of all my friends, and one of my games collapsed from a sheer lack of players. Oh, we attempted to bring in new blood, but they didn't understand the balance that we had worked so hard and long to create. We finally decided that it was easier to simply let the chronicle end. Another game came to its natural conclusion, and we sadly let those characters and that story go.

And then there was *Wild Cards*.

It's traditional in gaming circles to bore and delight your friends with stories of your campaigns. I'll listen to yours if you'll listen to mine. Well, in the name of upholding tradition, and in the interests of showing just how much *Champions* brought me back into touch with my inner math geek, I present a story from my campaigns.

I was coming up on the end of my first year of college when one of my long-time GMs announced that he was going to be moving to Washington to pursue his own higher degree. All of his campaigns were going to be concluded, including the *Wild Cards* game that I'd been playing in for the past four years. He scheduled times for our final two sessions, and we all showed up, eager and afraid of what was going to happen next. There were six of us in the game. Keep that number in mind: it's going to be important.

Wild Cards is a superhero setting based on a series of shared-world anthologies. George R.R. Martin is a *Wild Cards* author, as was Roger Zelazny. I grew up reading the Wild Cards books, and I love them almost as much as I love *Doctor Who* and the X-Men. In the *Wild Cards* setting, everyone's superpowers are triggered by a virus. Anyone can catch the virus. Ninety percent of the people who catch it die; this is called "drawing the Black Queen." Nine out of ten survivors will be horribly mutated, becoming Jokers. That last person, that one in a hundred, will get fabulous power and become an Ace. From there, grand adventures can unfold.

Our group consisted of three Aces, two Joker-Aces (Jokers whose mutations were accompanied by useful abilities) and one Deuce (an Ace whose ability was generally viewed as useless under normal circumstances). I played the Deuce. Her code name was "Redraw," and she was a micro-telekinetic. With sufficient time and focus, she could "draw" the effects of the Wild Card virus from someone and trade them with the effects of the Wild Card virus from someone else. This was a difficult power to use. She had to be protected during combat, since she had to be able to focus. It took several phases to fully activate her powers, and anyone touching her skin while she was trying to perform an exchange risked triggering an uncontrolled release of the cards she was "holding." It was, in short, more trouble than it was generally worth. I spent a lot of sessions with my character either waiting in the car or picking off our enemies with a sniper rifle.

In our next-to-last session, our little team of heroes had been called upon to rescue a senator's daughter from the Jokers who had kidnapped her. They had taken her deep into Jokertown, the portion of New York that had been given over almost completely to those who had been mutated by the virus. If we didn't get her back, her captors were going to intentionally infect and probably kill her, setting back Joker rights and relations more than a decade.

We went into Jokertown. We found the girl. We fought our way to freedom, and we ran... only to find ourselves caught between a rock and three hard places. We were at a four-way intersection. The kidnappers were coming from the south. The police, who thought we were responsible for the girl's abduction, were coming from the north. A Jokertown gang that had a score to settle with our team leader was coming from the east, and a group of Aces who also thought that we had kidnapped the girl was coming from the west. If we didn't get out of there, we were going to be trapped, and worse, we were going to lose the senator's daughter.

Remember when I said the number of characters in our party would matter? Here's where it happens: our teleporter, Off-ramp, was a Joker-Ace who looked exactly like a classic Cadillac convertible. He could teleport, but only with as many passengers as he had seatbelts – two in the front, three in the back. With the addition of the senator's daughter, we had six potential passengers.

Character death is a horrible thing. I think all gamers avoid it whenever possible. But character sacrifice can be amazing. I looked at my stats, did some quick math and announced, "Redraw looks around and says you should go on without her."

A vicious argument followed, during which the other characters tried to convince her that there was another way, while the other players looked at me like I had lost my mind. In the end, Redraw convinced the others to go only by threatening to shuffle their cards if they refused. They climbed into Off-ramp's seats, buckled their belts and were gone.

The GM looked at me. "Okay," he said. "What's your plan?"

"I want to reduce the time required to shuffle cards by spending Stamina."

"All right. How much?"

"All of it."

There was a pause. And then, slowly, he started to smile. "Then what?"

"I want to increase my area of effect by spending Willpower."

"How much?"

"All of it."

In the end, I pumped all my available Willpower, Stamina and Health into a single massive roll of the dice. "Massive" is meant to be taken literally, here: when the GM finished totaling my adjusted stats, the final roll came to something on the order of ninety-eight d8s to initiate the effect, one hundred and sixty-six d10s to determine its scope. Redraw shuffled six square blocks of New York City before she was killed by the strain... and, thanks to my having done the math, the effect was permanent. We ended that game session knowing that we'd saved the girl and changed the world at the same time, even if that change wasn't necessarily for the better.

And we did it all with math.

It's been years since I played a game of *Champions*. I had to look up some of the rules before I could properly explain them. But I'll never forget those games, the sound of ludicrous numbers of dice hitting the plastic gaming mats... and the joy of a teenage girl being reminded of her true and undying love for numbers. It wasn't an academic setting. It was the *right* setting, and I am forever grateful to everyone who played with me, GMed for me and put up with me during those occasionally hyperactive high-school sessions.

No matter how far away from that table I get, part of me is waiting for the next combat round to start, and when the cry of "Broadway on deck!" comes, well...

You know I'll be ready.

Look Behind You!
A Three-Headed Monkey!

L. M. Myles has written for *Doctor Who* in prose and on audio. She co-edited the Hugo-nominated anthology *Chicks Unravel Time* and the forthcoming essay collection *Companion Piece*, and can regularly be heard saying very sensible things about *Doctor Who* on the Hugo-nominated *Verity!* podcast. She still mourns the death of her Commodore 64, and blames *Knights of the Old Republic* for all her current gaming addictions.

When I was five years old, I played *The Secret of Monkey Island* for the first time. MIDI soundtrack (bleep! plonk! blip!), VGA graphics (a heady 256 colors) and the promise that, no matter what silly thing I tried to do, I wouldn't die as I embarked on the epic quest that all five-year-old girls dream of: to become a pirate.

Sadly, it's a quest unlikely to be undertaken by the children of today, at least the way I did it, for *The Secret of Monkey Island* (*tSoMI*) belongs to that genre of games known as the point and click adventure, and, in the late 1990s, the point and click adventure game died an ignoble death. Sure, there've been a couple of attempts to revive the genre (Telltale's excellent output and the wildly successful *Double Fine* Kickstarter) and they've done well in and of themselves, but they were brief flickers of life zapped into an otherwise cold corpse. There's an argument that the adventure game has simply morphed into other genres, but no, no, there's nothing today where you explore a world or follow a story by puzzle-solving; sticking the Towers of Hanoi in the middle of an RPG doesn't count.

The premise of the adventure game is simple enough. You move around a world, look at things, pick stuff up and talk to other characters. You encounter puzzles that block the way to whatever your goal is, and you use what you find and learn to figure out the solutions.

It sounds so simple, but, like many simple things, it's extremely difficult to do well. It gets trickier, for elegant puzzles are merely the foundation upon which to build your compelling storyline (or vice-versa), since the reward for the puzzles is to push the story forward. If the player doesn't care about what's happening, why should they bother finding out what that amber fish on a string is actually for?

That's a much more convincing argument for the death of the genre: not enough gamers cared, because the puzzles or the story were no longer good enough. Once upon a time, however, LucasArts excelled at creating crafting these games. *The Secret of Monkey Island* and its sequel, *LeChuck's Revenge*, were the very best of them. Hugely popular at the time, and still beloved decades later.

I am Guybrush Threepwood, Mighty Pirate!

It's a rather bizarre, often funny, occasionally scary and quite brilliant world that you're thrown into in *tSoMI*. You play the stupendously named Guybrush Threepwood, who appears without explanation at the lookout post of Mêlée Island, somewhere deep in the Caribbean, and declares that he wants to become a pirate. As the adventure progresses, you master the art of insult sword-fighting to defeat the Swordmaster of Melee Island and are rewarded with a T-shirt; encounter a three-headed monkey as you escape from a cannibal who's wearing a giant lemon on his head; and meet the fabulous Governor Elaine Marley who you must rescue from the ghost pirate LeChuck by descending down the throat of a giant monkey head.

The instant appeal of the game is the humor. How is Guybrush to become a pirate? Why, naturally, he's to head to the local pirate bar to ask the Very Important Pirates (capitals mandatory) what to do. It turns out there're three trials he must complete to win the acceptance of his grog-swilling peers: dig up some treasure (X marks the spot), master the art of insult-sword-fighting (no *actual* fighting in this game, but you do have to develop a healthy respect for a terrible pun), and nick something cool from the Governor's mansion (while avoiding her piranha poodles). You'll discover the use for a rubber chicken with a pulley in the middle, how to read a treasure map that gives you a dancing lesson and the extraordinary things giant mechanical banana-pickers can be used for (spoiler: it's picking bananas).

If it were simply cartoonish nonsense, it would be fun enough, but it's not, and that's part of what makes these two games so compelling. The anachronistic humor and Guybrush's frequent bumbling exist alongside some genuinely scary stuff.

Just take the opening moments of *LeChuck's Revenge*: Guybrush undergoes a rather humiliating robbery at the hands of Largo LeGrand, former henchman of LeChuck's. After divesting Guybrush of all the fabulous wealth he's carrying around in his inventory, LeGrand adds insult to poverty by refusing to believe Guybrush killed LeChuck back in the first game. Guybrush proves he did in the only sensible way open to him: he pulls LeChuck's still wriggling undead beard from his trousers. Ah, light-hearted whacky shenanigans! Largo, naturally, steals the beard too, but as he leaves there is a moment of fearful anticipation as Guybrush realises he may have just done something extraordinarily stupid.

LeChuck is pretty scary, y'see. Guybrush is a bit of a fool, but the rest of the characters are played straight, and LeChuck is a pirate that scares other pirates, even when those pirates are dead themselves. The scenes of him on his ghost ship were nerve-wracking stuff and, at the tender age of six, LeChuck's revival into a zombie pirate was as scary as any moment from *Terminator* I'd sneakily managed to watch.

As well as the scares, there was the inspiration, in the form of the sublime Governor Elaine Marley, who I still wish to be when I grow up. She's a pirate, a politician and effortlessly brilliant. Yes, she gets kidnapped, and our inept hero feels he must go and rescue her, facing countless dangers and working his way through numerous fiendish puzzles to find his way to the wedding between Elaine and LeChuck. Except he needn't have bothered. By the time Guybrush gets to the church, Elaine's substituted three monkeys for herself in the bride's gown and has got the magical root beer needed to defeat LeChuck. At her moment of triumph, Guybrush rushes in to mess things up. Oops...

Then there's Carla, the Swordmaster of Mêlée Island, whom I blame for my own love of sword-fighting. There aren't a lot of female characters in these games, but having one of them be the greatest swordfighter in the Caribbean was a delightful revelation for my young self. Also, Carla is tetchy, short-tempered and lives in the middle of a mysterious forest; there's a lot I can sympathise with there.

On the less sympathetic, more intensely annoying side, there's Stan; a second-hand ship salesman with as loud a checked jacket as you can get with 256 available colors, and an insatiable sales patter. Stan talks. A lot. And waves his hands and taps his feet, and you get the distinct feeling that he's taking you for a sucker. (Well, you did stick a pot on your head, and then let yourself be fired out a cannon as a safety test; he may be right.) In the sequel, he's back, and he's selling second-hand coffins. He really wants to sell these worryingly macabre things to you, and is eager to convince just how comfy they are to rest in for eternity. He gets inside the coffin. He shuts the lid to prove how roomy it still feels. You might have nails and a hammer in your inventory. Stan's still yammering. And he is *extremely* annoying. And he did sell you a really rubbish ship. What would happen if you were to use the hammer and nails on the coffin?

Oh, yes, you nail him in the coffin. And it's immensely satisfying. And now you can nick what you need from his shop, hurrah! (Don't worry, he survives; in fact, you let him out yourself in the third game.)

That's but one example of a healthy vein of delightfully morbid humor that the games cheerfully mine away at. There's plenty more: a spot of necromancy is required to recover a missing map piece (and a valuable lesson is learnt about always turning the oven off), a little body-snatching from a very old grave nets you a piece of bone for a voodoo spell and a very weird dream that involves dancing parental skeletons hints at the real Secret of Monkey Island™ that nobody ever gets to find out, since a completely new team made the third game.

That's the Second Biggest Monkey Head I've Ever Seen!

The pleasure of solving the puzzles is the glue that keeps all the pieces of character and story stuck together. There's a particular sort of skill and imagination needed to come up with good adventure game puzzles. It's easy to come up with *difficult* ones, but that's not the same thing. Many an adventure game went for making things more challenging by pixel-hunting (a particularly frustrating sort of puzzle, where you have to hover the mouse over precisely the right tiny spot on the screen to find what you need) or combining inventory items in arbitrary ways, so what you make works, but the how and why of it doesn't really make any real world sense. That's not an advanced puzzle, that's artificially upping the difficulty level via annoyingness.

The *Monkey Island* games don't do this. The solutions aren't generally obvious, but they do make sense, and the objective is clear. Adventure games are slow-paced things, and the magic of a great puzzle happens when you're given enough clues for your mind to gnaw it over, and then have a dawning realisation ("I couldn't look up the location of the ship-wreck in the library, could I?"), followed by excitement as you try out your new solution ("By gum, there's a book called *Great Shipwrecks of our Century* in here!"), and the triumph – the delicious mouth-watering triumph – as it works ("I've found a sunken monkey head! At last!"). It's an immensely satisfying feeling. It's what makes an adventure game great: when you can replicate that level of difficulty over and over, when each time the triumph of solving a puzzle feels earned.

Of course, it's not always going to work like that, even in the best of games. Some puzzles just won't be as good as others, or, disaster, your own skills of imagination and reasoning may not be up to the task. That's when you fall back on the old adventure-game strategy of Try Everything. That means wandering around, using all the objects in your inventory with everything you see, and with each other, until something works. It can be terribly frustrating, and there'll be no triumph at the end, but a sense of relief. There is, however, the secondary prize: if it was a good puzzle, you'll kick yourself for not having realised the solution earlier. How could you *not* have used the monkey on the waterfall pump? He was doing the exact same thing with his tail on top of the piano! You'll shake your head and tut at yourself and spend a moment admiring the elegance of the puzzle. Possibly. It may not sound like much of a prize, but it feels considerably better than randomly coming across the solution and wondering what the dickens the designers were thinking when they came up with that bloody nonsense.

There are a few of the less good moments in this *Monkey Island* duo. Which bits they are will, of course, vary from person to person (though I've yet to meet anyone who was anything more than unthrilled with Monkey Kombat – yes, with a k – in the dreadful *Monkey Island 4*). For me, it's the spitting contest on Booty Island. Working out the right combo of drinks to thicken one's spit? Noticing the wind blowing at the right moment? Swapping all the little flags again? A tedious chore, and nought but relief when I could move on and never have to think about it again. The only other puzzle that came close was finding a replacement for cartographer Wally's eyeglass. In the model of the lighthouse in the library? Maybe I just don't know enough about lighthouses, or maybe looking for a magnifying bit of glass in a model lighthouse was a touch on the arbitrary side.

The vast majority of the puzzles, however, are a delight. Ranging from the amusingly simple (tossing a red herring to the troll guarding a bridge) to the mind-bogglingly brilliant, by which I mean *LeChuck's Revenge, Part II: Four Map Pieces*. The objective is straightforward, one which is easily discernible based purely on the title, but the finding of those map pieces, ah, 'tis an enigma wrapped in a labyrinth, tossed into a bottle that's floating somewhere around the Tri-Island area. Which is where you have to go to look for them: three islands, four map pieces, dozens and dozens of interlocking puzzles that push your quest onwards step by step in strange and wonderful ways. I've two clear memories of playing through this section. Once, when I was very young and found it constantly frustrating but glorious. It was epic and exciting and there was so much to do that clearly the adventure will never end! The second time, I was a teenager, and there was an echo of the unfathomable epicness, thanks to nostalgia, but it felt *solvable*. I did need to randomly try stuff; I could work things out! In fact, given enough time, I could work almost everything out. And I could see how all the puzzles fitted together and built upon one another, and marveled at the minds that put together such fiendishly clever delights.

And I could enjoy such delights while exploring a world filled with drama, excitement, witty humor, characters I cared about and a bizarre yet intelligent storyline. Marvellous.

If There's One Thing I've Learned, It's This: Never Pay More Than $20 For a Computer Game.

The *Monkey Island* series continued on after the first two games, but the team making them had changed and it was never quite the same (though Murray the Demonic Talking Skull alone made the third one worth playing).

The first two games had been a part of an adventure games Golden Age. The makers, LucasArts, made great adventure games quite a lot in the early nineties: *Indiana Jones and the Fate of Atlantis* (AKA the Real Fourth Movie), *Sam & Max Hit the Road*, *Day of the Tentacle*. These were the computer games of my childhood. Jumping plumbers and speedy blue hedgehogs were strange, frightening creatures controlled in strange, frightening ways. It was with a nice comforting keyboard, in the warm glow of a PC screen that megalomaniacal time-travelling tentacles were defeated, Atlantis was destroyed (again) and homicidal ghost pirates were killed by the awesome power of root beer.

Chicks Dig Gaming
So You Want to Start a Fight

Since writing her last biography (for *About Time 7: The Unauthorized Guide to Doctor Who*, another fine product – she writes freely, of her own volition – of Mad Norwegian Press), **Dorothy Ail** has been working on the inevitable *About Time 8*, several Sci-Fi stories and the history of the world. Also her chess game, Agatha Christie's bibliography, online RPGs and the manufacture of the perfect Yorkshire pudding. She can be found online at "Life, Doctor Who & Combom," where she regularly writes up amusing *Doctor Who* news.

These days, any fandom worth its salt has a cutesy, schmaltzy nickname for itself. Trekkies, Whovians, Bronies... if you're reading this, you can probably think of half a dozen without taking a breath.

And then there's grognards. They've named themselves after the flower of Napoleon's army, the Old Guard veterans who served in all his campaigns – they were a special unit whose job was to defend the Emperor himself, and famously never broke in battle (even at Waterloo!). So: a fannish nickname that's a nineteenth century in-joke about men who honed the act of killing to a fine art. Welcome to boardgame wargaming.

It's a funny corner of geekdom – never as popular as the fantasy role-playing games that would supplant it, often unabashedly militaristic, pedantic and passionate about historical details. And massive piles of games (miniatures are a related but separate hobby, worthy of someone else's essay). These days, it's a small but passionate group of fans who keep the flame burning – doing it justice in one essay was a bit of a trick, but enjoy.

The discipline began on the opposite side of the Rhine, ironically enough. In 1812, a Prussian rejoicing in the name of Baron von Reisswitz came up with a way to simulate warfare, by moving small counters (wooden blocks, in the days before die-casting) over fictional maps, using dice to simulate the uncertainty of gunfire. He presented it to the Kaiser, who greatly approved. Soon the Prussian military was using *Kriegspiel* for practice, and other armies soon adopted it. By the end of the century, people were playing it for fun, too – H. G. Wells came up with his own intricate system for playing with his collection of toy soldiers and real miniature cannons. The photographs in his book *Little Wars*, with formally dressed Victorians gravely setting up their blocks and miniature houses, are a hoot.

Fast forward to the 1950s, and a US veteran named Charles S. Roberts, who'd come up with some technical exercises for practice when he was in the military, turned it into a board game and called it *Tactics*. It was a complete flop.

A few years later, Roberts tried again, with a rejiggered edition and a new name, and so Avalon Hill released *Tactics II* in 1958. It was the making of a company, and an industry. There were ups and downs, but after it got onto a sound business footing in 1963 (far-eyed creditors saw a business opportunity), Avalon Hill would spend the next three decades publishing hundreds of games. Including a lot of sport and general-interest board games, incidentally; their version of *Football Strategy* came out before John Madden was even coaching.

Meanwhile, Albert Lamorisse was busily inventing *Risk* in France (Parker Brothers put out an edition in 1959). You may have heard of that one, and indeed it's a solid if simple example of the genre – each player gets some armies to move around on a mapboard, they fight according to carefully specified rules in which pure skill is interspersed with whoever gets luckier die rolls, and when you wipe your opponent off the map you win. This is, crudely, how pretty much any wargame works. The fun lies in the complications.

In Roberts' case, he envisioned the use of gaming for educational purposes. The bulk of Avalon Hill's wargames would be simulations of actual historical events – along with *Tactics II*, other early games were *Gettysburg* and *U-Boat*. World War II would become far and away the most popular setting – its complexity and the surplus of historical information available meant that designers had their pick of situations. Everything from the naval conflict (*War at Sea*, of which more anon), and the diplomatic-economic side of things (*Third Reich*) to the German campaign on Russia (many, many examples, but *The Russian Campaign* remains quite popular) and attempts to simulate an entire campaign down to the last detail (*The Campaign for Northern Africa*, which always warrants a mention in articles of this sort for its sheer complexity – 1800 game pieces and a suggested playtime of 1500 hours).

That last one was a game from Simulation Publications, Avalon Hill's main competitor. It was founded by James Dunnigan, who made a few games for Avalon Hill before going into business for himself. These days, he's an advisor for the Pentagon and writes straight-up histories of warfare. Avalon Hill's biggest attempt in that line was *Advanced Squad Leader*, a massive project for playing out WWII battle scenarios at the company level. New scenarios are still coming out today, and, by the time it's finished, you'll probably be able to use it to refight the entire war. But that's just one conflict – Avalon Hill would produce games about everything from Roman legions to the Gulf War.

The hobby would be aided by the publication of *The General*, the in-house Avalon Hill magazine. Part advertisements, part historical essays, with a good measure of fanzine flavor to boot – it's immensely fun reading, even for games and time periods you're unfamiliar with. Company designers were the mainstay writers and would do long, complex articles explaining the way they had gone about creating a game, justifying their choices by showing they'd done their homework. Just one example: Japan held one side of Papua New Guinea during WWII, Allied forces controlled the other, but neither side managed a successful overland invasion due to the massive mountains in between, though they both expended time and effort doing just that. Designer Richard Hamblen distilled years of warfare into one simple rule – he declared it an impassable barrier for his game *Victory in the Pacific*.

One popular feature was the articles that simply chronicled a game's play from start to finish, with both players and a neutral commentator providing their thoughts. This could prove unexpectedly hilarious if one player got lucky with the dice and the game went off the rails early. Old games would be dusted off and given new scenarios, with fresh rules to increase realism or to simply add further hilarity. One ridiculous optional rule for *Victory in the Pacific* involved the Allies being able to counterattack the Japanese at Pearl Harbor (the US code-breakers had sent a warning that showed up a few hours later due to mishap, so there's a basis for it in historical fact – though it throws off the gameplay no end). The balance between playability and plausibility was a fond topic: gamers liked intricate systems that could model the historical events accurately, but also appreciated balance and what the *The General* surveys referred to as "excitement level." *Stalingrad*, an early Avalon Hill product, was less accurate than *The Russian Campaign* and they covered roughly the same historical situation, but people still enjoyed the earlier game for its punchy gameplay.

A passionate, often irreverent, letters page added to the fun – particularly serious fans might write articles outlining winning strategies they'd found. The line between a particularly dedicated fan and a maker of games was minimal, if you had the talent – Gary Gygax started off his gaming career with articles for *The General*, and graduated to making wargames before heading off to found TSR and *Dungeons & Dragons*. It wasn't the only such publication, either – Dunnigan started Simulation Publications largely to preserve the magazine *Strategy & Tactics*, still running today but originally an Avalon Hill fanzine. The 70s was the high water mark for all this: aside from the fanzines, there was lots of play by mail (you could write in to *The General* and be matched with someone else who wanted to play the same game, and conduct the whole game by post – today people use email, naturally) and even conventions. If you've ever heard of *Origins*, it started as a wargaming get-together.

Come the 80s, it all started going sour: fantasy role-playing games started taking over the market, video games made for an entirely new sort of competition and TSR muffed their buyout of Simulation Publications rather badly. (Dunnigan was better at making games than making a business, while a lot of designers ended up going to Avalon Hill – his version of the story is available in his excellent *The Complete Wargames Handbook*.) Avalon Hill kept going until 1998, when it was bought out by Hasbro and effectively ceased to exit. Though Hasbro has published a few of the old standbys, and hope springs eternal for further reissues...

Especially for the simpler, user-friendly games. Such as, ooh, my personal favorite, *War at Sea*. Originally published by an Australian company called Jedko Games (who're still around, actually – they made *The Russian Campaign*, too), Avalon Hill bought the rights and it became quite popular. It's essentially a simulation of the naval war in the Atlantic Ocean during WWII – that *Victory in the Pacific* game was designed on the same general gameplay system, so if you combined both games, you'd have a basic simulation of the whole of naval warfare in WWII. There were several articles in *The General* explaining how this might best be done.

Here's an example of the *Bismarck* sinking the *Hood*, the best ships of the German and British fleets, respectively – you can recreate the Battle of the Denmark Strait with all the capital ships that were historically present, if you like. The *Hood* is a small green counter with 447 printed on it, and the *Bismarck* is a blue counter with 496. The first number stands for the number of dice you roll when attacking, the second number represents defense and the third speed – these latter two diminish when a ship has been attacked, naturally enough. Once the defense number goes to zero or below, the ship is sunk.

When rolling the attack dice, the British player wants to roll a five (which disables a ship and sends it back to port) or a six (which means the ship has taken damage – you roll that die again to determine how much damage is taken). Any other die roll is meaningless. It's much the same for the German player, though for the sake of balance an undamaged German ship gets a plus one to its rolls, making a four a disabling five and a five a damaging six. The German ships need some sort of advantage, as otherwise the much larger British fleet would simply overwhelm it – it's that plausibility versus fun gameplay question again. The heart of wargaming lies not so much in the rules as in the exceptions.

So the British player goes first and rolls for the *Hood*'s four attack dice. Unfortunately, they are all twos. Nothing happens. Then the German player rolls for the *Bismarck* and gets three threes and a five – that means one hit, so one die is rerolled to determine the extent of the damage. Say it's another three. This number is subtracted from the Hood's defense and speed, so its defense decreases from four to one, and its speed is decreased from seven to four.

The *Hood* can try to retreat, but since the *Bismarck*'s speed is greater (six to four), the German battleship can sail fast enough to keep up. (Conversely, a large but slow British battleship – such as the *Rodney*, a 553 – wouldn't be able to catch an undamaged *Bismarck* that had decided to retreat. Which is more or less what happened to the *Bismarck* in real life: the *Sheffield*, a light, fast cruiser, damaged the *Bismarck* so that it couldn't sail, then the heavy battleships came in to finish it off.) But as for our example: another round of combat, a lucky six for the *Bismarck*, a German damage roll of five and the *Hood*'s sunk.

That sounds simple enough, but now multiply this basic gameplay by all the other variables – there's several dozen ships, representing the British, German and Italian fleets, plus a few American and Russian vessels for good measure. These gain Points of Control (POC, otherwise known as your score; the scale goes up to ten in either direction) by controlling the map. There are six different sea areas, and whichever side is still afloat after battle wins – unless there are U-boats left alive, which prevent the British from taking control (because, as in the real war, it means that the British have failed to control an area securely enough to protect the shipping). Then you have further complications: one aircraft counter apiece, which can knock ships out of combat before they ever make it to battle. Convoys: fragile but worth three POC apiece, so whether they make it to Russia intact can make or break a game. Various ports, with different repair facilities: Germans can use French ports, but only when they're Vichy. Speed rolls: if you want to move a ship an extra sea area away from port and it doesn't have a speed of at least seven, which most don't. The main exception is the small light cruisers, and you can see how the tactics are piling up.

Do you dare move a fleet of fast ships without much firepower to control an area alone, or do you play it safe and sail cruisers with the heavy battleships as reinforcement? Do you save the aircraft for the sea or deploy it in air raids against the ports? Retreat to save a crippled battleship or stay to hold the sea area? As a historical model, it's not particularly sophisticated – there are lots of dice and plenty of variability. (Russian ships only sail on the roll of a five or six, in the basic rules, so you can have an entire game where the Bear does absolutely nothing.) So it moves quickly if you know your way around – perhaps an hour and a half, no more than an involved game of *Monopoly*.

But as a way to think about the trends of the war, it's surprisingly effective. Throw in the optional rules and it really comes alive – try reading Churchill's account of politicking with Roosevelt about whether an invasion of North Africa is really a good idea, then play a game with the Torch convoy and watch with bated breath to see whether it survives a sea full of Italian ships, to score game-winning POC. Look up the disproportionate British response to the appearance of the *Bismarck*, then ponder that defense factor of nine again. It's not even sinkable on your first roll for damage, so if you want to be certain you've finished it off, you have to use disproportionate force and even then you may be unlucky... A good wargame serves as a kind of mnemonic; it takes the basic facts and shapes them into memorable images. It's an illustration of history not quite like any other.

Of course, that's traditional textbook history and not forward-thinking feminist reappraisals, which leads us back to the topic of this book – you'll have noticed the complete absence of women from this account, and, to be honest, that's because there weren't any. The major players, often ex-military from before women were taken seriously in the armed forces, were all men. The closest that those 70s *The Generals* would come to talking about women was a tedious running gag about wives who didn't understand their husbands' silly hobby. For obvious reasons, the subject matter deals entirely with men. There is simply no satisfying womanist moral to be found in this story at all.

It's frustrating, because I'd prefer my hobby to be in line with my feminism, but it's not. That's simply how wargaming evolved, and the small, conservative fanbase isn't undergoing a drive towards political correctness. But the cure for amending something you love and criticise in the same breath isn't to hold back apologetically and wait for improvement, it's to charge in with both barrels. Carve out a space for yourself at the table. Start a conversation and make sure you're in it. If you find something you enjoy, stick with it for its merits, even as you're aware of its flaws. There's much to enjoy about wargaming, and I'd like to think this article inspires someone to go try one out for themselves; Napoleon had a New Guard, too.

Go on.

Fight the good fight.

Who in the Hell
is Carmen Sandiego?

Teresa Jusino is an independent pop-culture writer at Beacon (beacon-reader.com/teresa-jusino), and her writing has appeared in such outlets as *Latina Magazine, Jezebel, Slate, Ms. In the Biz* and *Tor.com*. She is the writer/producer on *Incredible Girl*, an upcoming web series based on the short film of the same name, by Celia Aurora de Blas. Follow her on Twitter (@teresajusino) and keep up with her at her blog, The Teresa Jusino Experience (teresajusino.wordpress.com).

I can imagine that the way I experienced computers when I was a kid in the 1980s was the way kids experienced televisions in the 1950s. They were these shiny new things that I'd heard of, and maybe even used at school, but were slowly working their way into the homes of my friends. They were big, and expensive, and, as my parents were of an older generation (they actually remember the invention of the television), they didn't deem a home computer a priority.

We had a typewriter. I'm sorry; a word processor, on which I, um, processed words.

I first started learning how to compute on an Apple IIe. I remember referring to a cursor as a "turtle," because I was using Apple Logo and I used the "turtle" to help me draw lines. I remember taking computer class in second grade, where we learned how to use a mouse and move the turtle and we played educational computer games like *The Oregon Trail*. It made me crave more.

Then, one after the other, friends of mine started getting home computers. I used my friend Dawn's the most. Now, Dawn was one of my best friends from elementary school through high school, so I would've been at her house anyway, but I'm not going to lie. The fact that she had a personal computer in her room and a pool was pretty damn sweet.

Whenever I was over, I spent more time on her computer than she did. While I was at her desk playing some game, she'd be at her Atari console playing ColecoVision's *Cabbage Patch Kids: Adventures in the Park*. Yes, there was a Cabbage Patch video game, and we played it.

Anyway, she'd be playing that, and I'd be on her computer playing more *Oregon Trail*, or the Remote Control video game. You know, the one based on that MTV game show where their seats would flip them backwards if they got eliminated from the game? Yeah, that was pretty fun.

But there was one game that I played more than any other. One game that, when I was in elementary school and junior high, kept me riveted to the computer monitor. One game that appealed to my love of knowledge, my vivid fantasy life, *and* my soft spot for puns.

Where in the World is Carmen Sandiego?

The game debuted in 1985. And, as the player, you are an ACME detective who needs to follow clues all over the world in order to track down members of a criminal organization called the Villains' International League of Evil (V.I.L.E.), which is led by "the Miss of Misdemeanor": Carmen Sandiego. The player gets a time limit – they have to find the perpetrator of a crime by, say, Sunday at 5 p.m. – and, if they find the criminal by the deadline, they move up a level until they are eventually assigned to find Carmen herself. If they capture Carmen, they win the game and end up in the ACME Hall of Fame. They also end up knowing a lot more about geography than they did when they started!

I loved playing *Where in the World is Carmen Sandiego?* as well as subsequent games in the franchise – *Where in the USA...?*, *Where in Time....?*, *Where in Space...?* – because I've always been a sucker for trivia and facts. Not only did I love learning things, but I loved winning games by asserting things that I knew. My dad taught me to recite the 50 US states in alphabetical order, and I did – mostly enthusiastically. It was a party trick, and whenever my dad and I were at any sort of gathering he would inevitably call me and say, "Tell them the 50 States!" The performance aspect of it embarrassed me – I felt a bit like a parrot – but then there was the part of me that was proud I knew stuff. The part of me that would "lament" what my dad would "make me" do at parties, while secretly being proud of it, because I knew none of my friends could recite all 50 States in alphabetical order. Ha!

The fact that this wasn't exactly a fashionable skill to have wouldn't be made apparent to me until much, much later.

So yeah, I was proud of the knowledge my brain contained, and I loved using it to win at games. But there was something else about the Carmen Sandiego games that made me love them so much. It was Carmen herself. When I played, even though I was playing as a detective, even though I was supposed to be tracking down criminals in an attempt to take Carmen down, I never saw her as a villain. She was a badass!

She wasn't just a criminal, she was a criminal mastermind who stood at the head of a worldwide criminal organization. She stole monuments. And when she stole, it wasn't about money or power. She stole, because she could; because she was better at it than you and she wanted to make sure you knew it. She amassed great wealth and worldwide power, but that wasn't her objective. To her, this was also a game, and she was going to win. She was never ashamed of her skill, or her intelligence.

And neither was I. Especially not when I was playing games.

Sadly, that didn't last. Right around eighth grade, I started to care very much about how people saw me. I wanted people to like me, so I made an effort not to lord my intelligence over anyone. I wanted to fit in, so I tried not to blurt out answers to things, or be too enthusiastic about loving things like literature and space travel. I say I tried, because I wasn't very good at it. When you love knowledge that much, it's difficult to not spout off the things you know and be actively curious about the things you don't. Curiosity is a tap that, once opened, is difficult to shut off. However, that curiosity can also be a cause of shame, because, apparently, there is such a thing as "knowing too much," or "being too enthusiastic."

I spent my high school years (and most of my college years) caring deeply about what others thought of me. I didn't realize it at the time, but, looking back, so much of what I did and didn't do was based on the opinions of family, friends and teachers. This isn't entirely a bad thing. I mean, these are people that I know had my best interests at heart, and many of them are people I considered role models and whose respect I wanted to earn and keep. However, I didn't have Carmen Sandiego's inherent confidence in my own worth and ability. My confidence was entirely dependent on the approval of others, and that's the not-good thing.

By the time I got to my early twenties, I had come into my own in many ways. I was more confident about what I knew and what I believed. I was also becoming more conscious about representation in the media, more aware that the images I was seeing of women – and Latinas in particular – were at best incomplete or wrong, and at worst non-existent. It had been years since I'd played any Carmen Sandiego games, or watched the TV game show based on them (on which I dreamed of being a contestant), but suddenly the thought occurred to me whenever I thought of the Carmen Sandiego games:

Why does the criminal have to be Latin?

I'd say it sarcastically, as a joke. Like Ha-ha! Of *course* the head criminal is Latin! But then I started to wonder... is this serious? Is this character that I looked up to as a child actually harmful? After all, Latino drug lords and gang bangers are a dime a dozen in mainstream media. So are Latina prostitutes and gang girlfriends. Those on the right side of the law are generally maids and gardeners. Sometimes, they're even law enforcement. Shows like *NCIS, Dexter, Castle, Brooklyn Nine-Nine* and *The Wire* all have Latin characters in law enforcement. Many of them of high rank. Sometimes, they even have the spotlight placed upon them. Yet they are generally found on ensemble shows, one of a group designed to further the story of a (generally) white (usually) male protagonist.

What we don't have very many of yet are Latin protagonists. Media in which a Latin character is the central character, in whose journey the viewer or reader is supposed to be invested. Regular, normal people under extraordinary circumstances. Multi-faceted, flawed, brilliant protagonists that we get to follow over the course of an entire story.

It's been years since I've played any of the Carmen Sandiego games, but recently, when I was thinking about the lack of nuanced Latin characters in mainstream media, I thought about her. I realized that despite having played several games with Carmen's name in the title, I knew nothing about her. She was always just the goal, the big boss to be defeated at the end. At first, this bothered me. I thought back to how impressed I was by Carmen when I was a girl, and I was almost ashamed that I was taken in by this bone I was being thrown. Oh sure, she had a Spanish name, and she occasionally popped up throughout the game with a cryptic, punning message, but what did I actually learn about her? Not a whole lot. At least, not when I was playing the games as a kid.

So, I looked into it, and I discovered there was more to her than I even realized that had been developed over the course of the entire franchise. Which is understandable. After all, most video game characters from the 1980s didn't start out with elaborate back stories. It's only perhaps within the past decade or so that consumers even started to care about things like characters in gaming. It used to be that people just needed a game to have a puzzle to be solved or a task to be accomplished. Now, people expect A Story. They want someone with whom they can identify.

Carmen Sandiego is no exception. There are variations in her backstory over the course of several games and shows, but there are a few basic facts that seem to have congealed into something resembling a canon. Her full name is Carmen Isabella Santiago. She is generally portrayed as a brilliant ACME detective gone rogue. Catching criminals began to prove too easy for her, so rather than continue on as an ACME detective, she decided to start outsmarting ACME for the greater challenge. This being the case, she's often portrayed as a "thief with a conscience," and ACME detectives often have mixed feelings about capturing her.

Rather like I did as a child.

However, there are other intriguing elements of her character that change depending on how you're interacting with the character. For example, *Where in Time is Carmen Sandiego?* involves crimes like Stealing the History of Medicine which, if not set right, could cause the deaths of a lot of people! While it's never said outright, this points to a certain level of heartlessness in Carmen's personality that doesn't quite jibe with the "thief with a conscience" portrayal. In the *Where on Earth is Carmen Sandiego?* animated TV show, Carmen (voiced by Puerto Rican actress Rita Moreno) started out as an orphan who was given a home by the Chief at ACME Detective Agency, where, by age 17, she'd solved more cases than any other agent. And in the *Where in the World is Carmen Sandiego? Treasures of Knowledge* game, a more serious version of the original, Carmen was a child prodigy who won a huge amount of money on a game show called *It's a Wise Child* when she was ten years old, and used the money to travel the world until she was 12

This is why being the protagonist of a video game franchise is so important, and why Carmen Sandiego is so important. It isn't about any one game, it's about the world. It's about the possibilities. It's about the fact that, if a game is successful, its protagonist will live on through various mediums on various media – indefinitely. For example, Jennifer Lopez is currently attached to produce a live-action *Where in the World is Carmen Sandiego?* film for Walden Media, which is a huge opportunity for the character to be not only introduced to a new generation, but given even more depth and definition.

So when I think about Carmen being a criminal and whether or not that perpetuates negative stereotypes and is, therefore, harmful, my current opinion is... that doesn't matter, as long as the character is nuanced and has agency. After all, *The Sopranos* is all about a white guy who's the head of a criminal organization, but Tony Soprano is a fascinating character, because he isn't just a mobster. He has depth and nuance. He loves his family – and little ducks. *Breaking Bad* is a show about a white guy who's an egotistical meth kingpin and has few qualms about causing the deaths of those who stand in his way. But Walter White is a fascinating character, because of his reasons for doing what he does. He is a cancer survivor who uses his brain rather than brawn to climb the drug-trafficking ladder.

Carmen Sandiego *is* Walter White. Or she could be. The ingredients are there. And, whether she sees new life in a feature film, a TV show, or in newer games, her story can, and should, only grow and become more well-defined from here. Gaming needs a female, Latin anti-hero. Gaming needs Carmen Isabella Sandiego.

An Interview with Lisa Stevens

Lisa Stevens is the founder and CEO of Paizo Publishing. She led the group that published *Dragon* and *Dungeon*, the official *D&D* magazines, and also published *Star Wars Insider*, *Undefeated* and *Amazing Stories*. She launched paizo.com, a gaming website that sells more than 20,000 different gaming products and PDF downloads. Paizo's Pathfinder Adventure Path brand has become one of the hottest in the adventure gaming industry, spinning off *Pathfinder Modules*, the *Pathfinder Campaign Setting*, *Pathfinder Player Companions*, *Pathfinder Tales* fiction and the *Pathfinder* RPG. In addition, her company launched its *Planet Stories* line of books, bringing back the classics of fantasy and science fiction. Lisa received her MBA from the University of Washington. She has won numerous awards, including Origins Awards for the design of *Ars Magica* and *Vampire: The Masquerade*, as the assistant editor of *White Wolf Magazine* and for the graphic design of *Magic: The Gathering*. In addition, she was honored by Advertising Age in 1995 as one of the Top 100 Marketers of the Year for her work on *Magic: The Gathering*. Lisa loves to play the guitar and has an extensive collection of *Star Wars* memorabilia that threatens to engulf every room in her house. She lives in Seattle with her significant other, Vic, and her three cats, Jake, Marvin and Amiri.

Q. In your early days as a gamer, you found a safe haven in a store named Computer World. What was so accommodating about that environment?

A. Computer World was a brand-new branch of something called Sound World, which was your typical store that sold stereo units and televisions, stuff like that. Every time I got a new receiver or tape deck or turntable, it all came from there. My dad loved that place, and he'd go all the time just to look at new stuff and fantasize about buying it.

My dad wasn't the biggest computer person, but I was just getting started with some of the computer stuff in high school. We got a computer system when I was a junior – it was a big old IBM System 36 computer, and, since I was kind of a brainiac geek, I volunteered to help program it.

Then, the first personal home computers came out. Computer World sold some of those early IBM 80-86 machines, but I'm sure that the first time I went there, it was with my dad to look at the latest speakers or whatever. It's what we would do on a Saturday. And they'd take us to this little showroom that had a couple computers on display running *Akalabeth*. There was very basic figure, and a rat who was lunging at them, and the file said, "Touch this to do this." I started typing and beat their ass.

It was a computer and it was right in front of me, not something that filled up five rooms at a university. I was a big science-fiction and fantasy nerd – I read all the classic fiction writers when I was a kid, and spent my summers just devouring book after book after book. *Akalabeth* was right up my alley, a fantasy game. I just started playing, and the sales people noticed that customers would see me playing and say, "That looks pretty cool, tell me about that computer." All of the sudden, they had big sales off of me playing that game, and asked if I wanted to stop by and do that more often.

Q. When you transitioned from being a gamer to someone who makes games – basically, when you helped to launch a gaming company, Lion Rampant – did you stop and think that it would be more sensible to work for someone else, or did you just take a screaming leap and not worry about the consequences?

A. When I left college, I was pretty cocky about how I was going to be accepted into grad school. I had majored in marine biology; I wanted to get a Ph.D. and be like Jacques Coustou, on a boat, diving to study sharks or whatever. It sounded pretty cool.

Anyway, I was just like, "I'm great, I'm going to get wherever I want to go." So, I only applied to two grad schools: Wood's Hole MIT and University of Miami, Coral Gables. Wood's Hole had one position open a year, and Coral Gables had two. But I didn't work too hard when I was taking my GMATs. I didn't study that hard, so I didn't get into grad school.

So here I am, graduated, and I got nothin'. But, I was hanging around with some friends in Northfield, with some guys I had met at St. Olaf College [Jonathan Tweet and Mark Rein-Hagen]. One of them was playing in my *D&D* game, and I was playing in a *Runequest* game the same time as the other one. They basically decided to make the game that became *Ars Magica*. They heard me talk about how I was a pretty good editor, and they were like, "Can you edit this book?", and I was like, "Sure, why not? It sounds like fun."

I wasn't thinking about it as a career or anything. It was just me helping out some friends. The first copy of *Ars Magica* I got was when I was going home for summer break, and it was like, "Here, take this with you when you're gone." I've still got that copy of it – it's horribly written. It needed a whole lot of work, but it was so exciting, because the game was so cool.

When I didn't get into grad school, I was like, "Well, now I don't know what the hell I'm doing. I thought my life was going to write itself." But this game company was there, and I found myself working on it more and more. I just went up and literally slept on people's couches or wherever I could find a spare piece of floor.

But, two years later, I did decide to go back to grad school. I took my GMATs, and this time I studied for them. I'd actually gone and visited different schools and met the professors there. I applied to about 12 schools, because there was no way I was going to miss out. I actually got into all of them except one; I even got into Coral Gables. I got a spot that was fully paid, with a stipend I could use for rent and food and stuff, and my books were paid for. It was full ride. So, that was awesome.

The summer before I was supposed to head off down to Florida to my Ph.D. program, I had a quarter-life crisis. I saw a dream of myself getting my degree in my 30s – because biology, it takes about six to eight years to get a Ph.D. I was 25, imagining what I was going to be like at 33. I'd been talking to professors who kept saying, "Yeah, the government's not giving money like it used to, and we're having trouble getting grants now. You may not get to do what you want to do...", so I kept having this dream where I was delivering pizzas at age 33 with a PhD in marine biology. And it just kinda scared me.

I went to my dad for advice, because I was terrified to go to grad school. The alternative was this gaming company where we weren't yet making any money, but I could see it going somewhere, sometime. My dad suggested that I delay my entry into graduate school and see how things went, so I told them I was going to defer a year for personal reasons. And then Lion Rampant took off.

The thing is, my mom was very upset with me. She said: "You stupid kid, you have this awesome opportunity with grad school, and you're hanging around with your do-nothing friends making no money, living on floors and basements and whatever." My dad stayed supportive, but my mom carried a lot of weight in their house. She'd been helping me with money while I was living with my "no-good loser friends," and she cut me off. She told me, "You've got to float your own boat. If you're going to throw away your life, you're going to deal with the consequences of doing that."

I had basically one month to find a job, but I'd never really had a job in my life. I got one at the University of Minnesota, and, for about two and a half, maybe three years, I had a schedule that was just crazy. I literally got up at 3 a.m., showered, got dressed, drove to Minneapolis from where I was living in Northfield, worked eight hours plus a lunch hour, and then drove home and worked on Lion Rampant until I couldn't stay awake any more. A lot of times, that was 11 p.m. or midnight. Then I went to sleep for a few hours, got up and repeated it.

Q. What was your day job at the University?

A. I was an editor for a doctor in the Department of Surgery. I'd pull articles on stuff he was researching and edit his articles as he got published. I also got the job of running the computing for a lot of the department. Computers were kind of a new thing there, and, while I had a background in computers, I kinda lied my way into the job. I told them I knew what I was doing, but really didn't. I learned BASIC on the fly. One time, they told me, "Hey, we're thinking about networking these computers up, can you present us with our options tomorrow?" And, between the time they asked me and "tomorrow," I learned everything I could about networking and presented it to them. It worked. When I left, they were devastated.

And then, fortunately, Lion Rampant took off.

It worked, but in some ways, it didn't. Lion Rampant would never have made much of a company for me. When we merged with White Wolf, that became something of a career path. And then I joined Wizards of the Coast.

Q. You were a vice-president at Wizards of the Coast when *Magic: The Gathering* was developed. Were you aware it was going to be a massive paradigm shift in gaming, or was it all a happy accident?

A. This will sound kinda funny in retrospect, but... you have to remember that the year before we came out with *Magic*, Wizards of the Coast had about $30,000 in total sales. So we weren't very big. And I remember seeing *Magic* and saying, "Guys, this is going to be huge. I bet we make at least a million dollars."

Then I got scared beyond belief, because while I knew how amazing this new game was, we didn't know how to make it – how to actually manufacture it. It needed to be playing cards, but the playing-card companies didn't do randomized decks; none of them had technology for randomizing. And the guys that had randomizing technology all made trading cards, which you couldn't play with.

On top of that, even though the decks needed to be randomized, they still needed to be playable. Each deck of cards needed the right kind of manna, etc.

I'd been printing role-playing books, and there were all these things I had no experience with. We finally caught a break because of Luc Mertens, who worked for Carta Mundi – a printer who now has a huge operation in Texas, but at the time was only in Belgium. Luc was at Gen Con the summer before *Magic* came out and had been talking with my ex-company White Wolf. I had asked them if they knew of any card printers, and they brought him by our booth and said, "Hey, there's this guy from Belgium, maybe he can help you out."

Sure enough, he was the key to the whole thing. His company had the technology, and they sent their main guy over to spend a week teaching us how to lay out sheets of the cards. They put a lot of money and resources and time into a little nothing company that was in the basement of [Wizards CEO] Peter Adkison's home. And, of course, they reaped the rewards when *Magic* took off.

Another problem was that we didn't have any money to get all the artwork we needed. At that time, I could probably get a color cover for $500 or something like that, but, for *Magic*, we needed artwork for 302 cards. I had a huge Rolodex of artists I'd dealt with over the years on various role-playing products, so I spent a lot of time convincing them to do... well, it wasn't full-page art, like you'd have on a cover, but it was a full-color illustration for which we offered them $50, plus $50 worth of stock in the company and a shared royalty. I think we set aside 10% of the sales to divide amongst the artists, so many of those guys became millionaires.

But, at the time, those artists were facing being paid $50 per piece of art; that's what was tangible about the whole thing. There was no guarantee that you'd get any royalties, or that we'd sell the company for a ton of money. So, yeah, those guys made out like bandits – but hey, they at first agreed to do color illustrations for $50 each. A lot of the artists we used were in art school at Cornish College in downtown Seattle and had never had a paying gig. Their first thing was *Magic*, because one of our guys was going there, and he convinced all of his art friends to get involved.

So *Magic*'s development was a lot of happenstance. And we had to raise money for other things besides the artists, thousand dollars by thousand dollars by thousand dollars. Peter Adkison... if you said "hi" to him at the drive-through window, he probably made a pitch to you. He hit everybody, anybody, for the smallest amount of money.

Q. Do you regret that you didn't have Kickstarter to grease some of those wheels?

A. I would have been petrified, absolutely petrified, to use Kickstarter because we were so worried that if TSR or an established competitor got word of what we were doing, they'd beat us. I knew the key was to be first to market with this. But we didn't have the money or the knowledge base. It was like knowing there was a spot of land that had a diamond mine, and that if you can start diamond mining, it's yours. But you've never mined diamonds in your life, and you have no money to buy equipment. It was like that – trying to raise that money without letting anyone know the diamonds are there. It was scary. It was absolutely terrifying.

Q. How long did you live in fear before you hit that point of, "Oh God, oh God, this is actually going to work"?

A. I was starting to breathe easier by the time we got up to the release of *Magic*, because I knew that if someone figured out what we were doing, they weren't going to be able to move fast enough. We were in the home stretch. I think we showed off some of *Magic* at the GAMA Trade Show, and we teased it with ads in the winter of 1993, right before it come out. At that point, I knew we were at least going to be the first to market.

Q. These days, you're CEO of Paizo Publishing, which among other things developed *Pathfinder*. How much of your job entails making the wheels of business turn, and how much of it is hardcore story development and writing?

A. Right now, it's about 80% business and 20% creative. It's one of those things where, as your company gets bigger and you hire more people, you have more to keep track of. But I always make sure that, whenever there's an opportunity for brainstorming for an upcoming book or something, if I can fit it into my schedule, I am at that meeting like white on rice. You gotta keep up your creative skills. And I still GM a *Pathfinder* game every Monday.

Q. As part of your workday, or something you do at home?
A. I do it at my house with friends who don't work for me.

They are some lucky friends.
I'm lucky to have them. It's as much fun for me as it is a little bit of work too.

Q. Do you stick to what's in release, or do you GM *Pathfinder* materials in development?
A. It's mostly stuff that's out. I have been known to play-test the core rule book for *Pathfinder*. I'm not against [testing things in development], it's just that it takes a long time to get through a campaign.

Q. Much of the need to create *Pathfinder* came from Wizards of the Coast canceling some of your licenses and surprising everyone with the release of *D&D* Fourth Edition. As you developed *Pathfinder* as – shall we say – a compatible departure from *D&D*, were you worried that you splitting the gaming community in half? Or was the overriding concern, "We have to do this to keep our doors open, we really don't have a choice"?
A. I think it's the latter. Nobody wants to split a fan-community in half, but when Fourth Edition was being announced and play-tested, we saw that the community was already fracturing. A lot of people were saying, "I won't go [to Fourth Edition], I'll just go play the old game." In the history of *D&D* through its various edition changes, that's always been the case. That's the good and bad thing about new editions: you get to sell a bunch of books to people all over again, but some won't come along for the ride.

So there were a sizeable number of people who were going to stay behind whether we did anything or not. For us, it was a matter of surviving.

Q. With *Pathfinder*, you made the core rules and setting information available in wiki form. At the time, did that seem like a big risk? Was there any disagreement about whether that should be given out freely or kept proprietary?
A. We definitely talked about it, but things keep changing in the world. You have to look at reality, and say, "Information is going to get out there." You could spend all of your time fruitlessly playing Whack-a-Mole to try to stop people from posting information about your game

system or whatever, or you can embrace it and come up with rules and guidelines to govern that information. We have a Use Policy that tells our community, "Here's what you can do." We also have a lenient policy for publishers who want to publish our rules. That way, we don't have to squash a bunch of violations – which you have to do, if you don't give people permission, or you run the risk of losing your copyright or trademark.

This way, it helps to build the community and engage the customers rather than fighting them. It's turned out to be a really positive thing for us. I don't think it's affected our sales at all – in fact, it's probably increased our sales.

Q. Do you have a sense of what percentage of the *Pathfinder* players are women?

A. I have anecdotal evidence; we think it's probably around 20 to 25% women.

That's a hell of a lot better than, say, *Eve Online*.

Well, *Eve Online* is a toxic, testosterone-filled MMO. I hated that. They *want* that.

I think the number of women in gaming has definitely gone up. Nowadays, with Gen Con, I feel like it's more equal parts women and men. There are many couples, and they're bringing their families in. It really doesn't match society in numbers, but it's getting there pretty quick. Being a geek and a girl, it's something that's no longer frowned on. Back in the day, if you were a geek girl, oh my God, you might as well just curl in a ball and die, because you were going to be bullied and picked on for being that geek. Nowadays, it's crazy.

Q. In January 2013, you used Kickstarter to raise more than $1 million for *Pathfinder Online*. Two months later, producer Rob Thomas raised $5.7 million on Kickstarter for the *Veronica Mars* film, and he wound up writing the script very differently than if a studio had stumped the cash, because he felt a moral obligation to the fans who were paying for it. Would *Pathfinder Online* have been developed in a different way had it not been Kickstarter-ed?

A. Yes, it would totally have been.

Here's the thing about Kickstarter... it allowed us to be beholden to the fans, to say to them, "You guys get to tell us how to make this game." If we didn't do that, some investment banker or someone like that would have come in and given us the money, but they would have said, "I want you to make as much money as possible, to make as big a profit as you can, and to build it up as quickly as possible. In five years, we'll sell it to somebody and we'll all make a big payday." Which investors do, right?

There's nothing wrong with that, but it's a different way of doing things. You're focusing on the money and making a return on the investment, because that's your primary responsibility. With Kickstarter, we were able to say, "Hey, guys, you are our investors. What *you're* doing is giving us the money to make a game for you and us. The game that we want to make involves some decisions that aren't the best at making the most money the quickest, but it's in the interest of making a game that everybody wants to play and has longevity."

So, with *Pathfinder Online*, we're ramping it up slowly. We weren't looking to get a million people in during the first month, we were looking to get 20,000 people. We could grow the community slowly, because we didn't need to make money fast so we could flip it.

Q. You're renowned for being a *Star Wars* expert, but I understand that you also own some impressive items from *Doctor Who*?

A. My husband is a huge *Doctor Who* fan, and he's made me a pretty big *Doctor Who* fan. I can't talk about the show like he can; he knows everything about which companion did this and that. I was never a big *Doctor Who* fan growing up, but David Tennant is my Doctor now. We'll watch some of the old episodes, because he's got them all and a bunch of the re-creations for the ones that are missing.

We also own a screen-used TARDIS and a screen-used Dalek. I think we're the only Dalek and TARDIS in the United States. The Dalek is from the late 80s; it was a white Dalek, but they repainted it black and gold. They had it in an exhibit that went around the UK for a while, and then they closed the exhibit down and auctioned off a lot of the stuff in it for charity a couple of years back.

Q. What decade is the TARDIS from?

A. It's actually Christopher Eccleston's TARDIS. I'm told they had two TARDISes; this was the main one, and another was a back-up. It's made out of wood; it was heavy to carry around and put together, so they redid the TARDIS in fiber-glass to make it lighter when they moved on to Tennant. This TARDIS was also in a charity auction. We also have a Matt Smith Doctor costume too.

Q. Here in 2014, what do you know now that you wished you'd known in the 80s with Lion Rampant?

A. There's one thing I've always said in my life – I guess I intuitively knew this, but it would have helped me a lot more back then to know this – and it's that the key to success is surrounding yourself with good people. It doesn't really kind of matter what you're doing; if you have good people around you, you'll find ways to be successful.

The other thing is being customer focused. I had a moment in my life in the late 90s: when I was at Wizards of the Coast, we went down to take a class at DisneyWorld. They'd just started this thing called Disney University, and it was the first time they'd run a class on customer loyalty. So, we spent the week at DisneyWorld – which didn't suck in and of itself – and we got to go behind the scenes with the employees.

I saw this organization had one huge focus, which was on the customer. They had a thing called Magic Moments. Every single person from the bus driver to the wine cook to the maid to everybody, the whole puppeteers, they had a laser focus on providing Magic Moments for good customers. It was absolutely mind-blowing to talk to someone who was just some guy waiting in the yard where nobody even comes and talks to him. You could talk to him, and he would tell you about the times he'd traded Magic Moments. It built up customer loyalty for DisneyWorld.

To realize that when you focus on your customers to that level – if I'd have known that, I think we would've been more successful earlier. I still keep a course-book from the class in my office at all times. That single course changed how I do business for the rest of my life.

Q. Some sectors of the gaming industry have gender parity, roughly, but some remain the domain of men. Do you have any advice for female creators trying to get their start in the industry?

A. You have to get yourself out there, you have to get yourself noticed, and you have to take advantage of every opportunity. That might be tough for some women to be the aggressor, to go out there and say "I'm good" as a designer or whatever.

It's mostly in design that the women aren't there. Editorial, yes. There's definitely women in this industry, but designers – we don't have enough female designers.

Q. Why do you think that is?

A. I think it's because there aren't that many jobs in design, so you have to promote yourself, to say to people, "I'm designing good stuff, you should read my stuff, and here's why." I look at the men who are successful at becoming designers, and it's because they were aggressive at it. They worked for no money and pumped the products they'd done for no money, so that people saw them until they got jobs where they could make some money.

At Paizo, we do a thing called RPG Superstar: a contest in which anybody in the world can submit. Our fanbase weighs in and gets the entrants down to the Top 100, then celebrity judges take it down to 32, and they compete against each other until we get to the RPG Superstar. And this year, a woman won. Actually, the first year, a woman won too, but she didn't do anything with it.

I always tell the RPG Superstars: "You've won this, you're going to have a published module with your name on it, grab that bull by the horns and [leverage] the fact that you're an RPG Superstar. There are other publishers that would die to have stuff from you. People now know your name, and this is your chance to do something with it."

Every year we have a winner, and with some of these guys, their names are known all over gaming now. Other people have disappeared into the footnotes of history. You worked your ass off to win the thing, now do something with it.

But, you have to enter. This year, we had a couple of female judges on the judging panel; we wanted to try and make it more appealing for women to get involved, to put themselves out there and submit, because a lot of times, they think they can't do it. They think it's not something they're good at, or they think, "Aww, I won't win." Because they look around, and there aren't that many women designing games, so they think they can't do it. And all the famous designers are guys.

You've got to believe that you're going to be that person. You're going to be the next famous designer.

Chicks Dig Gaming
Intuition, Gaming
and the Laboratory Scientist

Kelly Swails is an editor and writer whose work has appeared in several anthologies. An avid gamer, her current favorites include *Settlers of Catan* and the ever-popular *Munchkin*. When she's not wrestling with words or playing a game, she knits, plucks at a guitar, and watches cult TV shows. There's an unsubstantiated internet rumor she sleeps on occasion. You can find her online at www.kellyswails.com.

I am a clinical laboratory scientist. Folks like me analyze blood, body fluids, and/or tissue samples to help doctors diagnose disease. That time you had strep throat in the third grade? Someone like me waded through the bacterial jungle that is your oral flora to give your doctor that information. Have high cholesterol, diabetes or take anticoagulants? Someone like me analyzes your blood. If you get into a car accident and slice your spleen open at three in the morning, my brethren will be working our asses off in the blood bank making sure you have the blood products your surgeon needs to keep you alive.

When I worked in a clinical laboratory, I was a good medical technologist: hard working, quick on my feet and able to politely explain the difference between a prothrombin time and a mixing study to internal medicine residents who shouldn't be allowed to write orders yet. In short, I had skills. Lots of them. But I lacked the one thing I needed to become a truly great technologist: critical thinking.

I Muddled My Way Through...

I had a little critical thinking, you understand. I wouldn't have graduated from my college program if I didn't. Like most techs, I also cultivated it throughout my career. Critical thinking is absolutely essential for a laboratory scientist – it's the gut feeling that a patient's electrolyte levels are critically high, not because they're in crisis, but because a nurse drew the labs through the same IV line that infused saline. It's intuition on steroids. Some people have a natural aptitude for it. I didn't.

Looking back, I attribute this partially to my inherent gullibility as a human being. I grew up in an "obey your elders" sort of environment where questioning authority wasn't encouraged or, in most cases, even tolerated. At a very young age, I learned to do what I was told. I also learned that when an authority figure says something, they're right. Don't question it. Even if they're wrong.

Which brings me to the lab. Most departments use sophisticated analyzers to test blood samples. This equipment undergoes rigorous daily, weekly and monthly maintenance to keep it in peak condition. Quality-control samples are analyzed once a shift to ensure the instrument is providing correct results. Quality-assurance programs monitor the analyzers as well as the techs that run them. These machines cost hundreds of thousands of dollars, and perform hundreds of precise calculations an hour. An analytic analyzer is the ultimate authority figure.

Still... an instrument can turn out erroneous results for a myriad of reasons. Tubing gets crimped; reagents run dry; you're unwittingly testing plasma instead of serum; or vice-versa. It takes a knowledgeable technologist to catch these idiosyncrasies before a patient is diagnosed with, say, an anemia they don't have. This is where critical thinking comes in; an expensive analyzer is just a piece of machinery that performs a specific task. Humans must determine if it's functioning correctly, and if those results are correct.

One evening, early in my career, I had been assigned to the Chemistry department. The section where I worked was quite automated – a conveyer belt uncapped the specimens before putting them through the analyzers and storing them in a large refrigerator. The analyzers "spoke" directly with the computer system and automatically released normal results so that the technologist only had to manually verify abnormal results. As long as the instruments worked properly (which they did most of the time), working in Chemistry meant I'd have a quiet night.

That night proved to be less than quiet. About halfway through my shift, I noticed three abnormally low potassium results in a row. Low potassium levels aren't that unusual, especially when dealing with hospitalized patients, but three in row? I smelled trouble, so I checked the reagent level. The analyzer said the reagent was at 50%, and a visual check of the container corroborated that. I checked the tubing that ran from the jug to the analyzer, but didn't see any anomalies. It wasn't until I checked the tubing around the apparatus that funneled the patient specimen into the analysis chamber that I found the problem: tubing had somehow become pinched between two moving parts. I fixed the tubing, re-analyzed the potassiums in question – the results were normal

– and continued my evening.

Where's the problem, you might ask? I failed to think the problem through all the way. The apparatus with the pinched tubing also measured three other analytes (carbon dioxide, sodium and chloride). The "normal" range for potassium is quite small, and so it made sense that this analyte would be the first to show analytical error. However, since the other analytes were within the normal range, I assumed they had received the proper amount of sample. I assumed wrong. When I told my supervisor the problem, he asked me to repeat the other tests on those patient samples. Sure enough, the chloride, sodium and carbon dioxide tested higher the second time. Still within the normal range, and so the patients hadn't been affected by the slightly lower results, but they were still wrong. A patient outcome could have easily been affected by an erroneous electrolyte result.

It's those sorts of critical thinking decisions a clinical laboratory scientist must make multiple times a day. While my experiences over the years helped hone that skill, I never got as good at it as I wanted.

... Until Gaming Showed Me the Way

I had always been a closet gamer waiting to be discovered. While my father was into science fiction of all kinds (everything from *Doctor Who* to *Mystery Science Theater 3000*), the only games we played were the usual mundane suspects: *Clue*, checkers, rummy and perhaps the occasional game of spite and malice. In high school, I had guy friends who played *Dungeons & Dragons* and *Magic: The Gathering*, but, when I asked to join them, they told me "girls weren't allowed to play." It didn't occur to me until years later that I wasn't the problem.

During college, I met my husband – an avid gamer who not only thought girls *could* play games, but *should*. He walked me through making a *D&D* character, taught me to play *Magic*, and got me interested in fantasy literature. It took me several years to become invested, but, once I decided to pursue writing professionally, I dived in. What self-respecting science-fiction and fantasy author doesn't play at least a few games on the side?

My forays into gaming started slow. A game of *Munchkin* here, a few hands of *Magic* there, and every now and then a board game to break it up. I had fun, but didn't usually win. I wasn't used to thinking three or five turns ahead or trying to deduce what my opponents had in their hand based on how they played. Once again, critical thinking got the better of me. I slowly got better, though, and soon enough I started to make a decent showing. After I started to win some of the games we played, we decided to break out the big guns and start a D&D campaign.

I found *Dungeons & Dragons* a bit intimidating: the thick rulebook, the history the other players had with each other, the way my husband remembered his dexterity bonus without looking at his notes. Everyone in the group welcomed me, but I knew I was the weakest member. This became apparent during our first session...

# # #

Rob, our illustrious gamemaster, started off by putting us in (you guessed it) a tavern. We accepted an adventuring offer from a shady man in a cape, and we took off across the countryside to try and find a relic in a castle.

"You walk up to the castle and see a set of large double doors lit with torches on either side. You—"

"I open the door," I said.

Rob blinked at me. "What?"

"I open the door," I said. When no one responded I said, "Oh, sorry. Lorilai opens the door."

My husband Ken nudged me. "You might not want to do that."

Rob said, "Do you want to check it for traps?"

I glanced around the group. Everyone had expressions ranging from defeat to anticipatory glee. It occurred to me I was about to experience my own version of the "... and then I set off a trap" D&D story that I'd heard people tell over the years. I peered at my notes. "Can I do that?"

"Not well," Ken said.

Rob looked around the table. "Does anyone want to help her?"

I held up my hand. "I don't need help. I walk over and grab one of the torches."

The tension at the table became palpable. "I take five steps back," everyone else said.

"I join them," I said, "and I throw the torch at the door."

Rob rolled a few dice and smirked. Someone – I don't know who – at the table groaned. "The door catches fire and you hear a small 'pop' before a cloud of gas escapes. The fire turns green and becomes intense before it burns out, leaving nothing but the empty doorframe in its wake."

"That's one way to find a trap," Ken said.

"Lorilai's a little bad-ass that way," I said.

# # #

This encounter did two things. One, it set up Lorilai as a devil-may-care character who loved fire and eventually became a lot of fun to play, and, two, it taught me the biggest lesson in gaming: *question everything.*

The proverbial light bulb had gone on. Once I started investigating potential traps in the gaming world, questioning the status quo in the real world became second nature.

Fast forward a few years. I left evening shift to specialize in microbiology on the day shift. I became a clinical laboratory scientist in large part because of my love of microbiology. I loved uncovering the secret bacterial world we all carry around with us. Microbiology isn't black and white like chemistry or blood bank; there are a lot of shades of gray to discern. A coworker liked to say we were bacteria farmers – I preferred to think of us as bacteria detectives, sifting through a patient's normal flora to find the pathogenic agent.

Take blood cultures, for example. Blood cultures are typically sterile, but they can become positive for a variety of reasons: contaminated blood draws, transient septicemia or true septicemia. It's up to the technologist to help the doctors determine which it is, and we do that by identifying the bacteria recovered. Skin flora such as *Staphylococcus epidermidis* suggests a bad collection while a blood culture with *E. coli* concurrent to a urine culture with the same organism suggests the septicemia is transient and will resolve once the urinary tract infection is treated. Positive blood cultures can usually be attributed to another infectious process somewhere in the body, like pneumonia or an infected wound.

I had been assigned to work on blood cultures for a few days when several blood cultures on Patient X went positive. Over the course of the next few days, I recovered several organisms on this patient that didn't make sense. For one thing, patients usually only have one organism in their bloodstream, such as *E. coli* or *Staphylococcus aureus*, but Patient X had several. One culture had a species of Streptococcus that was usually oral flora; another had Propionibacteria, an anaerobic organism that is usually skin flora; another had *E. coli*; yet another had a mix of organisms.

I could justify the Streptococcus and the Porpionibacteria as contaminants; perhaps the blood culture bottle or the patient's arm hadn't been cleaned sufficiently. But that little voice inside my head wouldn't let it go, so I delved a little further and looked in X's chart. I discovered he had been a sheriff injured in the line of duty. His injury caught my attention: Patient X had been shot in the abdomen and undergone emergency surgery upon admission.

I paged the infectious disease doctor on call and discussed the case with her. She agreed that things didn't make sense. She investigated further and called me back later that day. They'd performed a CT scan and discovered the patient's colon had been perforated during the surgery to remove the bullet and that he was in surgery again to repair the tear. She thanked me for calling her, because they wouldn't have known to look for anything if I hadn't questioned the results.

Would I have made the same call had I not been a gamer? Maybe. My experience in the lab and the microbiology department might have been enough. However, I like to think that all the hours I spent throwing cards, rolling dice and asking questions helped me give that sheriff a fighting chance. Maybe slaying a few dragons has helped me save a few lives.

Chicks Dig Gaming
Saving the Galaxy in Cute Shoes

Zoe Estrin-Grele is an aspiring writer living in New York City, like thousands of other aspiring New York City writers. She started gaming in her pre-adolescent years and has been murdering her way across hundreds of fantasy worlds ever since; she plays tanks almost exclusively because she likes to be taller than she is in real life. These days, when not writing novels and dreaming of publishing them, she spends her time baking muffins, playing *Guild Wars 2* and getting lost on the subway.

I was in a bar in Manhattan last week talking with a self-proclaimed nerd who, over his bourbon on the rocks, asked me if I played video games. My entire face must have lit up like a Christmas tree, because I hadn't been able to talk video games – my often embarrassing passion since discovering *Neverwinter Nights* at age ten – since moving to New York three months before. "Yeah," I said, attempting to sound casual and not as though I was going to vibrate off of my barstool at the very thought of discussing gaming as a story telling medium. "Yeah, I do."

"What kind?"

"RPGs mostly," I told him. He nodded knowingly.

"Why those?" As a writer/gamer talking to another writer/gamer, the story element of Role Playing Games would have been obvious as a draw.

I took a sip of my Whiskey Sour, because I was about to sound like kind of a nut and was worried about it. "I like being able to play through a story, you know? And uh... I really prefer to play women over men. It makes me feel like feminism is getting somewhere."

People keep asking me why I always play a girl. It's true; given the option, I will play a woman. But I mean, it's not even because I'm super girly (I'm your classic 90's tomboy, more male friends than female, am 22 and still buy most of my pants in the men's department), but I always play women. It's not because I'm trying to play myself in video games either, because I'm not at all, more that I really appreciate the option. Any game to me is more interesting when, instead of lady non-player characters being overly sexual at a boring square of male player character, it's just a couple of girls casually chatting about how they're going to save the world.

It's also great in games when you have no character choice but you aren't defaulted to male; *Portal* comes straight to mind, where I shocked myself the first time I looked through a portal at myself and went, "I'm a girl?" And while it's wonderful that that's not treated like a big deal and that there's no sort of sexy idea behind it, it's better at least for me to see my character talking, interacting, happy, sad, whatever and witness that women are just as capable of killing dragons and space robots and evil gods as any man.

To that end, I've always been an RPG fan. I like to have the freedom to really create a character. And, frankly, choosing gender is a great thing. See, in an RPG where the player has control over character customization, the dialogue and story have to be written in such a way that it'll work for different genders. Therefore, it really doesn't matter who you are or what you look like, you've got to be treated like a real person who does things just as well as the male character. Your character can't be sexualized, can't be marginalized, because they're saying exactly the same thing to an NPC[4], saving exactly the same people, and having exactly the same hardships.

If you marginalize one, you'd have to marginalize both. And that's just not going to happen with such a large, vocal, straight, male fan base.

Of course, there are still some games that don't quite live up to what you want. Because there's always a downside, right? One of the things I hate most is that part where you get in and you're making your character and she looks like she could probably eat bullets for breakfast and you're feeling great about yourself, like, "Yeah, me and my lady here are gonna take over space...", and then you *see what she's wearing* and it brings you to a screeching halt. Because it's going to be really difficult to take over space in a metal g-string and half a bra. How are you supposed to revel in the fiery destruction you can rain down, when you just know that everyone is just going to be staring at your ass?

Don't get me wrong: when I take over space, I want to look cute doing it. It's just that there's a line, and that line is breastplates that show my nipples.

Within a video game, the player's character obviously becomes an extension of the self. Everyone has different ways of doing it – some people actually re-create themselves in the game, while others create characters that can do things they would never do in real life, crafting an avatar to fulfill their need to destroy or control or save the world, who

4 A game-controlled *Non-Player Character*.

knows. I'm one of these latter players, and I love being able to revel in the escapism of being an absolute maniac. What's important is that, in some way or another, the character and the player are connected, especially in RPGs where the choices one makes really influence the world. More and more RPGs are becoming story-driven, with moral choices and even interpersonal emotional connections with characters. When I create my characters, I spend forever making sure they look and "act" and sound the way I want, because I'm going to watch this person for hours and hours and I want them to be just right.

So, after I put all this effort in, I don't want to be slapped down by someone else's fantasy fulfillment about what women should look like. And, by being proud of being a gamer, am I subtly allowing this to continue to happen? Am I becoming the very thing that I hate by buying games and supporting creators who will continue to do weird stuff with their ladies?

Well, yes and no. There are some games, some RPGs, that are so heinous I can't even play them. But, for the most part, when I buy a game and support something, I'm also subtly saying, "Yes, women are here too. Women are playing your game. Women are a part of your fan base, your player base, we give you money and we invest time and effort. We're going to want something back too. And that thing that we want is a sweater or something. Even the option for a sweater. Or massive shoulders, I don't care, give me exactly the same armor as that hulk of a dude over there and I'll be happy."

We are saying that we are here, we are vocal and we are going to save the world, whether you like it or not.

On the other hand, though, there's a lot of stuff out there that's really cool about what I wear to the apocalypse. More and more games these days are starting to register the fact that women are playing them – something that's just heartwarming all the time – and now there are options for some really kickass women. Sure, it sucks that they can get to us with their skimpy armor and weird sexualization stuff, but, on the other hand, in an RPG, that's the *only* way they can get to us, right? I mean, they can't change the story, the dialogue or the interaction. They can't make female characters lesser through statistics or classes (because hey, men play women too, and they'd make a stink if there was a penalty like that – we hope). So the only way they can seek to undermine women is through the way they look. And there are so many games out there that don't do that, that really, all they're going to do is hurt themselves.

And it's not just the player characters. As a big fan of BioWare games, my list of *Mass Effect* characters who could break anyone I know with their pinky is actually mostly comprised of women. And they're all different. Hell, alien engineer Tali is completely covered, even her face, for the entire three-game series and we still love her, and probably fear her; that girl is crazy sometimes. And then there's science experiment Jack, literally wearing a band of leather across her nipples, and still somehow managing to not be conventionally sexy. Interesting, well-developed female characters of different looks, backstories and personalities abound in some titles, in surprising places – the middle aged healer Wynn in *Dragon Age: Origins* who is maternal and protective, but also sometimes cruel and judgmental, comes immediately to mind.

The way games are written these days, these sorts of characters mean a lot more than people realize. We have girls in video games who are sweet *and* badass, sexy *and* effective, delicate *and* destructive. And having a player character allowed all the character depth that would be accorded for a male is wonderful. I can have my gun and my armor and my cute haircut too.

Maybe it seems like I'm making a big deal about this, but when I grew up and was getting into video games, it was predominantly male characters, no choices. Female characters were relegated to sidekicks or party members – almost always mages or sorceresses, non-combat-heavy roles. We still live in a world where male characters dominate box art and developers are told that female characters can't carry a game, which is absolute madness because some male characters don't even talk and are hardly seen but can still carry one. *Bioshock 2* had the major female character relegated to the back of the box, while *Mass Effect 3* – a game I love and have already praised to high heaven – featured the generic white male solider type that is default Commander Sheppard (instead of spritely ginger fem!Shep who is beloved by fans, male and female alike).

I like playing women, yes, but also I see it as a statement of purpose. If I want to play a tank, I'm going to play a tank, but she's going to be a petite Japanese girl with a sledge hammer as big as she is. Because video games break the rules of physics left and right – and why can't we as women use *that* to our advantage in order to really say what we want, get what we want, play who and how we want? It seems to be such an easy step to take. And RPGs give you that option, right up front. Chose your race, your class, your gender. It's that easy to take the whole gaming industry, everything I hate about it, every stupid uninformed sexist comment I've ever received, and turn it on its head.

#

Why do I play girls? Because I can. Because I want to. Because video games are escapism and I want to escape to a world where a girl can be anything. Because I should be able to see myself in everything I play and read. Oh, I could play a male character, and he could be just as relatable and wonderful and whatnot; playing a man in a game does not make you less of a feminist or anything. But it's that option, it's that ability to say yes to being female – be that traditionally feminine, armor-clad or terrifying or any combination thereof – and to push that boundary and see ourselves as women be just as effective as men.

So play what you want. Play who and how and with whatever weapon you want. But the point is that, no matter what, I still want to be able to say, "I, a pretty girl in fabulous shoes, saved the galaxy; yes, thank you, please throw all roses right here."

The Silence of the Games

Sarah Groenewegen was born in Sydney, Australia, but now lives in London. Her features and reviews have been published in periodicals such as the *Sydney Star Observer, Lesbians on the Loose* and *SFX*, and her essays have appeared in anthologies including the *Time, Unincorporated* series and the Hugo-nominated *Queers Dig Time Lords*. Her short fiction has won the Scarlet Stiletto Award, 2002, and been published in Big Finish's *Doctor Who* line, including the award-winning *Short Trips: Zodiac*. She blogs at http://nyssa1968.blogspot.co.uk. She is currently working on a science-fiction novel trilogy when she's not out walking in the British countryside and sampling the fine ales and whiskies of that land.

It's the music's fault. It wormed its way into my cerebral cortex like some kind of parasitic creature. The notes littered like lice eggs attached to my neurones, and then refused to let go. They hatched every now and again, smaller than microscopic versions of the eggs that spawn aliens. Their progeny slithered and skittered spider-like through my brain, and then burst forth into my memory. Hijacked my propensity to hum tunes roughly approximating pop songs or movie soundtrack themes to incorporate their musical payload.

Whenever that happened, it took me a little while to notice, to understand where the odd bars had come from that shifted my musical trajectory.

They came from the computer games I played obsessively for a few years. The ones I became addicted to. The ones I played non-stop for hours – days, even – at a time.

#

I should have known my relationship with computer games was problematic from the way it invaded my dreams.

The soundtrack in my dreamscape was a full orchestral version of the snatches of music played through my PC's speakers. In my head, the plinky-plonky little theme played lush, deep and by the best symphonic orchestras in the universe. Heroic riffs for each of the little guys whom I put in harm's way like I was their god. Their little jerky fidgety movements oddly hypnotic as they waited for instructions that inevitably resulted in their deaths.

"Go forth, little guys, and drop that stone on that nuclear sub I've got circling your little Stone Age island."

Some of them grunted their allegiance and set off on their doomed mission, then grunted again and shouted as they pushed their big rock to the cliff edge, dropping it into the sea below. Bullseye as the rock hit the sub. Then the boom of the explosion and the magnificent flowering of the radioactive mushroom cloud and ubiquitous Tchaikovsky-esque finale that would wake me up.

That, or the dawn sun streaming through my window after I'd stayed up all night gaming again. Only stopping in the pre-dawn cool to rest my eyes, my head on the computer desk. To shake out my mouse hand from the tension built up from creating the computer world for my people. Bleary-eyed and having to stand, shower and drink loads of coffee before heading into my office to do a full day's work. The music beaten back to the electronic pastiche of the score, occasionally roaring to life as I completed yet another email.

# # #

Age of Empires is probably my favourite computer game. I played the PC version obsessively in the early 2000s. I spent all night setting up ridiculous scenarios like cave men versus nuclear submarines and World War II US infantry units. Or pitching knights against Romans in a vaguely scientific study of which battle tactics would win out.

Who am I kidding? It wasn't at all scientific. It was *fun*.

When I first started, I played *Age of Empires* the way it was meant to be played. It's a strategy game a bit like *Civilisation* – I tried playing that game once, but didn't find it nearly as fun. Too many rules. Too strategic. Too divorced from the human level.

Most importantly, I liked the way the soldiers in *Age of Empires* moved their tiny CGI bodies to the tune of the music. As best as I can recall, *Civilisation*'s music wasn't quite as funky, wasn't quite in my groove, and the soldiers in that didn't have the moves in quite the same way.

Age of Empires had a lot of rules, too, but I learned to circumvent them fairly quickly by limiting the power of the computer's control over my opponents. The nuclear option tended to kill a game off pretty quickly, so eliminating that imperial development became my first move in setting up my game options.

Part of the reason for doing that was a futile attempt to force myself to get some sleep, especially on weeknights. The problem was that I had an often-stressful job, and taking out my frustrations in a harmless computer game proved effective. Or so I argued to myself at the time. Maybe a first-person shooter would have been better, but I'd had a bad experience with one of them. Too many negative associations.

A colleague suggested *Flight Simulator* might help. He used it to ease his stress levels. I considered it, started saving up to buy a copy, but then this happened... Our team had a particularly rough time of it, and my colleague had been home playing *Flight Simulator* to distract himself from the real world. He piloted his imaginary 747 to successfully crash into the World Trade Center in New York City. Apparently quite a difficult manoeuvre, and the first time he'd done it. Feeling better, he switched the game off and turned the news on. The date was September 11, 2001. He never played that game again, and I never bought it.

I played *Age of Empires* a lot that year. I stopped when I swapped my desktop PC for an Apple Mac laptop and resisted buying the Mac version.

# # #

I blame Nintendo Game & Watch handhelds for all of this.

My family and I discovered Game & Watch in Singapore in the early 1980s. We were there on holiday at a time when electronics were cheaper in Singapore than my native Australia. I had *Parachute* and my brother had *Octopus*. We would occasionally swap, which is a nice way of saying that I as a 13 year old would bully and boss my ten-year-old brother around until he gave up playing his.

They were both the first "widescreen" versions of hand-held devices that combined a digital watch and alarm with a game. The forerunner of the Nintendo and Playstation games, I guess, that took the world by storm a few years later. They had all the hallmarks. The way you held the units with your hands and your thumbs manipulated the buttons to react to music and motion. Bleep-bleep-bleep, bleep-bleep, bleep. Bleep.

Parachute wasn't exactly highly complex. Essentially, it was all about catching parachutists in a little row boat before they fell into the water to perish. The slightly more difficult version allowed the parachutists to get caught in trees, where they could also die. If you lost three, if I recall correctly, you had to start again. If you "won," you got a little fanfare. The sounds were so simple, they must have been incredibly annoying to those not engrossed in the gameplay. The graphics were simple, too, but mesmerising. Soothing repetitive movement that required a bit of thought and dexterity on a machine that was small and quiet enough to smuggle under the covers at night with a torch.

I loved my Game & Watch. I don't remember how long mine lasted, but evidently long enough to discover just how difficult it was to get lithium batteries at the time. I had to go to the jewellers. Had to watch patiently as they changed one exhausted battery for a fresh one. Paying over the amount. Anything to keep getting that little victory fanfare.

# # #

Timing matters a lot.

Computers arrived at my high school in my final year. We learned a bit of BASIC, and it seemed a lot of fuss just to get one computer to say "Hello" to another. It was the mid 1980s, and the future had yet to arrive.

At the time, I read SF obsessively. Computers in SF were great and could do the most amazing things. They could calculate space travel for generation star ships and combat craft. They made robots more human than human. They could even talk and have "breakdowns."

They did *so much more* than painstakingly say "Hello" to each other.

Home computers weren't entirely out of my family's budget, but my parents didn't really see the point of them. My university got a batch of Apple Macs in my final undergraduate year, but they only had word processing programs on them. Unless you were doing computer science (like I wasn't), you couldn't easily get computer games. The BBC Radiophonic Workshop experimented with computers making music and I loved what I heard on the telly shows they accompanied. But that was so far out of my reach, it may as well itself have been science fiction. I never even thought about how electronic music could become part of a computer game. The revolutions going on in computer gaming passed me by.

Which actually suited me fine at the time. If I was gaming, it was RPGs with real live people, but that's a whole other story.

# # #

After university, I moved out of home and into a house full of geeks. As inevitable as the soft drink cans and pizza boxes piling up, so was the household computer. One of my housemates had an Apple Mac loaded with monochrome, silent versions of some arcade classics like *Space Invaders*. When he wasn't playing them, I'd have a go.

Timing again. When those games were everywhere, I was just that little bit too young to go to where they were and play them. Just as well, because they probably would have wiped out my pocket money. Then, when I was old enough and had more finances, they had pretty much disappeared into places full of loud kids full of attitude, and rock music replaced the electronica I'd always been drawn to in those places.

The Apple Mac version of *Space Invaders* was enough to keep me entertained.

Then my girlfriend and I moved into our home together and we bought a PC. She was younger than me and had grown up with computers and computer games. We bought a few games that she liked, and I tried them out. None of them really grabbed my fancy. Anyway, they were her thing and she'd play them. I was busy writing.

We had dial-up internet at home and colleagues at my work excitedly spoke about *Doom* and some of the other of those first games that you could play with strangers or friends online. I don't know why, but we didn't buy them or even try them. Maybe it was because we were doing lots of other things. Building a life together. Making fanzines. Having fun with my friends who had become her friends.

I was a huge fan of the *Alien* films. My girlfriend bought me the *Alien Trilogy* PC game, probably knowing I'd play it obsessively and not notice how she was wooing new friends. She knew me better than I knew me, and so it was that I whiled away many, many evenings blasting aliens, chest bursters and face huggers like I was demon possessed, while she played the field, got me to agree to "a break" and then fell in love with the woman she's been with for over ten years now.

Ouch. Yes.

I played it first because I loved it. Loved how I could "be" Ripley with her pulse rifle and flamethrower. Hunt down those aliens in their various states of being – face hugger, chest burster and full-grown warrior – and shoot them dead, dancing away to try to avoid the acid rain of their blood. The music, which was a version of the soundtrack to the films I knew so well. My imagination and memory supplying what it didn't.

When the real world leaked in and I worked out what had happened (yes, I really was that clueless), I played the game for different reasons. It wasn't as crude as me imagining the aliens as her new friends, nor even her. More a distraction as my brain worked out everything. Understood her motives, and understood that my own feelings for her had shifted from lover to friend, longer ago than she had really noticed. I was angry at her at the time for not telling me, but angrier at myself for not getting it. My anger drove me to kill, kill, kill those aliens. The music ceased to be a thing. It was all about the killing.

She met and fell in love with the woman she is still with.

When she moved out with her stuff, I bought myself a way better computer and kept shooting at those face huggers. Blam, blam. Splat. Sometimes, they would fall back like spiders and wave their legs in the air. Then leap back up to attack. I'd often miss them and the screen standing in for my face would be hugged in that adorably fierce way face huggers have.

Spiders.

I have always been a touch arachnophobic, which made growing up in Australia particularly entertaining. Huntsmen spiders are rather large and entirely harmless, unless you're a cockroach or some other insect. There is something about the way they move, when they choose to move, that creeps some people out. Me included. I particularly don't like it when they flip over onto their backs, even if it means they're on their way out.

But, while spiders like huntsmen scare me, it's (mostly) an irrational fear. My fear does not mean I want to wipe all spiders from the planet. Not even huntsmen. Huntsmen are great at getting rid of other nasties and they are harmless to humans. While I would prefer it if they didn't meander into my bedroom, I was generally happy to share the planet with them.

... until I started to play the *Alien Trilogy* first-person shooter. Something about the unholy alliance between the repetition of the game play getting into my head, linking the creep-creep-leap, blam of the gun and then splatter of face huggers I'd shot dead in the game with huntsmen creep-creeping into the fear receptors of my brain. In real life, I didn't have a pulse rifle with grenade launcher that could stop those face-hugger-like spiders in their tracks.

It became a problem, so I stopped playing that game.

Actually, it was also because I resolved my differences with my ex. I recognised true love when I saw it. They are a real family now, and we are all friends. Her new friends became my friends, and our old friends became friends of us all. Yes. Really.

# # #

The Sims (2000) was my gateway drug to *Age of Empires*.

My ex-girlfriend's new friends introduced me to it. At first, I was hugely sceptical. My girlfriend had liked various versions of *Sim City* where you construct cities. I couldn't really see the point of that, and the options to destroy what you'd built were limited.

The Sims was a bit more interesting because you got into the lives of the characters whose towns you built. It had a jaunty little soundtrack, too, and it was fun to set up houses to fail or to fight with each other. Ultimately, though, I quickly lost patience with it. Whiny teenagers not wanting to take the garbage out and whiny 30-something men not wanting to go to work were all just a little bit too real-world. The music was just that little bit too saccharine pop pastiche for me, yet it wormed its way into my brain and my dreams. My dreams, once a great source for my music and my fiction, now consumed with the banal stories of gently swaying ordinary people and their pastel rom-com theme tunes. Too far to the sweet after the militaristic violence of the *Alien Trilogy* game.

Then I discovered *Age of Empires*.

# # #

Buying a new computer involves so many parts to the decision-making process. I'd had a PC for years; my last, a custom built one to accommodate my experiments in making electronic music and my *Age of Empires* addiction. But, travel beckoned. I needed a laptop that could withstand travel, and deal with my music. I did the research into all the PC laptops within my budget, and none suited what I needed. They seemed to be built for spreadsheets.

Someone suggested an Apple Mac. I checked them out. The model I wanted and could afford was compact and could deal with music *or* games. Not both.

I loved music and I loved games, but only one of them was keeping me awake all night. Eating up my writing time and social time. The repetitive little riffs sapping my creativity. Draining my attempts to make my own music.

It wasn't really a choice at all, and I haven't touched a computer game in over ten years, even though I've wanted to. The number of times I've stood in the Apple store looking at *Age of Empires*, debating the wisdom of giving in. Smiling as I remember the heroic riffs of my little guys doing the impossible.

Resisting the siren call of computer gaming gets easier over time, thankfully, and the music that once incessantly provided the soundtrack to my own dreams has faded into silence.

Almost.

Raising Gamers

Filamena Young is a professional writer, working as both a freelance and independently published game writer for more than five years. She's written and character designed for award-winning games including *Shelter in Place*, winner of the 2011 Judge's Spotlight ENnie. She is a cofounder and contributor to www.GamingasWomen.com, an award-winning blog that features women's voices in the analog gaming world. Her credits include the *Smallville High School Yearbook*, and books for the Vampire: The Requiem, Shadowrun, Dragon Age and Mistborn ranges, as well as numerous fiction anthologies. Currently, she's co-owner of Machine Age Productions. Fun game. There, she publishes major releases such as *Farewell to Fear*, many free games and games for young gamers such as *Flatpack: Fix the Future!*

I'm raising girls who dig gaming. My mother raised a girl who became a woman who digs gaming. In her case, the methodology was more of a pleasant happenstance; in my case, I'm doing it with intent.

So far, it's going along swimmingly. Like a mad gaming scientist, I'm having as much fun as I can raising my girls in an environment that encourages them to create, imagine and play the stories in their heads.

So how did my mom do it? How am I doing it? I'm so glad you asked!

The giant robots outside were decorated in roses and daisies, the light glinting off of their freshly polished chrome, that light streaming through the great round church window where I stood in a long gown with an even longer veil extended out behind me for about half a mile. I forget who I was marrying at the time; the groom was unimportant in the story, just one of the other robot pilots. This was about me. And when the invaders from… wherever they were from, exploded through the brick wall of the church on my *wedding day with their weapons and their sneering derision, I looked* awesome *destroying all of them from the cockpit of my giant robot in my wedding dress with daisies and roses flowing everywhere.*

Of course, this scene didn't actually happen. But I can remember it in my mind's eye as clearly as I can remember graduating from kindergarten, or my first day of first grade. Maybe more clearly. This particular game of pretend happened somewhere between age six and age eight. My mother had helped me with a veil made out of crocheted afghan, inspired by pictures I'd seen of my mother's hand-made hippie veil when she was married all those decades before.

My parents, both creatives, never batted an eye when I wanted to watch *Voltron* (which is where I got the giant robots, if you were wondering) as much as I wanted to watch *Strawberry Shortcake*. I was not only allowed to explore my creativity, I was encouraged. Sometimes my mother would ask me about the games of pretend she saw me playing. She did a great job of feigning interest.

When I first heard about roleplaying and *Dungeons & Dragons*, my parents picked up on it. They found me a box set that was older than I was, and my mother made cookies for the boys I invited over to play. I was allowed regular access to computers, to *Pool of Radiance*, to fiction and genre movies. They bought me a Nintendo and *Final Fantasy*. My mother (and father in some ways) created a girl who became a gamer.

From age two, my oldest wanted in on gaming. She, like me, was already playing pretend with dolls and tea sets. Common things for kids to do. But she also wanted to play the games we were playing. She wanted to roll dice and move miniature monsters and characters, and loved when we pretended to be people we weren't. She loved when we dressed up and LARP'd. In particular, she loved the guy who showed up dressed as a monster, a nicely suited green-skinned, red-eyed demon who spoke only in whispers. Whenever she saw him before the game got started, she'd run to hug him. As she got older, she started giving me roleplaying advice.

She's six as I write this, and, between watching her retell *Sailor Moon* stories by acting them out and playing store with her little sister, I got the idea she was ready for roleplaying.

I'm a gaming creative by trade these days. I write and design them for hire, or design a game from the ground up. So, naturally, when I sat down to play a game with my daughter, I had all these ideas in my head about what would make a good game for her. I was going to design a game for six year olds. Girls especially. What I didn't realize was, everything I knew about game design wasn't going to work here (not exactly), and I had entirely new things to learn and discover as we played.

Who's in Charge Here?

Now, I spend a lot of time in dirty hippy indie gamer land, where people experiment with all kinds of narratives in gaming, from GM-less to multiple GMs to all variations in-between. Still, I assumed that I was going need to take a heavy hand and guide the story. I thought I'd need to set scenes and guide plot and handle the non-player characters, and in many cases leave just the illusion of choice for her to have the most fun.

Boy, was I dumb.

I apparently forgot, from the years I spent telling children bedtime stories off the cuff, that I am not in charge of any story I tell a child. Never have been. Never will be. It is a child's very nature to tell stories, and they need an excuse, not a guiding hand.

It went something like this:

I set the scene. She had already defined some important things about her character. (She lived in a crystal cave with, apparently, a very nice kitchen set up.) I asked her what her character wanted to do today. She said, simply, "Help people." Well, that was illuminating on its own.

She told me there were bad guys who wanted to rob people. She told me how their parents hadn't raised them right. She began to tell me how she'd solve the problem and rush on to the end. I hurried after her, trying to get her to give me a second to build challenges for her character in a game sense.

She had no time for such silliness. The story was very clear to her from the get go, and, to be honest, the story was a beautiful one. So I just chased after her, asking questions where I could, and suggesting she roll dice along the way. That was our first attempt; it sent me happily flying back to the drawing board, and her off to her room to replay that story with her younger sister in tow.

Sucking, Well, Sucks

I stared at the dice. I thought about the stories we'd told while trying to game. For example, currently, my daughter tells us, she's actually from the future. She used a machine to go back in time and become my kid. She is also probably a robot. People in the future don't have internal organs and other squishy parts, but skeletons are okay. The future is very boring where all you do is fight monsters. She was, naturally, the best at fighting monsters. I assume she traveled back in time to stop that bleak future from happening; she claims it's just because there is no Disneyland in the future. She's very coy about her heroics. This is roleplaying: it's a thing all kids do, if they're allowed to. She's pretty creative, but not exceptional, in her desire to tell these stories.

But I was stuck on the dice. I was stuck on the game part of things.

We sat down to play again. I had a character sheet now with three traits. The traits were based on animals, and choosing which trait to use was based on the activities the animal favored. Smarts for the owl, the bear for acts of bravery, that sort of thing. I handed her the sheet, I explained it, she got the idea. I asked her, "What is your character okay at, what is your character great at, and what is your character no good at?" I had a whole thing in my head that she'd get tokens to spend when she tried things she was bad at. I'd reward her for taking risks. It would be great fun.

But she was stumped. She stared at her choices. She asked me to explain them again. I did. She told me her character wasn't bad at any of those things. She said her character was great at everything.

Which, for a six year old, makes sense. Why waste time in your story having a character do things they aren't good at? How do you get to the end if you don't do things right? She understands pretty well that in real life when she fails at something, that means she's learning, and she'll do better next time. That's pretty much the main conflict in her life these days. A world full of *things* to do, and she's not very good at most of them. Why would she want to emulate that in a game? In pretend-fun time, she wants her characters to succeed and do it with style.

How could I blame her for that? This, again, sent me back to the drawing board.

Respect the artifact that is the game pieces.

The next time we played, her three-year-old sister wanted in on the action. The little one had long been interested in what we were doing. She, like her little sister, loved dice and tokens. We use poker chips or sometimes glass aquarium stones. They cannot get enough of them.

So when we sat with a pile of dice and tokens, the little sister was immediately drawn our way. I told her she could help. I told the oldest she could spend a token, and that her little sister could act as a helper, adding dice to the pool.

Somewhere between tokens and extra dice coming into the challenge, it was magical. We told a story about a girl and her dragon. Dramatic deeds were done. I was onto something. And that "something" was the artifacts of the game appealing to the girls and drawing them to the game side of roleplaying.

There's magic in dice and tokens. They must have some kind of power, or else why would we keep using them? Why did we start using them? Why are there so many kinds? Sure, there's math in the answer, statistics and probability, but also magic, the artifacts of the game. I feel like you can make a game, play a game, with as many or as few artifacts as you want.

Math Problems

I had an okay system, I could have built a game on it, but I wanted to keep tinkering and see what else the girls could teach me. My six-year-old was learning math in kindergarten. Apparently, adding and playing with numbers struck a chord with her. As did Fudge Dice; that is, six-sided dice with pluses and minuses on their sides instead of numbers. She'd set up math problems for herself, using the dice to work them out. She was doing this unprompted. She was doing this because it was fun for her.

Girls are bad at math? Phooey.

I figured she was on to something again. I sat her down, handed her some tokens, her sister some dice. We talked about resolution. She was going to play Sailor Moon in a typical episode of *Sailor Moon*. I let her set up some other characters, some enemies, some conflict. Then I told her, as she came upon problems in the story, to solve math problems to get through them. She was *delighted* by this plan. Math was something she loved. Telling stories was something she loved. Spending time with mom and her sister was something she *really* loved. Put all of those in the same pot, cook 'em up and I've made her favorite meal.

At one point she told me: "That's not how it happens. Can I solve a problem and tell you how it happens?" You know I let her. In that moment, she leveled up as a gamer. Or maybe I did. I think I'll just call it a party win.

Yesterday, I was accidentally raised as a roleplayer.

Today, I'm telling you about the girls I raised to love gaming.

Tomorrow, I'll spend more time leveling us all up. I know our numbers are growing. Everyday, more and more of us are growing up to dig games.

Game Change

Linnea Dodson is a technical writer who has been in fannish culture since 1976. Her *Doctor Who* publications are the short story "God Send Me Well to Keep" (*The Qualities of Leadership*, Big Finish, 2008), and the essays "Greatest Coulrophobia in the Galaxy" (*Outside In: 160 New Perspectives on 160 Classic Doctor Who Stories by 160 Writers*, ATB Publishing, 2012) and "Conscious Colorblindness, Unconscious Racism" (*Doctor Who and Race*, Intellect Books, 2013). She also reviewed much of the Big Finish Doctor Who catalog for unreality-sf.net. In other fandoms and genres, she has published "Doctor Watson in the 21st Century" in *The Watsonian* #1 (JHW Society, 2013), "From Russia With Love" in *The Watsonian* #2 (JHW Society, 2014) and over 190 mystery novel reviews for reviewingtheevidence.net.

"Want to play a game of *Night of the Ill-Tempered Squirrel*?"

Admit it – that sounds a lot more interesting than "Want to play a game of *Trivial Pursuit*?" doesn't it?

Let me rephrase the question: is it more fun to spend an hour and a half of your life collecting rental fees a la *Monopoly*, or collecting political points by chopping off the right heads a la *Guillotine*?

When the commercial tabletop game businesses want to pander to fans, they slap photographs of familiar faces and props on the board, the cards, and the box. But with the possible exception of a specifically tailored card or two, the underlying game is exactly the same. *Star Trek Trivial Pursuit* plays like any other *Trivial Pursuit*. *Harry Potter Uno* is still *Uno*. *Sherlock Cluedo* may have British spellings, but it's otherwise indistinguishable from American *Clue* (which has not turned away the chance to adapt American media to its purposes; see *Scooby-Doo Clue*). And sometimes it's pretty clear that the big companies think that fans will fork over cash for *anything* as long as it has the show name on it. *Doctor Who Monopoly*? What possible connection is there between the Doctor and the game of blatant capitalism?

On the other hand, *Squirrel* and *Guillotine* are just two of the many tabletop games that, for lack of an official designation, could be called "artisan." The ones often crafted by a tiny company that only exists in the owner's basement and are sold by word of mouth or convention dealer's rooms. The ones that can dare to be totally different.

#

My first personal experience with an artisan game came at about 1:30 a.m. one January 1st – which gives you some idea of how easy *Cosmic Wimpout* is to play. All you do is keep rolling the dice, add up your score – and hope you don't wimp out and lose everything in that turn. That less-than-sober New Year's Day taught me that there was so much more out there to play than the same old titles that have been selling for decades. And I wanted more.

For years, I collected anything that fit my rules: it ought to have a smallish box (preferably one that could be tucked into my purse), provide fast play, and it absolutely *had* to have a compelling name. *Fishing for Terrorists*, a political rewrite of *Go Fish* that was wildly popular in the Washington DC area when it came out (from SlugFest Games). *Guillotine*, "The game where you win by getting a head," is a card game where you play an executioner during the French Revolution. You have three days (i.e., three rounds of condemned prisoners) in which to manipulate the execution line and thereby gain the most points for offing the most politically important victims (Wizards of the Coast). *Fluxx*, where the rules are... wait, has anyone played a rules card yet? We can't finish the game until someone plays a rules card! (Looney Labs). In *Night of the Ill-Tempered Squirrel*, you compete to make the world's worst B-movie; the best games end with not just a numerical score, but a recap of the failure of a flick (Alien Menace). *Captain Park's Imaginary Polar Expedition* is "imaginary" because the furthest he traveled was to an antique shop for fake proof of a false adventure, and you need to beat him and buy the stuff yourself without being caught (Cheapass Games).

Quite a change from standard tabletop games!

Then I discovered the tie-in games. Not the commercial tie-ins, but small-business tie-ins. *Chez Dork* by Steve Jackson Games was another collect-it-all-first competition, only this one is based on the group of fans starring in John Kovalic's webcomic *Dork Towers*. *Girl Genius: The Works* by James Earnest Games is a puzzle based on Phil Foglio's *Girl Genius* webcomic. By purchasing these, I was making a small difference directly for the people who created the things I enjoyed. Oh, it's a small investment in a small company – but contrast that with working with the big-box boys. When I buy a fannish game from the commercial producers, I'm not really supporting the show I love, I'm just tithing to the licensing departments of Hasbro and the BBC, and hoping some of it trickles down. Now, for a change, I had an option that allowed me to directly support in a tiny way the actual people producing what I liked. What a change!

Unfortunately, such support could be a sporadic, anemic thing for the game creators. With the "print first and hope someone buys it" marketing model, producers ran the risk of sinking their life savings into a game that then didn't make a profit. Cheapass Games was possibly the most blatant about attempting an end-run around this problem. They earned their name by selling a minimal package at rock-bottom prices. For less than $10, you got a black and white board, the rules and a list of "what you need" printed on the back of the box. Rather than asking you to spend money repurchasing dice, money or tokens with every game, they simply didn't include them. You had the choice of making a one-time purchase of the extras at Cheapass or simply scrounging the materials from what you already had on hand.

It was an innovative model for an innovative company (many of their games won industry awards), but it wasn't enough to save them. Cheapass collapsed in 2007, at which point it went even cheaper – many of their original games are still available on their website free for anyone willing to print their own copies.

It was Cheapass' revival five years later that introduced me to Kickstarter. Kickstarter, Indigogo and the rest of the internet crowdfunding sites changed the rules of funding. By making sure that producers could gather sufficient public interest and investors did not pay a penny until the entire project was fully funded, the potential for financial disaster was greatly reduced.

It also gave surprising power to game collectors like me. In the crowdfunding model, instead of spending the price of a game and just getting the game, I can spend the same amount and be part of a group that decides if the game ever gets to exist in the first place. But crowdfunding isn't just about spending the minimum to buy a minimal return. It includes increasing levels of incentives to tempt people to invest heavily in a product – and, in the case of tabletop games, those incentives include everything from public recognition to the ability to affect game play.

# # #

Cheapass' first foray into crowd funding was a deluxe version of *Exploding Cow*. (It's a card game where English cows with mad-cow disease are being run around French pastures to trigger leftover ordinance from the world wars. It's... rather hard to describe after that.) If you paid enough money, you got your name in the credits; if you paid more, you got to help name a cow.

Their second foray was *Deadwood Studios*. (You play an extra in a spaghetti Western factory trying to make enough money to get rich without being fired, injured, or upstaged.) The middle-tier Writer's Package incentive let you write one of the cards. The premium On Location incentive promised that the game creators would actually come to your house to play, leaving you with both the memories and an on-location sketch by artist Phil Foglio.

I didn't buy the On Location package. Nobody did, presumably to the relief of Phil Foglio and James Earnest. But several people bought the writer's package.

The third Kickstarter was *Kill Doctor Lucky*. (You want to sneak up behind him and kill him. You don't want anyone else to sneak up behind him and kill him. You don't want anyone witnessing it when you sneak up behind him and kill him. It is actually not that easy to sneak up behind him. He's named Lucky for a reason.) This was so popular that it not only reached target funding, but started reaching stretch goals (read: can we get even more money than we originally asked for?). The latest stretch goal promises to make a brand new prequel game, populated solely with characters chosen by the investors.

Crowdfunding is, quite literally, a game changer. And, with this new funding model, my status as a consumer of artisan tabletop games leveled up.

It leveled up for the game creators too, because it puts fans on an absolutely equal playing field with any other small-time producer. One of my next investments was in a card game called *Slash: Romance Without Boundaries* – a card game of the fanficcers, by the fanficcers, for the fanficcers. (It plays much like *Apples to Apples*: people lay down the names of characters and one player decides which two make the best couple.) As I write this essay, the Kickstarter Games page shows pitches for games tied to SF conventions, movie universes, dragons, mythology, zombies and time travel. (And that's just the games. The food category includes a pitch for someone wanting to produce police-box-shaped candy sprinkles.)

Up until this point, I haven't talked much about my gender. Artisan tabletop games don't tend to *be* gendered: the *Wimpout* dice don't care whose hand throws them; the *Guillotine* chops male and female alike.

But many commercial tabletop games *are* gendered. In the same manner that the big gaming companies assume that as a fan I will buy absolutely *anything* with a TARDIS printed on it – a misconception; I will merely buy *almost* anything – they think that the way to make me rush to buy a gender-neutral object is to make a girlie version that's 3 / 4 the size and painted Pepto-Bismol™ pink. "Shrink it and pink it" has been a marketing strategy for decades because, apparently, to a roomful of executives, no matter how much a girl likes strategy and intelligence games, at heart she's just a six-year-old pretty, pretty princess. Even more insultingly, at the same time they are treating adolescent players like little girls, they are treating little girls like sexualized women. Look at the changes of the board art in Candyland over the last 30 years: Princess Lolly has gone from an eight year old with a lollypop crown to an 18 year old with a lollypop-decorated strapless boob tube. At this rate, in another 30 years, she'll be Princess Lollita wearing a couple of pasties on sticks.

It's enough to make me reach for the Pepto Bismol for an entirely different reason.

And that's when crowdfunding changes the playing field again, because money is the ultimate equalizer. Just as fans can compete on an equal footing, so can feminists. And fannish feminists in particular are flooding to crowdfunding projects to provide viable alternatives for themselves and their children. When Anita Sarkeesian asked for funding for her movie project *Tropes vs Women in Video Games*, she was subjected to a vicious sexist backlash and became a rallying point for gaming feminists. Both rape threats and full funding came to her by the end of the day the project was announced. The Kickstarter for *Goldieblox*, a mechanical engineering toy meant for girls aged four to nine, didn't create such violent pushback, but it did generate a lot of controversy over gender presentation. Is it good enough to have a toy that teaches girls to build something without focusing on domesticity, or was Goldie's pink box and blonde hair enough to condemn her as another antifeminist stereotype?

Considering that fans are willing to argue over the details of a TV show for 50 years, a little controversy isn't going to scare women or our feminist allies from the market. At the time I write this, Kickstarter has concluded successful campaigns for such female-friendly fannish projects as *Miskatonic School for Girls* (build your opponent's deck in the Cthulu mythos), *Girl Genius and the Rats of Mechanicsburg* (an iOS/ Android gaming app based on the *Foglio* webcomic), *Fake Geek Girls: The Show* (a new webcomic) and *GTFO: A Film About Women in Gaming*.

True, Hasbro, Milton Bradley and Parker Brothers are hardly shaking in their shoes. The Lego Friends line keeps expanding. *Candyland* continues to have sweet sales figures. Disney Princesses march like a conquering army though *Monopoly, Trivial Pursuit* and so many more. These all sell at profitable numbers, because they wouldn't exist in the first place otherwise. Commercial companies are not sentimental. It's all about the bottom line.

But still, that bottom line has fundamentally changed, and changed in a manner that benefits the niche, the fannish, the feminist. It is now just as easy to go online and "preorder" an artisan game by funding a Kickstarter as it is to go online and preorder an upcoming commercial tabletop game. The money even gets charged to the same Amazon account! This will inevitably change the relationship between purchaser and producer, in ways that can't even be predicted yet. Crowdfunding is too new a concept for long term prognostication: Indigogo launched in 2008, Kickstarter and Fundly in 2009, GoFundMe in 2010.

I can't promise an upcoming fannish feminist utopia, in tabletop games or anywhere else. The market is a volatile place and crowdfunding itself is vulnerable to pressures and competition; FundAGeek barely lasted two years before failing. But I can promise that right now we're a lot closer than we've ever been to one. When we talk of the Golden Age of science fiction and comic books, we call them past eras, a history of the time when all things were possible and the market was booming. Well, the Golden Age of tabletop games is *right now*. Now is when you are so much more than just a passive consumer. Now is when your idea has equal footing. Now is when your investment makes a difference.

Now is when you are an equal voice in the marketplace. As a producer. As a consumer. As a fan. And as a feminist.

Chicks Dig Gaming

The Evolution of a LARPer in Three Acts

Johanna Mead has been writing and running RPGs for longer than some of her players have been alive, and she's not sure how she feels about that. Her other interests include costuming, writing and SF/F fandom. She lives near San Francisco with two cats, three sewing machines and almost too many books. Previously, she has contributed to *Chicks Dig Time Lords*, *Geek Girl Crafts Podzine* and *The Gazebo*. She invites you to read more of her LARP thoughts at www.johannamead.net and to follow her on Twitter as @ Britgeekgrrl.

Id

OMG! I have the coolest character idea ever! No one has ever done anything like this before! The other players will fall about me in amazement, gobsmacked by my awesomeness! I'm wearing bunny slippers and blowing a bubble pipe; *of course* my character is funny and interesting and everyone will want to talk to me!

Hmm, the gamemaster is paying an awful lot of attention to those players. I bet they're important to the plot! I think I'll go hang out around them and hope that some of the plot will rub off onto my character. Riding coattails is a legitimate approach to plot, right?

Those shoes are *so* my character. That skirt, too. And epaulettes are *in* again, I swear! C'mon, I'm pretty, isn't that enough to get your character playing along with mine? I know we're *supposed* to be enemies but, look! Epaulettes! And cute shoes!

This was not the most edifying period of my life.

But nor was it *all* bad, either...

New players! Hiya, new players! I'm a new player, too! Let's all play together! You don't know what to do? I'll find something for you! Look! I found a slice of plot pie! Would you like a bite? It's delicious! Let's all nom on the plot pie!

In fact, looking back, it wasn't unlike being a Labrador puppy. A lot of fun in small doses, but with a tendency to tear up the furniture when it feels like it's being ignored.

After the *pay attention to me!* phase came...

Ego

If I can't solve every mystery I encounter, win every challenge and unsnarl every plot-tangle my character comes across, I've failed as a player. Oh, sure, the game isn't a win-or-lose thing. But if I haven't *won*, doesn't that mean I've *lost*?

Every single character I play *must* have a fully realized history. I know where they grew up, their childhood hobbies, what they dreamed about in school. The highs and lows of their life to date must be recorded in significant detail. Not only that, but I can tell you how they dress, what they like on their pizza, how they felt when the local team won the pennant. And I will painstakingly craft a dozen "kick me" signs and place them on my character's back, hoping the GM will find just one of them useful when reaching for an idea.

(It took me a while to grasp the notion of quality over quantity when it came to character creation. In fact, I'm still getting the hang of it.)

I'm smart. I've got ideas. I can run a better game than that guy. I can create more compelling settings than any other GM in my vicinity. Just watch me. The more players in my troupe, the more successful I am, right?

If I can't keep every single player happy all of the time, I have failed as a GM. And then I will bend over backward trying to keep everyone happy. You *really* want to play that character that is so far outside the game boundaries that they can't be seen with a telescope? Oh... alright. You're going to quit if I don't retcon that undesirable outcome for your PC? Oh... alright. You want your new-to-gaming significant other to have a character with just as many points and just as much plot-pull as your veteran PC? Oh... alright.

My first LARP campaign fell apart after two years because I had confused *gamemaster* with *doormat*.

But, like the newt in *The Holy Grail*, I got better.

Failure makes a character more interesting. If the first rule of LARPing is *get into trouble* and the second rule is *get into more trouble*, then the third rule is *be willing to fail*. Some of my best moments as a player have happened because I botched a rule, or even because I *volunteered* to blow it at a critical moment, just because I thought it would make for a more interesting story. It usually did.

Players need boundaries to fully enjoy the game. If I declare that I'm running a complex political drama based on the work of Frank Herbert,

I'm within my rights to say *no* to the guy who wants to play something out of *Spaceballs*. That player might think he's hilarious, he might even have a good time, but the other players won't and I certainly won't. *Because I said so* is a valid ruling.

Both players and GMs have responsibilities to the game, and many of them are held in common: a cooperative spirit, a willingness to accommodate a change in plans, good gamesmanship and even punctuality. As a player, I agree to abide by the spirit and the rules of the setting, to not have a tantrum when I don't get my way, and to offer constructive feedback in a timely manner. As a GM, I will endeavor to entertain my players for a few hours with a coherent plot featuring balanced NPCs and sufficient in-game challenges. I want the players to feel like they've really done something at the end of the event.

However...

That time I ran a game and made that guy cry, in-character? The guy who's known for being the hardest-bitten LARPer west of the Rockies? The same game where the players threatened me with their therapy bills? I know I *said* I was sorry for the trauma, but actually I wasn't. I'm pretty certain my repentant expression post-game was not entirely unlike that of Orson Welles "apologizing" for the *War of the Worlds* broadcast.

And then I realized that there was still more to learn.

Superego

I firmly believe that a LARP isn't about winning or losing. But, to be honest, I'm a softie and when I'm running a game, I want the players to "win." That isn't to say I don't I often end up wishing I could have challenged the players a little more before they made mincemeat of my plot! As mentioned earlier, my primary responsibility is to entertain the participants for a fixed amount of time, and, classically, a lot of that entertainment relies on unraveling the plot. I think I've presented them with a Gordian knot, and the players have the sword of Alexander under their trench coats.

Oh, dear. The plot survived exactly two hours' interaction with the playership. Can the other GMs please talk to me, so we can figure out where it goes from here? We can't have them sitting around singing *Give Peace a Chance* for three more hours, can we? Who just made the suggestion that the sweet schoolteacher is actually an avatar of the Creeping Evil? You're awesome! Run with it! No, never mind what I had in mind – it clearly wasn't going to work out, anyways.

My players have saved my plot's butt more often than I should admit, simply by coming up with a twist I didn't anticipate. Much to my relief, I know I'm not the only GM to admit this.

I have a meticulously crafted list of personal victory and defeat conditions for my character. If I don't meet those then, clearly, I'm a dreadful player and I should just never... what's that? The Big Bad did *what* to my character? That's really dreadful and... um, kind of cool, actually. Let me go rig an eye-patch and borrow a crutch from the infirmary. I can make this work!

Yes, I have meticulously picked out every single thing I'm wearing and every piece of jewelry means something to my character. You don't care? That's cool. You don't have to ask about it if you don't want to. Hey, what's the deal with that pocket watch you look at all the time? Can you tell me? You can't because it's cursed? Why is it cursed? You're not sure? Let's find out!

And I'm back to the puppy phase again. But this time, I'm housebroken.

Black Windows

E. Lily Yu received the 2012 John W. Campbell Award for Best New Writer. Her fiction has appeared in *McSweeney's, Kenyon Review Online, Clarkesworld* and *The Best Science Fiction and Fantasy of the Year* among other places, and has been nominated for the Hugo, Nebula, Sturgeon and World Fantasy Awards. She has written for the Bungie game *Destiny* and for Tale of Tales.

I was 11 or so when my friend Lei introduced me to a text-based MUD called *Cardea*. My first task, once I had been born into the white-lettered world, was to retrieve a stick for a character who was essentially a sentence on the screen. Said character elongated into a paragraph if you looked at him.

I had to bring him his stick by typing in a baffling sequence of *w, e, s, ne, sw*, which Lei reeled off to me, then *get stick*, then *give stick to*. Very quickly, I discovered that the stick vanished if you left the game, as did various other desirable items, pearls and dead rabbits and so on – which was depressing, if educational.

Lei walked me through the basic actions and demonstrated how to skin, cook and eat a rabbit. This was only the word *rabbit* in white on a black screen. But the word changed as it went from a living rabbit (unsympathetic to my newborn hunger and dispatched with a cudgel) to dead rabbit to skinned rabbit to cooked rabbit (put into a fire, which required tinder and flint). You could do things to this word, *rabbit*.

I ate my rabbit. And for all that it was a word and a shred of code, I could taste it.

Without my friend and guide, playing alone on a computer in the public library, I got hopelessly lost. On my own, I racked my brains to figure out where and how to buy a cudgel, clothes and a backpack, and how to put one's gold talons and specific objects in one's backpack. The game required a specific syntax and was unforgiving of errors. After a short struggle, I left *Cardea*. When I looked for it recently, I found out that it had died some time ago, as MUDs tend to do, like so many soap-bubble universes. But I remember my rabbit.

#

Not until high school did my family set up an internet connection. As soon as they did, I found an online index of MUDs and skimmed through them one by one, puzzling out syntax and basic mechanics and dipping a toe into each new world. The black Telnet window became a second home. I learned to parse the ASCII art and maps that at first had confused me: tildes were ocean waves; asterisks were cities, forests or scrub in a desert; roads were hyphens or equals signs; your character and your place in the world was an ampersand or an O.

I remember in particular one neon-colored world, my first encounter with ANSI colors, where the first thing I learned was a savage ability called *backstab*, executed by typing *bs*. The only way I could leave a mark on this riotously colorful world, I discovered, was by slashing at seagulls, then people. Some of them fought back. That was a short and bloody visit.

Materia Magica was the first MUD I stayed in. Its world was bewilderingly large, provided with oceans in which you could drown or sail, towns where you could buy and sell, twisting quests you could perform for gold and honor, and so on. I was enchanted at first by its sense of humor and tickled by its allusions to Terry Pratchett, from the existence of a skeletal horse named Binky to the possession of a Magical Luggage of my own. The game was based on killing NPCs over and over and taking whatever they dropped when they died. For a cranky adolescent, that was satisfying for a time. But bloodlust and perpetual errand-running eventually lost their appeal.

Thinking back now, having created and killed off so many characters of my own, I'm appalled at the carelessness with which I butchered guards, animals, crooks and citizens, characters with names and personalities, never mind that they were up and walking around again within hours of falling bloody at my feet. Characters ought, I think, to be murdered with more narrative consideration.

#

I arrived in Achaea next, looking for something deeper. There, I lived several different lives in different bodies, settling eventually on a priestess who blessed and healed her fellow citizens at the gates to their city. It was in Achaea that I learned both the delightfully efficient aliasing of combat commands and practical reflexive triggers, which were daisy-chained actions for dealing with pickpockets and assailants. The latter fired when the Telnet client matched one of several lines of text that signaled an imminent text. When someone tripped those reflexes, faster than I could read or react, my character fought free of snares and fled in any available direction, the adrenaline kick coming only after he or she had run several rooms away, as I was trying to understand what had happened.

By now, the geography of these worlds was no longer cryptic, but, in *Achaea*, the writers and players had put together dense, compendious political and religious systems, which were much harder to navigate than sequences of rooms. I acquired at least one inflexible theological enemy. The result of this depth of background and the worldwide agreement to strict roleplaying was a strange kind of immersion. There was the white text and the black screen. There was the sentence that was my character. And there was the lush and vivid world that was neither of these things, that existed nowhere outside of my head, but that sprang forth in rich detail in my mind.

My priestess bought and wore flowers, perfume, and ridiculous outfits in ridiculous colors, none of which I would wear in real life, none of which were more than a few words and lines of code, and yet I saw and smelled them. She was someone I wasn't. She said things I would never say and acted in ways I would never act. She got falling-down drunk in the game long before I ever tasted alcohol. (A delightful feature: after enough glasses the room would start to spin, any words you spoke came out garbled, you'd lose your balance and fall over, and, eventually, if you drank enough, you died of alcohol poisoning.) I reveled in all of it.

When I left, it was not because of boredom, or because the black-and-white dream had broken. I had a hunting partner who helped me bag game and level up, who happened to be sworn to all the dark and unholy powers. For a priestess of the pure and good, our friendship was politically incorrect. But he was pleasant to be around, patient and crackling with jokes. He seemed, suddenly, to be on the brink of declaring his love for my character. I was about 14, and I'd never been kissed by a boy. Since I myself had puppeted winged men and male druids, I knew there was no telling whether my hunting partner hid a 60-year-old woman or a 12-year-old boy.

Did I want my first romance, even if it was imaginary, even if was by proxy, to happen in this flat black world? Did I want to fall that deep and that far into other people's dreams? It might have been as harmless as falling in love in a novel through the protagonist's eyes. But there was no ending, and a game was not a book.

I put everything I had into a charity box, logged off and disappeared.

# # #

The next MUD I tried was *Armageddon*. I knew one of the staff, though we hadn't met in person, and I had been curious. The login screen had a vivid piece of ASCII art in the shape of an ant's head, or an insect like an ant, with elbowed antennae and mandibles. To play, I applied to have a character created, submitting a brief history and description, and waited for a staff member to approve it.

My male dwarf lumberjack eked out a wretched existence by felling trees, chop by laborious chop, then hauling the logs back to town to sell. The game made sure you felt the heft of the wood: dragging a log from place to place took forever.

Armageddon was designed to be a bleak, barren world. But I scraped along well enough for a while, until the day I left him idling in the woods to do something or other in the house. When I came back to the computer I found, in a scrolling recitation of white text on black, a moment-by-moment account of how halflings had caught my dwarf, poisoned and paralyzed him, dragged him through the woods, and then eaten him for dinner. He was awake and alert for all of this. The events were recounted to me in the second person, which was not a little disturbing.

Death was permanent in that world. There was no save point, no resurrection, no restart with a small penalty. I came face to face with the black, silent end of things. As in life, there was no restart. You were issued one entrance ticket, one and only one, and it might be ripped from your hands just as arbitrarily.

As I sat staring at the Telnet window, I could understand the desire to hand out multiple lives and endless restarts in any game with death in it. To do otherwise would be to imitate life in its most fixed and implacable aspect. A game is premised on play, and play naturally implies minimal consequences and reversible mistakes. In a game, there is the freedom to experiment without fear. A game incorporating permanent death departs from the idea of a game and approaches art, or philosophy, or something else altogether. It was too much for me.

Other MUDs have subtler but equally unsettling approximations of life. As in a kind of fairyland, time passes faster in most MUDs than in the real world, a feature that acts much like a cinematic clock with spinning hands, pointing to the real hours and days dripping away. I returned to Achaea once, more than a year after I left. By then, my character had become an old, old woman whose clothes had long since decayed, requiring a brief dive into the charity box for the sake of decency. I looked up my old hunting partner, out of curiosity. He was married now, and to all appearances prosperous and happy.

I logged off. I was 16, I think, but I felt much older.

#

When I went to college, I left all of those games behind. I studied; I wrote; I traveled; I worked; I lived. I all but forgot the black windows and white-lettered worlds I had wandered through.

One night in spring of my senior year, I ended up in Boston. I was staying for a couple nights at a friend's place; the same friend, incidentally, who had taught me to catch and cook rabbits ten years earlier. She had moved to the city for college and remained there afterwards. That night, I opened a short, plain e-mail informing me that one of my stories had been nominated for a Hugo Award. Life seemed briefly and shimmeringly unreal.

A great deal of time had passed since the day she helped me catch and cook and eat a rabbit made of white words. She was a gifted artist. She would shortly begin working at a local hospital. We talked about the difficulty of doing creative work for a living, the exigencies of life right out of college, the tensions between working for love and working for money.

When our conversation reached a natural lull, she pulled up on her computer a black window with white text and ASCII art in the familiar shape of an insect's head.

"Is that *Armageddon?*"

It was.

#

For the past nine months, I have been working at a game-development studio, writing names for artifacts, weapons, pieces of armor, ships and NPCs. There is no black Telnet window. There is no blinking cursor. Our game will be vivid, with microscopically perfect art and rousing music, as all console games must be these days. Most of these dreams fall between the gorgeous and the sublime. Little is left to the player's imagination. Even MUDs are slicker products now, with music and clickable buttons instead of a blinking command line.

There was a strange and satisfying freedom in the poverty of white text in black windows, which the imagination could render more brilliantly and persuasively than any physics engine. I miss it. But I haven't gone back. I couldn't tell you the name of that former hunting partner. I couldn't tell you the names of the characters I played. I've lost them on my way.

Chicks Dig Gaming

Another Puzzle Solved?: Professor Layton and the Passive Princess

Mags L. Halliday started gaming when you had to do all that business with loading them off cassettes. She has written for and about Doctor Who, Faction Paradox, Bernice Summerfield and Iris Wildthyme. She also helped to form a couple of female networking groups – one in *Doctor Who* fandom and one for creative women in her home city. She currently works as a civil servant, having given up being a scientific doctor's assistant. Yes, really. The hours were terrible. She lives in Devon with husband and fellow gamer Mark Clapham and their young daughter, who like playing *Mario Kart*. She can be found at magslhalliday.co.uk

Since I first scored a perfect Tetris on an arcade machine in the 1980s, I've been prone to getting addicted to puzzle games. The introduction of narrative puzzle quests suited me entirely, given I also played the Hitchhiker's game back in the days when you had to load it into a BBC Micro off floppy disks. And so it shouldn't be a surprise that I was initially smitten with the Professor Layton games on the Nintendo DS.

Then I started to have doubts.

Professor Layton is a hybrid adventure/ puzzle game format, in which the player explores a world within set parameters. Your mission is to find and solve simple puzzles, which in turn unlock the bigger "mysteries." As this is a DS game, exploring takes the form of tapping everything in sight until you find hint coins or puzzles. It also involves set conversations with characters you encounter and rather more tedious walking around than is necessary. There's some non-essential mini-games to collect as well, and the occasional cut scene.

The Layton world is also a stunningly lovely design job. Nominally set in Western Europe, it really belongs in the same Japanese fantasy Europe as a lot of Studio Ghibli films. It also recalls the grotesques of *Belleville Rendevouz* (the best animated film about the Tour de France ever). This is a Europe of tiny lanes and alleyways, steampunk trains, fairy tale castles and fog. It has accordion music in the soundtrack. The first time

I loaded it, I laughed out loud at the opening cut scene.

Professor Layton, the lead character, is an English don with a penchant for solving puzzles (and never removing his top hat). Quite how he makes a living is a tad unclear, but I've always presumed, given the relationship he has with an incompetent Scotland Yard inspector, that he is a consulting detective.

All consulting detectives need a companion, in part because otherwise your lead character has no-one to explain things to. Layton is accompanied by a young boy, Luke. Luke wears shorts and a flat cap, and rapidly becomes the second-most-annoying character in the series, with his endless cries of "Layton's Apprentice Saves the Day!"

That brings me on to the *most* annoying character in the series, the one who made me start questioning how comfortable I was playing the Layton universe. And how comfortable I might feel if my daughter picked it up.

Puzzle games are one of the more popular game genres for girls. They lay an emphasis on using brain over brawn, problem-solving over shooting things up. Unlike, say, *Grand Theft Auto*, female players are not expected to defend their playing of a game that is perceived as masculine.

You do get gender-stereotypes in your choice of character, though. Play as a male character and you can be all kinds of body shapes. Play as a female character, and expect cleavage and clothing that surely must chafe. For example, my warrior in *Puzzle Quest* wears both a semi-transparent face veil and skimpy armour. Which strikes me as not the most practical fashion choice for killing orcs and trolls.

There's Something About Flora

In *Professor Layton and the Curious Village*[5], the debut title, Layton and Luke arrive in a moated village loomed over by a dark and spooky tower. A treasure is said to be hidden within, and, after 120 puzzles and a battle against Layton's adversary, they reach it.

It's a young girl.

You can see the logic within the game's narrative: it's as much about fairy tales and ghost stories as anything, so a Rapunzel-style passive princess should not be a surprise. In fact, combined with the moustache-twirling villain and his balloon, the whole finale reminded me most of Penelope Pitstop. In itself, that could fit with the vague retro feel of the

---

5 The names used here are the UK ones, as those are the version I've played. The games sometimes have a different name in the US.

Layton world, but...

Flora is presented as totally lacking in agency.

Like so many characters that Layton meets, she loves a good puzzle. Yet she has never investigated how she's ended up trapped, nor how to escape her luxurious prison. I've been known to explain to my girl how Rapunzel could have cut off her own hair and escaped the tower. Penelope Pitstop frequently got herself out of trouble with her itty-bitty hairpin. Flora is rescued, but you do wonder if she's that bothered.

Throughout *The Curious Village*, the player is either playing Layton or Luke, and this role play is dictated by the game. The only way to progress the game, and the story, is through their actions. Flora, along with all the other characters, is not able to progress the story herself but is dependent on Layton and Luke.

As this is in line with all the other secondary characters in *The Curious Village*, it's not a series-killing problem at this stage. It's not great that a girl is presented as a valuable treasure to be locked away in a tower as a passive princess, but at least her non-playability fits with how everyone else is treated. No, the problem with Flora really kicks in when she returns in the sequel.

The second game, *Professor Layton and Pandora's Box*, was released in Europe in 2009. It opens in a Layton version of London, which, naturally, I loved. Layton and Luke set off on a train journey, with all the allusions to Golden Era European Detective fiction someone could wish for. It seems to be repeating the narrative structure of *The Curious Village*, with the detective and his sidekick off to explore the mysterious new location of Dropstone.

Rather to my surprise, Flora pops up on the train. She'd hidden away so she could come with them, despite Layton having said it was too dangerous. This seemed like a development in the right direction, I thought, as Flora has become active. She's inserting herself into their boys' own story, against their ideas about what is an acceptable role for a girl.

She sets about solving puzzles, effectively becoming a playable character and someone who drives the game and story onwards. Maybe not my kind of playable character, but still this seems like a positive development.

At which point, Flora is kidnapped by Don Paolo, the plain-dealing villain from *The Curious Village*. He then disguises himself as her and heads on to the next town with Layton and Luke, leaving Flora tied up in Dropstone. She has been forcefully kicked out of the story once more, incidentally demonstrating that puzzle-questing is too dangerous for girls.

Flora is again banished to being a pawn in the epic on-going fight between Layton and Don Paolo, someone who is patronised by the hero and assaulted by the villain. You could argue that anyone in the sidekick role in these narratives is at risk of being used by the villain to attack the hero, irrespective of their gender. But the better sidekick to have sidelined and then impersonated in this instance would have been Luke.

In 2010, *Professor Layton and the Lost Future* was released in Europe. It may tell you something about gaming and the gamer community that a major selling point was that Layton removes his iconic hat.

Layton and Luke attend the unveiling of a time machine, at which the inventor Doctor Stahngun and Prime Minister Bill Hawks disappear. Investigating, they find a clock shop that apparently contains a time machine that sends them ten years into the future and into a fully steampunked London. A future version of Luke explains that, in this reality, Layton has turned bad and is the head of a criminal gang.

After the usual running about being set puzzles, we discover future Layton is actually Dimitri Allen, who had also disguised himself as Stahngun. Allen, along with Layton and Don Paolo, had all been attracted to Claire Folley. Her death, before the events of *The Curious Village*, had triggered the bad blood between Layton and Don Paolo. Her younger sister Celeste is working for Allen, but switches sides to help Layton.

Future Luke is revealed to be the main villain, and is actually someone called Clive, whose parents died in the same accident as Claire. The steampunk future is, in fact, an elaborate underground lair that takes to the air. Layton and the others deactivate it by reversing the polarity of the neutron flow, or some such pseudo-science.

And, once again, Flora is annoyed that the boys are excluding her from their adventures. She follows them into the future and is kidnapped, this time by the arch-villain Clive. And, to the surprise of no one, she has to be rescued by Layton and Luke.

The fundamental problem with Flora is that she is shown as an ineffective member of the team: the two male characters are happy to ditch her, she's easily overcome physically and she spends way too much time waiting to be rescued. She's supposed to be Layton's other apprentice, but she is given no agency and no status. Luke appears on the covers of the games; Flora doesn't. She is nothing more than a pawn in the games.

Perhaps the only redeeming element to such a reactionary female stereotype is that Flora loves to cook, but isn't very good at it. It doesn't really balance out the fact that she'd been the worst kind of passive princess for 50 hours of gameplay.

Women in Refrigerators

The first three games do have other female characters. *The Curious Village* has a matriarchal aristocrat, Lady Dahlia, who seems remarkably unfussed that her young daughter has been locked in a tower by her dead husband. *Pandora's Box* has both a town founded by a woman, Sophia, and a secondary female character, Katvia. The flaw there is that the town's founder fled her original village when she discovered she was pregnant out of wedlock. And Katvia, despite also being on a quest, acts primarily as an exposition device and peacemaker.

The most significant other female character in the first trilogy is, however, Claire Folley in *The Lost Future*. Claire drives the story, and is revealed to have been driving the whole arc of the first three games. Claire, in case you missed it in *The Lost Future* plot summary earlier, is dead.

Claire was such a perfect woman that Layton, Don Paulo and Allen fell in love with her when they were all at university together. Her death, told through flashback, is the trigger to both Don Paulo's evil and his rivalry with Layton. It's also implied that her death drove Layton into being a puzzle-solving genius.

This plot device, the idea that the death or maiming of their love is a key driver for a male antagonist, is known in pop culture circles as the "women in refrigerators" device. This phrase was first used by Gail Simone in 1999, when she noticed that female superheroes in comics were frequently maimed, killed or depowered not as part of their own character's development, but to enable their male boyfriend's development. The phrase itself comes from the fate of Alex deWitt in the *Green Lantern* series, who was found, by the eponymous hero, dead and stuffed in a refrigerator.

Even earlier, female fans of male genres noticed "dead girlfriend of the week" syndrome: where female love interests were introduced solely so their death gave a lead male character something to brood about. Female characters who are denigrated and dismissed from the story for the sake of male characters' development are now referred to by feminist critics as having been "fridged."

In short, the existence of Claire as a motivator for Layton's character is not a surprise; it's entirely obvious.

Claire was a prize to be fought over in the past, her preference for Layton triggering the villainy of Don Paulo. As a crucial character who only exists in the past, her defining characteristic is her deadness. She can play no active part in the plot resolution, and has no choices open to her. She's been fridged.

Except, spoiler alert, Claire is alive. Her "sister" Celeste is, in fact, Claire. The explosion of Allen's prototype time machine, which was thought to have killed her, actually threw her into her future (our present). Layton's classic "tragic past" can be resolved if he can solve the puzzles. Claire/Celeste is another female character offered as a prize/reward (this time with added romance).

Even better, Claire/Celeste is offered a choice, which suggests she is being granted narrative agency. Except the choice is to stay with Layton and allow London to be destroyed, or to throw herself back in time to really die in that original explosion.

Oh.

That's not much of a choice, really.

Naturally, Claire/Celeste chooses to die. And it's at that point that the much-hyped hat-removal happens.

Emmy, We're Needed

So far, I've focussed on the problems in the first trilogy of games. The trilogy ends with Luke's family moving away, taking Luke with them and ending his apprenticeship. Still, that won't be the end of things, surely? The twice-heartbroken Layton can continue on his puzzle quests with his other apprentice, Flora, right?

The fourth release is, in fact, the first of a series of prequels set before *The Curious Village*. In 2011's *The Spectre's Call*, Layton and his assistant, Emmy Altava, travel to the mysterious village of Misthallery to find out what hideous monster lurks in the fog and why Layton's old friend Clark is behaving so oddly. Each monstrous attack is preceded by eerie unearthly music.

Layton and Emmy investigate through the usual series of games, mini-games and mind-numbing walking about a cityscape. They encounter Clark's young son, Luke, who loves solving a good puzzle and who has been taking notes about the monster's appearances.

They also meet a gang of young tearaways (a whole other essay could be written about the debt Layton owes to Sherlock Holmes), and an ill, anti-social girl, Arianna. It turns out that Arianna plays a flute that controls a gentle dinosaur-like creature, Loosha. They are defending the town against robots controlled by a mysterious new villain.

This feels like a reaction to the problems of Flora. By going back in time to answer an obvious question thrown up in the first trilogy (why is Luke Layton's apprentice?), the story can also give Layton a more active female assistant.

Emmy is a young woman rather than a girl. She is confident, and will disagree with the professor. She drives her own scooter about the place rather than being driven around by Layton in his 2CV. She's also physically capable: rather than being routinely kidnapped, she fights off attackers easily.

At last, we have a female character who actually carries a chunky section of the story when she goes back to London to carry out some research. During the big boss battle at the end, she has four puzzles to solve to disable the megarobot, compared to the single one Luke tackles.

And, finally, we get a female character as one of the leads on the box art.

This should be great. It should resolve the problem of the passive princess by creating a sassy modern woman who ticks all the boxes. That, in a way, is the problem. Although Emmy is given agency and much more puzzle-solving chances, she doesn't actually bring anything back from the London trip besides her creepy stalker detective from Scotland Yard.

And you don't feel Layton approves of her physical prowess. In *The Lost Future*, the Professor uses violence at one point and it felt uncomfortable. Layton sets great store in being a gentleman, being civilised and using brain over brawn. So his violence felt uncomfortable and Emmy, when she is introduced, also goes against the grain. It is possible to be an empowered, active woman without being Mrs Peel.

Another Puzzle Solved...

Why does any of this matter? The Layton series are games that promote brains and civility over brawn and snarky one-liners. It's a series that doesn't feature in mainstream media's stereotyping stories of games as triggers for real-world violence and crime. It's nice. Your gran might play it, or your young children.

And that is precisely why it matters. If you accept the premise that our culture both reveals our values, and embeds them in us, then an innocuous game that reinforces gender-stereotypes tells us more about our culture than is entirely comfortable.

It's easy to dismiss sexism in the triple-A titles. Of course various crime titles have women as strippers, prostitutes and drug-addicts, because that's the cultural genre they are in. The *Grand Theft Auto* series plays with the iconography of American gang culture, and all the possible sexist tropes within that. It's also easy to dismiss it on the grounds that the target market is adolescent boys and young men with lots of time and disposable income. Playing into their juvenile concepts of women is, if not acceptable, understandable.

Professor Layton insinuates gender-stereotypes into a much younger audience, creating in children – both male and female – the idea that women are passive characters in male stories. They exist to be rescued, kidnapped, pined for, killed or frowned at for failing to do any of that. They are punished for taking action, whether that's Flora being kidnapped after not listening to Layton or Sophia losing everything because she dared to have sex.

I've spent about 60 hours in the Layton series so far, which equates to nearly a whole US season of a TV series. That's a lot of time, and a lot of subtle reinforcement that women are either prizes to be fought over, delicate flowers or both.

This, fundamentally, is why my love of the Layton universe has become so tempered. I'd stopped playing *Spectre's Call* partway through, and only finished it so I could write this essay. I've not felt the urge to buy a 3DS to play the next instalment, and I'd no longer recommend the series to young gamers.

Chicks Dig Gaming
An Axe Up My Sleeve

Cheryl Twist is a mild-mannered bookkeeper with a first degree black belt in American Kenpo Karate. On weekends, she trades her ledgers for RPG rulebooks. She runs a good dungeon crawl and gives vivid descriptions of the death blows, even if they're not asked for. Keenly fond of dice and game tokens, she will often play board games just for the chance to organize them properly in their boxes. She can also deliver a roundhouse kick whilst quoting Tolkien.

We stood at the broken stone doors of the Desecrated Vault. We knew Blackfang the Dragon was in there and we had to go get him. The Ranger tested the string of his bow. The Wizard flexed his casting fingers. I, the Fighter, rested my hand on the hilt of my sword, shoulders back and chest puffed out. The Paladin was reassuring the wee gnome Druid.

We stepped in past the crumbling masonry. Time was short. We turned each corner dreading to see our quarry, disappointed when we didn't. We found a dagger, fought a Shadow, almost fell into a pit trap. I discovered a spell scroll, but hadn't the wits to use it. Last chance. The gnome druid was up. He toed his way into the next room. Evil eyes glowed in the torchlight. Blackfang the Dragon reared up and hurled his acid breath at all of us.

The sizzling fizzled away and the Gnome considered his options. No weapon. No attack spells. He had a dog, a blessing, a tome of knowledge and a spyglass. He also had us. The Wizard cast Strength; the Paladin added a Blessing; the Ranger drew his bow; my fighter's awe-inspiring presence gives anyone in combat a surge of battle-fury.

Backed and Blessed by his companions, the Druid hurled himself at the dragon and punched him in the eye, driving his fist into his brain. The dragon died. We won! We laughed, out loud and vigorously, full of shock and amazement that it had worked. No one had expected that the smallest and wisest member of the party could, or would, punch a dragon to death.

#

All this drama arose from a session of the *Pathfinder Adventure Card Game*. Our group usually plays the Pathfinder RPG, pen-and-paper style. It's a *Dungeons & Dragons*-style game. I am the dungeon master. My players say I fit well in the role. I suspect it's my cackling and wide grin when I'm rolling damage dice. That's what they see. Not seen is my dungeon master "laboratory." That's me on the couch, communing with piles of open books, customizing a magic item for their loot drop. It all takes time. And thinking. On the weekend.

The *Pathfinder Adventure Card Game* needs no dungeon master. It uses cards to set up the story. So I am free to play and I have a huge box of cards to look at. Each adventure has its own set of unique location decks. The Waterfront, Warrens, Nettle Maze and Treacherous Cave are all places you'll visit – but wouldn't, if you were smart. The cards are beautiful. Artwork, descriptions, statistics. Yes, statistics are beautiful. I will not concede that point.

Characters also have decks of cards. The Wizard has cards for spells and useful items. My fighter has cards for weapons, armor and for glaring at the idiot hogging an extra seat on the bus. Oh wait, that's not my Fighter, that's me. But that could be a fun card to have, in my real life. I want that card. There are others...

Card title: Stink-Eye of Severity
Artwork: There should be a pair of eyes in a seraphic face, three quarters profile. The far eye will appear normal. The near one will be alarmingly wide, with an arched brow. Twitch lines will denote frequent spasms.

Spell-Like Ability: Compulsion. Target creature receives Will Save against Difficulty equal to character's age plus the number of tote bags she is carrying.

Effect: Target feels the cold dread of prey under a raptor's gaze and moves her oversize purse from the seat to her lap.

That's the intended effect. But since compulsion effects only work against creatures with intelligence, public transit might not be a target-rich environment. The people I encounter might be stupid, but so far they're not trying to eat me, bite me or use a breath weapon. Hmmm, in fact, yes, breath weapons are a problem when you're packed in close with humanity. I wonder what would be a good defense card.

Card title: Shield of Face

(The standard spell is Shield of Faith, but the only thing I believe is that I might faint if I take a face full of malodorous breath.)

Artwork: A noxious green cloud with a nasty face blowing a cone of bad air against a fancy shield. The shield is a force effect, so it should definitely have some sparkles.

Effect: Bonus to Constitution saves against poison and conditions like stunned, staggered and sickened. It's an opposed check against the potency of the halitosis. If the spell fails, I just have to hope the card itself is large enough that I can hold it in front of my face.

My Fighter cards would be mostly useless. It's not socially acceptable to cleave one's way through a throng with a dwarven battle axe. So they say. I've learned during my commutes that interactions of any kind are best avoided. The people most in need of a Tongue-Lashing are also most likely to yell back or pull a knife. Useful information for the Location description. Even scarier are the Small-talk Trolls. They want to talk to you. About weather. Either way, my best bet is to keep my mouth shut. I'll need help with that.

Card title: Mask of Stoicism

Artwork: The comedy and tragedy masks of Theater, but with duct tape over the mouth areas.

Supernatural ability: Silence. Yes, I am serious when I say that silence is a heroic feat.

Target: Myself. It would be more satisfying to zap other people with a ray of "shut up," but I am trying to be heroic here, remember?

Effect: I press my lips firmly together against the barrage of words clamoring to run amok upon the air. With no reciprocal vocalizations, the Small-talk Trolls slow and sputter out entirely. That leaves the rude and loud people, the ones that need to be told a Thing Or Two. Nothing polite can stop them. You can only hope that there is a Blackfang the Dragon in their future.

Note: Mask of Stoicism allows use of the Stink-eye of Severity, but with a 30% miss chance.

The City Bus should also have its own location card. The equivalent *Pathfinder* Location that comes to mind is Treacherous Cave. The open maw of the bus door frames a murky hole with hints of slitheriness. High proportion of monsters. No loot. Succeed at a wisdom check to reduce the difficulty of challenges at this location.

Work is another primary location, but that would be a topic for an expansion pack. That leaves home and a small selection of public places where I acquire goods and services: the game store, the grocery store, the coffee joint.

Elixir of Life

Coffee shop location card: This easily equals a Potion Shoppe, except for the haggling. I'm happy that bartering is a mainly a thing of the past as it involves unnecessary human interaction. And charisma.

The Coffee Joint's main trait is a high concentration of Traps: chair legs, laptop cords and idiots. Also a high concentration of coffee.

I could burn through a lot of cards here. For starters:

Card title: Illusion of Calm

Artwork: A forest nymph, serene in her arboreal eden, supine in peaceful slumber. Just under the lush verdance lurks a fire demon pounding its fists against the restraining loam.

Target: Myself, again. I get worked up stuck in a line of people who don't know how to perform a simple retail transaction.

Effect: My temper may flare, but all they see is a small secret smile on my lobotomized visage.

Illusion of Calm is similar to Mask of Stoicism, but more powerful. The benefit is that you're starting your barista diplomacy check with a favorable attitude. The cost is that people might think you're a morning person.

(Optional) Card title: Read Magic

Artwork: A straightforward photograph of the coffee joint menu board.

Effect: If you're getting anything beyond the most basic cup of coffee, you will need to look at the board. You will also need to understand it. Now you can.

This would be a rare card in my deck, because I mostly get the basic cup of coffee. Even so, you must be cautious. There will be questions.

(Required) Card title: Speaking in Tongues

Artwork: The Tower of Babel.

Effect: Allows a pre-caffeinated person to make words that people will understand. Its duration is limited, however, and may run out at some point between spelling your name for the cup and explaining that, although you don't need room for dairy, you do need to be able to walk with the coffee without scalding your hand and staining your clothes.

(Optional) Card title: Gambit of Exact Change

Artwork: Two copper pieces, a plus sign, two more copper pieces, an equal sign, then four copper pieces.

Action: You open your palm to display the precise amount of money for the coffee you've ordered.

Effect: The cashier puts two and two together. The ceiling tiles open and a ray of golden light washes their face in beatific realization that no, you do not want a muffin or artisanal breakfast sandwich with that.

(Exit Strategy) Card title: Boots of Haste

Artwork: You might expect to see a pair of strappy boots with wings on them. My version has rocket boosters. Little ones, but still, rocket boosters.

Effect: You remove yourself from exposure to people at greatest possible speed.

Not-so-little Shop of Horrors

The Grocery Store Location: This card is pure black. A black so black that all memory of light is gone. Your stomach churns; you tremble. Attempt a Fortitude save versus fear to enter this location. Failure means you starve. Success means you face the horrors within.

You must be fully equipped before entering the Grocery Store. If you have spent all your cards just getting through the day, do not attempt this location. The effects of the cards we've talked about will also apply to the Grocery Store environment. For example, Read Magic will help with ingredients labels. Mask of Stoicism and Illusion of Calm are similar, but you can use them together. Stacking them will intensify their protective properties. In fact, once I sprayed my entire deck at the first monster, screamed real loud and ran for the exit. You get a huge power burst for using the whole deck at once. But then you're screwed.

The extra power comes from an all-purpose booster card that you can use to enhance any other card.

Card title: "You Got This"

Artwork: A boxer in full regalia, gloves, braids and shiny robe, surrounded by her entourage. Coach is in her face telling her that she can do anything.

Effect: Brazen it out. Whatever you're attempting, your bravado will help you along. You might still lose, but you will have the comfort of doing so with style and courage. I suggest keeping several copies of this card in your deck. You never know when you'll need to up the awesome.

Friendly Brick & Mortar

We have come to the game-store location. It is mostly a happy place. Friendly NPCs who want to talk about games. Knowledgeable gentlemen who will help you with your card-storage issues. One must consider carefully when choosing protective sleeves. Make an easy perception check when you enter to identify and avoid the rare troll, and all will be well. The greatest danger is to your bank account.

Card title: Aegis of Lead

Artwork: A leaden card sleeve exactly the size of a bank card or credit card. Protective runes adorn its edges and a sturdy padlock is etched in the center.

Effect: Protects your bank card from the scanning machines. Instills thriftiness with its imposing presence.

However, it is countered by....

Card title: Surge of Urges

Artwork: Fireworks of rainbows spouting from a unicorn's horn

Effect: Causes all the serotonin in your brain to flood your common sense. Bank cards are brandished, bereft of armor. The promise of fun is purchased in a celophane-wrapped box, painted with pretty pictures and filled with wonders.

A new card game. In this one, I am a Netrunner in the future. I am jacked into the system, and I have cards for programs and viruses and biotic enhancements. I am hacking the Corporation to trash their assets and sabotage their agendas. I look through all the cards, delighting in titles such as Aggressive Secretary, Neural Katana, Icebreaker: Wyrm.

These are really going to change up my Grocery Store strategy.

Finally, the best location of all: Home. I need no cards here, except maybe a Potion of Cat's Grace to avoid stepping on the one that sneaks up and stands directly behind me. It is game night. Friends are here and stories are told. Wine is poured. We each take our character deck, shuffling with hopes of a good first draw. Ready, we examine this scenario's locations, looking for the next dragon to punch...

A Chick Who Doesn't Dig Games Plays *Portal*

Fiona Moore was born and raised in Toronto, but has lived in the UK since 1997. She has a doctorate in Social Anthropology from the University of Oxford, and is currently Reader in International Human Resource Management at Royal Holloway, University of London. She has written academic articles on a wide variety of subjects, from the identities of Taiwanese businesspeople to the culture of drag queens, and is the co-author, with Alan Stevens, of a number of guidebooks on television series, most recently *By Your Command: The Unofficial and Unauthorised Guide to Battlestar Galactica* vols. I and II. Her fiction and poetry have been published in, among others, *Asimov, Interzone, On Spec* and the Aurora award-winning collection *Blood and Water*.

The basis of ethnographic research is for somebody who is an outsider to a particular culture to join it, participate in it and observe what its members do, and, from the experience, to learn what it is that makes it distinctive. I am an anthropologist, and ethnographic research is what we do.

I am also someone who wouldn't, under normal circumstances, be writing for this book.

Which makes me ideal for the current project.

The background to this experiment is as follows. I am a chick who does not dig games. From childhood, I've never really enjoyed playing games, and, when I do play them, it's generally been for the social activity (e.g., playing *Trivial Pursuit* at a party), or as a time-passing activity (e.g. playing computer solitaire when on hold). Video games, especially, are largely outside my comfort zone, the aforementioned solitaire games notwithstanding.

I've never particularly attributed anything gendered to my dislike of games in general, or video games in particular. I have plenty of examples of chicks who dig video games in my life: my sister, many female friends and so on. My parents, like many in the 1970s and early 1980s, took a very gender-neutral approach to child-rearing; I never recall hearing either of them use the words "girls can't..." or "girls don't..." while I was growing up, and I owned handsome collections both of My Little Ponies and Transformers. As an adult, I'm very gender-neutral in my choice of movies, TV programmes and reading: I like *Doctor Who* and *True Blood*, *Black Swan* and *Taxi Driver*; Robert A. Heinlein and Joanna Russ. I'm not afraid of computers; as a grad student, I supplemented my grant by working as IT tech support person and webmaster for my university department. When my partner played his way through *Grand Theft Auto*, *Max Payne* and *Call of Duty*, I watched with interest (though felt no real desire to join in). But, with discussions breaking out all over the fan world about gendering, particularly in games, I began to wonder: was I just in denial?

The nature of the experiment is thus for me, an outsider to game culture, to play a video game and determine whether gendering is, indeed, a barrier to my enjoyment.

The game chosen was *Portal*, on the grounds that, according to my background research with gaming friends and online sources, it appeared to be largely free of gender messages, and of the aspects of gaming which have been cited in the media as excluding or putting off female players. *Portal* is a puzzle game rather than an action-adventure game or a "shoot-em-up." Both the protagonist and antagonist are female, in presentation, anyway: the antagonist is a computer, but one named GLaDOS, and with a feminine voice. Indeed, there are no active characters at all who are, or appear to be, male: the only masculine presence is, first, photos of the company's founder briefly visible during Level 17 (and then only if you find the secret chamber); second, the Companion Cube (which, although GLaDOS refers to it as "he," is an inanimate object emblazoned with a rather girlish pink heart); and, finally, one of GLaDOS' personality cores, which, when separated from her in the final stage of the game, has what I initially took to be a masculine voice, although a second listen indicates it's actually GLaDOS' normal voice slowed down to a lower pitch. The "turret guns," laser-wielding robots that have to be defeated at various points in the story, have childlike, feminine voices, and there is a reference to "take your daughter to work day" in one of GLaDOS' periodic announcements.

More importantly, the gender of the characters is arbitrary in that there is no narrative requirement for GLaDOS or the human character, Chell, to be female. Chell's appearance and dress is not sexualised (she's also, arguably, racially neutral, having medium-toned skin and short dark hair); she has normal body proportions and wears an orange jumpsuit over a white tank-top. Indeed, since Chell is only visible to the player when she stands between two portals facing each other, it would be possible to go for several levels without realising that the character is female. It's a single-player game, removing the possibility of potentially gendered power struggles with other players. It was also not seen as a "feminine" or "masculine" game by my gaming friends, with both men and women recommending it.

So the research question is: if one removes the aspects of video gaming most criticised as prejudicial to female players – the masculinity of the characters, the violence of the scenarios, misogynous or sexist storylines, harassment from fellow players and the sexualisation or marginalisation of women – will I overcome my dislike of games? I also live-blogged the experience, using Facebook, to gain feedback from friends who had more experience of gaming than I do, and their comments have been incorporated into this article.

Portal, for the uninitiated, involves Chell working her way through a series of "test chambers" in a mysterious facility owned by a company called Aperture Science. In each chamber, she has to figure out how to combine and move the objects within it – principally boxes, moving or static platforms and balls of energy – in order to reach and unlock the exit. Her main tool is a "portal gun," a device that can shoot an entry and an exit portal onto different surfaces, allowing instantaneous travel between them. The game also involves a lot of what anthropologists call "tacit knowledge"; that is to say, information that is difficult or impossible to explain, but has to be learned through experience. The game builds on the player's knowledge, slowly developing a repertoire of moves and techniques through different exercises. While the purpose of the testing is unknown, it is hinted that there is a sinister secret to the facility, as GLaDOS (who I described to a non-*Portal*-playing friend as "sort of like a cross between HAL 9000 and Laura Roslin") utters cryptic phrases such as "cake and grief counseling will be available at the conclusion of the test." Some of the questions are contextualised, if not answered, by the final level of the game, in which Chell goes behind the scenes of the testing area, and finally encounters and defeats GLaDOS herself.

As a new player, I found the experience of game-play surprisingly satisfying; figuring out the puzzles, and then actually performing the moves to solve them (the game is as much about physical technique as about mental skills) was a lot of fun. I liked that, apart from a few puzzles with a countdown element to them, the game didn't try to keep me to time and allowed me as long as I needed to find the solution. I also liked that the game subverted the violent tropes of video games, by humanising rather than dehumanising antagonists (the turret guns perish with tragic cries of "Why?" or "No hard feelings..."), and making the gamer feel bad about violent acts (one level concludes with the player being made to feel ashamed for destroying an inanimate object, even though this is the only way to resolve the puzzle). I had an initial problem adjusting to the first-person perspective of the game, but got used to it after a while (though I still feel rather seasick when I try the advanced version of Test Chamber 15, which involves a vertiginous drop through multiple portals). I had a slightly more serious problem in that it was sometimes hard to tell whether one's failure to complete a puzzle was down to getting the answer or the technique wrong (since having the right answer to the puzzle was no guarantee that one could perform the moves successfully). All in all, I really liked the experience, enough so that I played the game twice and am, at the time of writing, working my way through the advanced bonus levels, the fan-made expansion maps and the sequel game, *Portal 2*.

So, if I played a game with the gendered aspects removed or neutralised and enjoyed it, does this prove the initial hypothesis, that my dislike of games has something to do with being a chick? I have to admit that, despite what I thought, that may be part of the answer. Since playing *Portal*, I've been noticing the gendering of video games a lot more: shopping for similar games has been an offputting experience, full of shoot-em-ups, RPGs and characters that seem calculated to give teenagers of both genders body-image issues. Reading a synopsis for *Half-Life*, a game I thought I might try as it is by the same people who made *Portal* and has some similarities, I found myself slightly put off by the fact that its (male) protagonist has to shoot at aliens, mutants and government agents as part of his puzzle-solving; it seemed a little boring and disappointing. It might be that the first-person aspect of video games brings these issues to the fore: I like gangster movies, but the difference between watching *Scarface* and playing *Grand Theft Auto* is the difference between passively watching Al Pacino beat someone up, and actively participating in the beating-up yourself.

On the other hand, that explanation is probably too simple. I also discovered, in the process of researching which game to play for this article, that I don't like the "virtual farm" or "dragon-breeding" type of game that a lot of my female friends do, even though those are also nonviolent and involve female characters doing creative activities. I put this down mainly to anxiety: this may sound crazy, but I don't doubt that I would feel terribly guilty if the virtual dragons were neglected or the farm failed, even though I know they're not real. It took me a while, on *Portal*, not to feel like I'd let Chell down if she "died," even though she instantly respawns. Likewise, puzzle games just for the sake of the puzzle itself – like *Sudoku* or *Tetris* – hold limited appeal, fun to play to pass the time, or as a brain-scrubber after work, but they don't have the narrative and constructive aspect that *Portal* had. I actually quite liked the more violent parts of *Portal*, like smashing up turret guns and the final "boss" fight against GLaDOS; I still intend to play *Half-Life* later on, in the hope that a game by the same team incorporates the same clever gameplay and wry humor. I doubt playing a male character, in and of itself, would be that much of an issue for me. So, clearly, it's not just gender that makes me not dig games.

Perhaps it's an issue of competition? Studies show girls tend to be discouraged, and boys encouraged, from competitive behaviour. I don't like competitive sports; I keep fit, but prefer going to the gym to taking classes and competing in events. For a while I studied karate, but again, tended to keep my involvement in formal tournaments to a minimum. However, I do work in a very competitive field (I'm an academic – and more than that, I'm an academic in a Management and Economics faculty), and have a hobby that does veer into the competitive sometimes (fandom). Also, there's definitely a competitive aspect to *Portal*, if only in that you're trying to outwit GLaDOS. So I have to conclude only that it may be part of the explanation.

Another interesting point is that *Portal*'s gender-neutrality seemed to be part of its appeal for a lot of the players. The fan-made expansion, *Portal: The Flash Game*, which has a second-person perspective, features a player character that is completely devoid of visible gender, and Google searches suggest that fan art of Chell is generally on the non-racy side. There was also, reportedly, a certain amount of complaint from *Portal* fans when the redesign of Chell for *Portal 2* (where she wears her jumpsuit with the arms tied around her waist, exposing the tank-top) made her look, arguably, more sexualised than in *Portal* itself. Significantly, this seemed to be the case for both male and female fans of the game, which suggested that the often-repeated idea that women don't like video games because they're made by men, for men, isn't entirely true. Although *Portal 2* includes male (or male-appearing) characters, their relationship with Chell is again gender-neutral, and the crucial dynamic in the story is still that between Chell and GLaDOS. Like *Alien*, *Terminator* and *Buffy the Vampire Slayer*, *Portal* clearly indicates that both men and women can enjoy a story with a female protagonist, which doesn't objectify, sexualise or victimise her.

So in conclusion: gender isn't the whole story when it comes to explaining why I don't play video games. That said, the experience of playing *Portal* also showed that the gender messages of games can have an effect in putting people off playing them: I'm not sure I'd've been as willing to try *Portal* if the game had involved shooting zombie hordes, or playing a busty Lara Croft-type fantasy figure, and clearly its neutral approach to gender is part of its appeal more generally. I still don't think I will ever try multi-player games with strangers, given some of the stories I've heard about online harassment, and given that I do prefer playing solo. Likewise, *Portal*'s gender neutrality seems to be a significant part of its appeal for all of its fans, male and female. If there's a lesson for the industry in my experience, it would be: don't get too hung up on gender in itself as a barrier to enjoying video games, but don't discount the effect of gendered messages – or, even, of deliberately non-gendered ones.

At the conclusion of the experiment, I've successfully made my way out of the test chambers, had my cake and eaten it, and am happy to redefine my status from being a chick who doesn't dig games to being a chick who digs at least one game, and is willing to try some more.

An Interview with Margaret Weis

Margaret Weis is the *New York Times*-bestselling writer who, as an editor at TSR, expanded upon the foundational *Dragonlance* series as developed by Tracy and Laura Hickman. With Tracy, Weis co-wrote key *Dragonlance* books including the *Dragonlance Chronicles* and *Dragonlance Legends*, and was the solo author of *The Raistlin Chronicles*. Weis is the author of many other award-winning and notable series, most recently *Dragon Brigade* with Robert Krammes. She owns Margaret Weis Productions, a publisher that has developed the *Serenity*, *Firefly* and *Battlestar Galactica* RPGs and more.

Q. How did you come to be involved with *Dragonlance*?

A. I was hired at TSR as a book editor. I'd been an editor at a very small publishing company in Kansas City, and I'd read about *Dungeons & Dragons* and played it, and I thought TSR sounded like a wonderful company to work for. So I sent in my resume – I applied to be a games editor, but they sent me a test, and [as I habitually know] nothing about rules, I flunked that.

What happened next was very serendipitous... my agent at the time lived in Milwaukee. He knew Jean Black [the head of the books department at TSR]. Jean said she was looking for an editor who also needed to be a writer, because they wrote a lot of in-house material. So she called my agent, who said, "I just happen to have this client who sent her resume to your games department." So Jean went over there, found my resume, called me and hired me.

My job was to edit the *HeartQuest* novels and then a new project they were developing called *Dragonlance*.

Q. At the time, *Dragonlance* was unusual in that it was jointly developed as an RPG and a book series. Did it seem strange to be working on a literary pursuit where the characters could be boiled down to a set of numbers and attributes?

A. Tracy [Hickman] was in charge of the *Dragonlance* team, and my job was to work with the plot that was set for *Dragonlance* and extended over 12 gaming modules. *Dragonlance* was the first to ever come up with a plot for the modules – it wasn't like, as Tracy used to say, "The [heroes] go out, find the dragon, kill the dragon, get the treasure, then the next time find the dragon, kill the dragon, get the treasure..." With *Dragonlance*, the players had a much more noble goal, and that was to save the world from the Queen of Darkness and her evil dragon.

It was also the first game that had pre-generated characters, because we needed characters to go along with the plot. At the time, TSR was doing the *Endless Quest* novels for kids. Those were like the *Choose Your Own Adventure* books; they were selling really well, just unbelievable.

So the head of the TSR books department and management decided that they wanted to do an adult novel to go with *Dragonlance* the game. My job was to take this giant plot and the characters and distill them down into a plot that they could give to an author to write the novels, so that's what I did. I had the plot, I had the characters, I knew what they looked like and what they did in the world. My job was to give them personality and life.

Again, remember: I don't know anything about rules. When I played *D&D* back in the day, somebody always had to tell me what dice to roll, because I was clueless.

When I started with Raistlin [one of the most popular *Dragonlance* characters], I knew he was a third-level wizard – and I knew what "third-level" meant, because I knew he was dressed at pretty much the low end of how wizards go. I knew what spells he had, and I knew what he looked like, because Larry Elmore did this amazing painting of him. I knew Raistlin had golden skin and hourglass eyes, and I knew he had this twin brother who was a real hunk, named Caramon. And so we were in the meeting, and I said, "Okay, I'm putting together Raistlin and Caramon, and I need to know – why does Raistlin have golden skin and hourglass eyes?" And everybody looked at Larry, and he said, "Because it looks good in the painting."

And so I had to come up with a reason. So I said, "It must have some- thing to do with his magic, as Caramon his twin is perfectly normal- looking." Then I said, "Well, he's a young wizard, what if he had to pass a test for his magic, because magic in this world is very rare and very powerful? So, what if the wizards said, 'Okay, anybody who wants to use magic, they have to pass a test that we give them. And not only that, they have to bet their life on this test. If they fail, they die'."

Then I thought, "What would Raistlin's big twin brother, who has obviously been his protector, feel about that?" And, suddenly, I knew Raistlin and Caramon. I knew their co-dependent relationship, their personalities and that Raistlin would bet his life on attaining the power that he'd never had. All of that, essentially, came out from Larry Elmore's painting.

Q. Once a character becomes hugely popular, like Raistlin, does it make writing for them more intimidating, given the heightened levels of scrutiny they're going to receive, or is it the same either way?

A. With Raistlin, it was the same, because I knew him, I knew his story, I knew what he would do. We wrote *Chronicles* and *Legends* in the space of maybe two or three years, so we were working very, very fast – it wasn't like these days, when I take nine months or maybe a year to write a single book. Because the first book sold really, really well, TSR wanted more, and they wanted them as fast as they could get them.

It was a little bit after the first book [*Dragons of Autumn Twilight*] came out that Raistlin started gaining in popularity. Probably the most popular character at first was Sturm, and people were so upset when he died. And then Raistlin became popular, especially with women. The majority of the readers at first were men, but the boys would give the books to their girlfriends and wives, and then the women started getting involved in the world and liking him. He was just fun.

Q. When did you realize that the *Dragonlance* books were going to be a huge hit?

A. We knew we had something special, but none of us had any idea that, 30 years later, these books would still be in print. There were times we didn't even think they would be published. Our distributor had never heard of Margaret Weis and Tracy Hickman. The books sat in the warehouse, and bookstores didn't know where to order them, so it was really kinda depressing there for a while.

What we knew was that when the books were actually sent out, usually to hobby stores, they were quickly bought up. Because hobby stores, they'd never sold novels. They'd have one copy by the cash register. Somebody would buy it. Our game modules were out, and people were playing the game. And then word of mouth caught on. We got the books into the bookstores finally, and the first one hit the *New York Times* bestseller list. And it was *then*, I think, we knew that we really had something amazing.

Q. Have you ever given any thought to writing a personal swan song for *Dragonlance*?

A. I know what I'd like to do with *Dragonlance*, although I don't know whether I'm going to get to do it or not. The first three novels especially were written to length, which means entire scenes and chapters were cut. I'd like to go back and put in all of the material that was cut out, kind of like Stephen King did with *The Stand.*

Q. Do you still have that extra material?

A. I don't have it written down, but it's in my head. I actually did some samples and showed them to Tracy, and he loved it. So he would be eager to work on that with me.

Q. What is the gender split among the *Dragonlance* readership today? Equal men and women, or is there still an imbalance?

A. I would say it's equal. It's just like we've seen at Gen Con, with more and more women coming into gaming. When I went to Gen Con in 1984, if you saw a woman walking down the hall, she had 20 guys following along behind her. Now, at Gen Con, you have women, you have families.

Q. Fantasy has a very patriarchal tradition. *Lord of the Rings* is brilliant in so many ways, yet there are scarcely any women in it. Do you feel that your interest in writing about women came from your being a woman, or was it an attempt to be more realistic about the world in which you lived?

A. I think it was because I am a woman. Even as a girl, I was very militant. I was really mad in third grade because they would not let me play softball with the boys, and girls were supposed to jump rope. I was absolutely furious. I went to play softball with the boys anyway, and they didn't stop me. I had to play in my skirt and petticoats, but I went ahead and played. And so, I've always been interested in working with strong women and promoting women. Not to the point of going overboard, because in writing, you need a nice balance. You have to have strong men and strong women. Just strong characters.

Q. You once gave an interview in which you mentioned a study that suggested women "study" men more than vice versa, which might explain why some men have difficulty writing female characters. Do you find yourself "studying" men in a manner that works its way into your books?

A. I don't know... I think that came from my reading background. When I was growing up, my family went to the library every week, and

I read voraciously. We were limited on TV time, so I read. And back in those days, if you read interesting books, you read books with male heroes. I was reading *The Three Muskateers* in the fourth grade, but there there certainly weren't any female Muskateers. The only thing written for women or girls at that time was *Cherry Ames, Student Nurse* and even *Nancy Drew*, which I thought was a little "blech." I was more drawn to Sherlock Holmes.

So it came not so much studying men as studying people in general, and then studying the way writers portrayed their characters.

Q. You've commented that at places such as Gen Con, rather than promoting women in gaming, you'd be more inclined to promote *families* in gaming. Why so?

A. The very first game I ever played was with my kids. In fact, I read about *Dungeons & Dragons* in *Publisher's Weekly*, and my first thought was, "My gosh, this would be such a great game to play with my kids, because it would teach them to use their imagination, to tell a story and to develop characters." That's why I used to get a little tired of everybody promoting women in gaming just for the sake of women in gaming. My thought was, "If you get women involved in gaming instead of these kids sitting there playing a game and Mom has no clue what they're doing, she looks at *D&D* as something evil."

Better to get Mom involved in the game. I played it, and my kids had a ball. My son thought it was the coolest thing to rush in and save my life – he got to save Mom from the Big Bad Whatever. And that's one reason why I, and Tracy too, would promote families in gaming.

Q. Nowadays, you are the big kahuna at Margaret Weis Productions (MWP), but you are still also a writer. What percentage of your time is spent as a businesswoman, versus being a hardcore story developer?

A. I earn my living as a writer; that's what I love to do. With Margaret Weis Productions, I have a great business manager, an awesome staff and a great team. I trust them implicitly to take up the ball and run on their own. We connect through the internet, so I keep tabs with what's going on. I actually got to write an adventure for [the] *Firefly* [RPG], which was my first adventure, and had a great time.

Q. Do you test any of the games that MWP produces?

A. When we did *Serenity*, I was really hands-on on that one. I pretty much helped to write the core book and did some editing. When we got

Firefly, I didn't have as much time because I was doing two novel series simultaneously, but I was involved in play-testing it. I played Jayne, who is my favorite character. So I do play-testing, and I love seeing the artwork and approving the artists. But I'm not so much on rules; the rules people do that.

Q. Here in 2014, as a hugely accomplished professional, what do you know now that you wish you'd known when you wrote your first book?
A. I wish I'd had a computer.

Q. You did it all on a typewriter?
A. All of my early books were written on typewriters. I was covered in Wite-Out. The advent of the computer was a godsend.

Q. Do you have any advice for young female novelists trying to get their start in the industry?
A. Just what I tell everybody, when they ask my advice on aspiring writers... keep reading, keep writing and keep your day job. I majored in writing in college, and I worked for ten years, writing at nights and on weekends while my kids were growing up, before I got my first book published. It was a biography of Frank and Jesse James. So, you have to work at it, whether you're a man or a woman.

I knew a woman who was drop-dead gorgeous – she was a beautiful blonde, and she had a great time writing male adventure novels under a pseudonym. And then I knew a man who wrote romance novels under a pseudonym as a woman. So just write what you love.

Q. You've been in the gaming industry a long time. Since you started out in it, what's the most positive development you've seen, and what's the most negative development you've seen?
The most positive development has been more and more women becoming interested in gaming. The negative would be that there was a downturn for a while because of video games and card games, which made role-playing games take a downturn. But we're starting to see role-playing games come back. I think people are realizing that sitting in front of a computer and playing a game is not nearly as much fun as sitting around a table with your friends and a bag of Doritos.

How to Design Games for Boys

Winner of the 2013 Interactive Fiction Competition, **Lynnea Glasser** is an independent designer who loves games for their ability to tell unique and amazing stories. With a background in Biopsychology, she enjoys applying rigorous science and self-examining philosophy towards her craft. She is currently enjoying working at BioWare, although she continues to release games independently. Lynnea believes firmly in the inclusive potential that games have to offer, and is thankful to be surrounded by encouraging and supportive people.

The video-game industry is ignoring a lucrative and untapped demographic: boys. Right now the popular and market-dominating games – makeover games, romance games, cooking games and animal-rasing games – are all very female-centric, leaving boys out cold. It's been argued that boys just aren't as interested in quietly staying indoors and playing in virtual worlds, preferring the more physically boisterous play that the outdoors offer. But it doesn't have to be that way: many of the more popular kinds of video games can easily be modified to appeal more to the more masculine among us. I propose that there is a potentially rich market in games designed towards boys: that boys can be just as ready to invest in video games as girls are.

First of all, I'd like to clarify that this is a guide on how to market towards "boys," not necessarily adult males. Adult men are unique individuals who have more diversified interests, and should not be treated as a homogeneous group. Boys do seem to have more targeted interests and needs, and these suggestions are about how to tailor to those needs.

Let's start with makeover games: how can these be modified to appeal to boys? Many developers have tried to take the easy route by just allowing male avatars as similar blank slates, but it's obvious that boys just aren't as interested in tone-matching their eye-shadow, getting a good blush spread or drawing straight eyeliner on their male avatars. These developers then throw their hands in the air when this modification doesn't sell well, but it was a design decision that was doomed from the start. I'd like to point out that the developers are missing one of the most important features that males have: facial hair.

Consider adding mechanics for shaving and trimming. Give unique patterns and interesting shapes, and add a variety of colors, braids and clips. I'd personally love to play a game where you can carefully carve out the iconic beard of Seneca Crane from *The Hunger Games*, and who wouldn't want to recreate the instantly-recognizable goatee of 2002 Olympic Gold medalist Apolo Ohno? Allowing these kinds of options will not only appeal to boys, but also remind them that there are important and interesting men in the world that they can look up to for inspiration. Girls won't mind these additional features, considering that most won't even select to play as men in the first place. But this inclusion will make a large difference to boys.

I'd also like to propose a second new kind of game mechanic: the application of (temporary) tattoos. This obviously complements the more clothing-focused makeover kinds of games. With this mechanic, players can select from a series of prefabricated tattoos that can wrap on the avatar's skin, and can be adjusted for the shape and color. This mechanic will give boys a more socially acceptable way to dress up their characters while still being as colorful as the girls. Not to mention that this mechanic expands upon content offered, and can increase the profitability of a game by offering more features to sell. It is a win for all.

Romance games are perhaps more difficult to adapt. Many developers have attempted to just slap on an avatar swap and call it a day: turning a game about a girl surrounded by boy classmates into a game about a boy surrounded by girl classmates. To be sure, in graphic novels this is a low-budget and easy addition to make that does help vastly broaden its appeal (although it remains rather heterocentric, but that is a topic for another day). However, I propose that boys are less concerned about what their avatar looks like than they are about other aspects of the game. Now certainly, offering male avatar options is important, but not as important as providing more stimulating surroundings. Boys would prefer romance games with more outdoorsy and exciting settings.

Consider creating romance games with a western setting, or taking place in the military, or amongst bank robbers, or fantasy troll-hunters, or even in space. More exciting settings will offer boys the adrenaline rush that they need to connect with the central game. For example, if designers look past the "trashy boy fiction" reputation, I believe that an age-adjusted adaptation of *Ender's Game* would reach many young boys, while still offering a full romance experience. There's no need to compromise on the rich character development, the realization of self or the unique choices along multiple romance paths when tailoring the game to boys. On the contrary, using these exotic locations can even enhance and tie into the main game story itself. I know some groups of gamers are concerned about women "losing" the focus on romance games, but I think that there are many women out there who would enjoy gaining more options and will appreciate the variety.

The cooking game is definitely one of the most untouched genres when it comes to reaching out to boys. One more innovative game introduced liquid nitrogen and flame-thrower cooking tools. While well-received, such an addition was still only a patch and not a comprehensive solution. Admittedly, this is much better than the typical approaches of frosting the pastries blue, or adding flame decals to the cooking utensils. These are blatant attempts to pander at a stereotype, and, while changing the graphics may make the game more visually palatable, it's not addressing the core issue. It's been found that boys prefer to first gather their materials before combining them into a final product.

Add an economy-based game play mode: somehow gamify the gathering of the cooking resources into a way that boys can enjoy and identify with: hunting or fishing for ingredients, refining sugars or mining salts. I realize this next suggestion might be risky among large-scale developers today, but imagine a mechanic of stealing cooking ingredients from neighbors or stores. Boys seem to enjoy surreptitiously collecting items from others, and they will get more satisfaction from the eventual payoff of combining those stolen goods into delicious dishes... which are then given back to the victims, or even to the needy. A Robin Hood or Shoemaker Elves of cooking games, if you will. Of course, these additions do not need to dominate the design of the game, merely offer additional ways to enjoy the game that already exists.

I thought I'd finish out the discussion of games with the most popular kind on the market today: animal-raising games. Horses, cats, dogs, birds; even gerbils, hamsters and turtles. It's very difficult to market these games to boys. Certainly, boys are not without empathy towards creatures (even Spock is moved to pet a tribble!), but the fact is that many boys are overwhelmed by the anxiety of assuming care-giving responsibility, and by the saccharine cuteness of the pet itself. Luckily, there are solutions.

First of all, offer scarier choices of animals to raise. Wouldn't it be fun to care for dragons: training them not just to be house-trained, but also to do flying and fire-spitting tricks? Or how about giant snakes, or sharks, or spiders? I think adapting the recent surprise success *Pacific Rim* into a Kaiju-raising game would do wonders for attracting boys into video games. Just imagine feeding it with virtual helicopters, playing splashing games with it, and training it to tread carefully along the coastlines: all for the reward of a glowing blue smile. I think this would make a satisfying game to all gamers, both girls and boys.

Second, realize that boys are not as good at picking up the subtle social clues, and as psychology continues to be dominated by the female gender, the concepts behind classical and operant conditioning are not as familiar to boys. Bottom line: boys need just a little bit of extra help. Add ways to monitor progress with numbers, bars and charts. This way boys can mathematically get feedback on their actions and get a better idea for what works and how to progress in the game.

Adding tracking numbers has the additional benefit of offering boys a way to compare their scores to the scores of average players, friends or top players. It's been found that boys are often encouraged and motivated by competition, and this can play into that. Now, I don't want to suggest that these number-driven mechanics become obtrusive: imagine a GUI where those features don't show up unless toggled. In this way, animal-raising games can be adapted to be less intimidating, and even appealing and motivating without sacrificing any of the visual appeal of the game.

Now, I've discussed how to adapt some of the more popular game styles to appeal more to boys, but I want to also take time to look at some of the more cutting-edge games out there. There is definitely interest, and, if big industry game developers don't court this growing market quickly, they may soon find themselves behind as some new upstart company nails down the market for them.

Of runaway indie success is the game *Shooting*, which has the unique mechanic of allowing the player to control one sprite that fires projectiles at other sprites who enter and exit the screen randomly, while simultaneously avoiding projectiles itself. A counter keeps score: hitting the colored sprites awards points (different amounts for different colors), while time spent "alive" adds to the score as well. The game is viewed from a top-down, two-dimensional grid with exaggeratedly pixelated sprites. The mechanics were lauded as interesting and novel, and certainly it has enjoyed indie game accolades, but most large-scale developers have their reservations. While claiming to draw its art inspiration from the early eight-bit forays into graphic novels, it has not escaped attention that the art style serves to abstract the many, many logistical problems with a game of this style.

Who are the enemies, and why are they enemies? Why do the

defeated sprites disappear into nothing? Why do they keep approaching the protagonist in the same manner as their fallen comrades? Why do they not mourn for those same fallen comrades? Where does the protagonist have her ammo? Why can she take so many hits, while the enemies can't? Why doesn't she need medical care? How can she continue to effectively fight while injured? It has yet to be demonstrated if such a gameplay style can be adapted to more realistic graphics. It is likely that seeing realistically rendered people engaging in such behavior will completely break the suspension of disbelief. One potential way to get around this is make it clear that the game is non-lethal, perhaps with a laser tag or paintball depiction. Or to make it set on a magical planet with targets and protagonists of alien physiologies. Time will tell if this success can be repeated, but it is still worth investigating. For a more detailed exploration of these themes, I recommend Gregory Weir's "Why So Few Violent Games?"

On the more academic side, consider *Exothermic*, winner of the Grand Jury Prize at the 2006 Slamdance. This research project explosion-simulator was the most realistic and dynamic game of its kind ever created. In it, you rig up different explosive material to objects of different shapes, sizes and densities, combined with options to add different accelerants, also in their own amounts. The game boasted nearly three million combinations that would each independently render its own explosion. While its physics simulation was lauded as groundbreaking (described as the "future of gaming"), the mechanic has yet to become commercially successful.

I propose that it just wasn't well-integrated with the kinds of game structures already familiar to players. I think this sort of explosion simulation could do very well if combined with a story-based game structure. Give the players a reason as to why they feel motivated to blow up particular structures. Perhaps they are fighting aliens trying to destroy the human race? Perhaps they are a warring faction? Or maybe the protagonist is the villain, attempting to rob a bank or jewelry store. Story-based motivations are critical for gaining and maintaining player interest. Otherwise, why are they fiddling with so many variables: just to see an explosion that is slightly different from another explosion?

Another way to approach a game like this is to put a "demolitions expert" or "scientist" skin over the typical cooking game. The obvious *Anarchist's Cookbook* PR disaster aside, the recipes would be too similar to one another, and it's not clear whether the game would be as satisfying without the colorfully appealing ingredients and dishes. A good way to salvage interesting colors would be to morph this game into a fireworks simulation, but I still am not sure how well a game like this would be received. Again, perhaps some developer out there will find a way to make it work.

I hope I've demonstrated that current games can be adapted to appeal more to boys, and perhaps offered inspiration for new kinds of future games. I'd like to point out that, while I consider my arguments a good launching point, it's important to ask and listen and discuss with reference to what men have to say about the issue. They understand and deal with this issue on a daily basis. During the course of designing my own games, I like to make a point of asking men their opinions to see if they have suggestions for how the game could appeal more to them. Half the population doesn't deserve to be ignored when it comes to gaming – a pastime that is fundamentally about having fun and enjoying yourself. I have hope for the future that we can become more inclusive and rounded out, and that boys can one day enjoy being themselves while gaming just as much as girls do.

The Grace of Dice and Glossy Cardstock

In addition to being an avid board gamer and RPG player, **Lucy A. Snyder** is the Bram Stoker Award-winning author of the novels *Spellbent, Shotgun Sorceress, Switchblade Goddess* and the collections *Orchid Carousals, Sparks and Shadows, Chimeric Machines* and *Installing Linux on a Dead Badger*. Her writing has appeared in a wide variety of anthologies and magazines. You can learn more about her at www.lucysnyder.com.

It's disconcerting (to say the least) when the game you see spread on the table before you doesn't match the description in the instruction booklet. Maybe you keep kicking down doors, but there's never a monster to fight so you can advance to the next level. Perhaps there's just never enough wooden track in the bag to build that rail from Madrid to Petrograd. Or maybe the book talks about the importance of curing the yellow disease, but the box only came with tokens for purple and green.

Growing up geeky and female in a male-dominated world can often seem a whole lot like playing a series of games with missing pieces. Or it feels like you've been consistently dealt one less card than your male tablemates, even though they claim everyone's hands are equally full. But the frustration of discovering that reality just doesn't match up with what we're told it should be is often worse when it comes to relating to other girls and women.

Friendships are important to everyone, we're told, but they're especially critical to a female's happiness because we're the nurturers, right? The common wisdom is that we as the possessors of double-X chromosomes are more empathetic, more sociable, more able to connect emotionally, more able to love, than males. We're supposed to effortlessly gain deep and lasting friendships with other females that we carry from grade school to college and beyond.

The reality? For me, female friends were often hard-won and easily lost. When I was a kid, navigating the world of female relationships seemed far more complicated than trying to get my *Mouse Trap* game to work. My stint in the Girl Scouts, despite all its emphasis on healthy outdoor adventures, sisterhood and friendship around the campfire, often made me feel like I was playing an unrewarding knock-off LARP of *Paranoia*. Many girls were genuine sweethearts, but others were cutely smiling sociopaths... and I was really lousy at telling the two apart. I learned about cliques, and hurtful gossip, and emotional manipulation, and – near as I can tell – nobody really won those toxic head games, but plenty of girls felt compelled to play.

I think I know where a lot of that social dysfunction comes from. Most everyone in our culture, male and female, grows up with some subtle and not-so-subtle messages that girls just aren't as capable and interesting as boys. Meanwhile, the adoring parents of many little girls raise their daughters to think of themselves as princesses (Disney is more than willing to help out on this ego-boosting project). I'll grant that a positive self-image is usually dandy. But what happens when a girl is brought up to think that she herself is a worthy and snowflake-special person (as long as she performs her gender correctly, of course, as a good princess must!), but that the other girls she encounters – especially the ones who don't look and act just like her – are stupid and inferior? Yeah. Nothing very good comes of the "I'm awesome, maybe, but you suck" mindset.

The rules of my gender performance and how I was supposed to go about making real, genuine female friends were conveyed to me and other girls through TV shows, movies and books. Girls were supposed to like gossip. Remembering the sting of being mocked by girls I thought were my friends, I despised gossip. Girls were supposed to love shopping for clothes and makeup and dishing about boys, failing the Bechdel test at every available opportunity. Faced with flimsy, ridiculous fashions and sneeze-inducing perfumes, I decided I hated shopping and that I'd rather just hang out with the boys and play *D&D* instead.

Through my twin skills of rolling up damn good characters and brushing off sexist jokes at the table, I successfully made myself into one of the guys. But I didn't stop wanting female friendship. Every once in a while, I'd meet another geek girl, and I'd have that glimmer of hope: maybe this time I'd found my BFF. But we girls who'd grown up in the lonely social outcasts' Siberia would eye each other warily, circle, then go our separate ways, unable to get past the walls we'd each prudently raised to defend against marauding princesses.

My own interests in science fiction, games and horror seemed so far removed from what society kept telling me I should be interested in by virtue of my boobs, and my own efforts at connecting with other girls such a failure, that I began to angst over whether I was a "real" female or not. I questioned the essential nature of my identity. So I got a lot of comfort from playing RPGs, because I could be whoever I wanted to be as long as our games lasted. My character's abilities, goals and the reasons for her existence in the world were all utterly clear. There's no existential angst when you're up at 2 a.m. hurling dice to take down Tiamat.

Once I got into grad school, my gaming fell by the wayside, largely because I felt I had to abandon it to be a serious student and, later, a serious writer. I had to focus on the work at hand, and all my mentors were telling me that games were a waste of time. That precious, precious time passed, as it does, and one day I woke up to realize that, although my writing career was going reasonably well and I had plenty of rewarding friendships with men, I had not one solid female friend. I had female acquaintances, sure, but nobody who really knew me or wanted to know me.

What happened? I had a geeky IT day job and, although I mostly worked with men, I did encounter the occasional double-X tech. But my female coworkers and I just never seemed to click. I went to conventions and conferences where I met plenty of other female horror and science fiction writers, but again, somehow I persistently missed the friendship mark with them. What was I doing wrong?

I took a long look at my situation and one night I had an epiphany: when it comes to bonding with other women, the game really *is* the thing.

I could look back at my grandmother and her sisters and see the truth in that revelation. God, those ladies hated each other. Or anyhow you'd think so from the way they squabbled about anything and everything. You'd think that adding competition would create a situation that was anything but friendly. But they'd sit down to play bridge on Friday nights, and all their anxious jealousies and arguments would fall away as they concentrated on the game. I remembered watching them when I was a kid, marveling at their focus, the air in the room blue from their cigarette smoke. As the night wore on and they fell into the rhythm of deals and auctions, they'd laugh and smile with a genuineness that I never saw otherwise. While the games lasted, they became real sisters working toward common goals.

I thought back on my relationship with my mother; my fondest memories of her certainly weren't when we irritated each other during unavoidable shopping expeditions, or when we argued over how late I could stay with my boyfriend. It was when we went out for miniature golf or played pinochle at the dining room table, the soft riff of the cards smoothing away the mundane stresses of our weeks and bringing us closer together.

I considered the erstwhile friendships I'd had with other smart, geeky girls. The very best of them had involved gaming. I met Dyan playing *D&D* in junior high; we stopped hanging out when her religious parents made her quit the game. At my undergraduate college, I met Carol and Alex, and we spent many late nights playing *Scrabble*. There was my friend Lisa, whom I hardly saw anymore because she was busy playing *World of Warcraft* and I politely declined to join in (I suspected I would love it like nothing else and my productivity would screech to a halt).

I still think avoiding *World of Warcraft* was a good decision in much the same way that I think turning down that offer of heroin at the indie film party in Austin was a good decision. But dropping gaming entirely? That was clearly a clueless move on my part. I love games, and so do my kindred spirits. Games let us shed all the petty bullshit that drags us down in the mundane world. In games, we're free to exercise our minds and imaginations and simply be ourselves. And through our shared joy of playing, in those shared worlds of imagination, those shared quests and battles and competitions, we geek girls can bond with each other in ways it's hard to do elsewhere.

The smooth cards under our fingertips. The rattling, jewel-toned dice. The beautiful boards and maps spread upon the tables. The promise of epic imaginative adventures represented in tiny, tiny figurines. Who wouldn't love that?

I asked myself, why are all those gorgeous games supposed to be less important to a woman than rummaging through racks of clothes at the mall? Why is laughing and conquering imaginary demons with your friends supposed to be inferior food for the soul compared to watching a tear-jerking chick flick at the theatre? Why is the game table supposed to be a less feminine place than the beauty parlor, particularly when all the older women in my family had homemade hairdos and a deck of cards in every purse?

I am absolutely not saying that you can't be a girl geek if you love frilly blouses and makeup and *Legally Blonde*; I'm also not saying you can't be a real geek if in your heart of hearts you think of yourself as a princess, because Xena and Merida kick ass. I hate that so many women have been accused of being "fake" geeks and turned away from their true passions by self-proclaimed tin-pot defenders of nerddom. If it's not hurting anyone, you get to love what you love, period. If someone else's rules are telling you that you have to abandon the games you adore or else you're somehow less of a legitimate woman, less of a serious artist or poet or whatever, throw out those rules and write your own. Follow your joy where it leads you.

I followed mine and dove back into gaming. *Ascension. Bohnanza. Catan. Dominion. Munchkin. Pathfinder. Ticket to Ride. Pandemic. Iron Dragon. Fiasco.* And, lo and behold, new friendships with like-minded women followed. I've got more real female friends now than I ever did back in my Girl Scouting days.

That joy I mentioned? It was the element missing from my female friendship equation. And frankly, I just can't work up loads of joy at the day job or even at a poetry slam.

So, if you're like me, and you find yourself saying, "Yeah, most of my friends are guys; I just don't get along with other women, I guess," then it might be time for a change of venue. Check out your local game nights; even if you don't meet any new friends, the games will be there, and you're bound to have a lot of fun.

Chicks Dig Gaming
THACO of a Gamer Girl

Jaleigh Johnson is the author of five novels and several short stories in the Forgotten Realms fiction line, published by Wizards of the Coast. She lives with her husband at the edge of cornfield in the wilds of the Midwest. You can visit her online at www.jaleighjohnson.com.

"Where in the remorhaz's digestive tract is the gem? Because maybe *that* part of the monster is still on *our* side of the portal."

Don't Dungeon Masters just love questions like that?

But it wasn't just the question. It was the whole situation, one of those classic players vs. Dungeon Master arguments that can only end in the DM throwing up his hands, popping two aspirin for his migraine, and giving us a 20-sided roll to try to accomplish whatever insane scheme we'd cooked up while buzzed on caffeine and cheese balls.

In other words, a typical Friday night.

We gamed in our friend Dex's – that was his character name – garage. A few months before we started playing, he'd enclosed the entire back section in wood paneling and insulating plastic. The floor was bare concrete, and our gaming table was composed of a large slab of wood thrown over two sawhorses. It sagged in the middle, and we'd covered almost every square inch of its surface with some type of penciled graffiti. Very classy. We'd scavenged old furniture to put around the table, so on any given night we'd be sprawled on faded, floral-patterned armchairs, beige couch cushions, barstools and folding chairs. *Advanced Dungeons & Dragons* Second Edition maps and posters covered the walls alongside hand-drawn continent maps of our homebrew campaign setting. Dex's daughter left her toys scattered around the room, so we had sock monkeys, plastic tea sets, roller skates and dozens of dolls at hand.

That room – with its improvised door kept closed with a piece of cloth wrapped around a nail – was a sweatbox in the summer and got so cold in the winter that we could see our breath and were entirely unsure if our toes were still attached or if they'd snapped off inside our shoes. But it was our place, our secret hideaway, and we loved it.

In the far corner, there was an old-fashioned gas heater, the kind where you could see an unholy orange glow dancing behind the grate.

If you stood in back of the heater and leaned forward, waves of delicious warmth flowed over you. All our good winter arguments and crazy planning sessions usually took place around that heater.

The remorhaz argument occurred when the ravenous thing swallowed a priceless gem – along with the adventurer carrying it. We attacked the monster and were holding our own just fine, but complications arose (they always do) when a rival adventuring band crashed the fight. The competitors went after the remorhaz, but things went south for them. Their wizard hastily opened a portal and escaped with the other survivors. Unfortunately, the remorhaz had found them tasty. It tried to sneak in one last bite and ended up getting itself sliced in half by the closing portal.

Now, for all the gamers out there shaking their heads and muttering: "That's not how portal mechanics work!", remember that we were playing Second Edition and we had many home rules, so hush. All that matters is that suddenly the remorhaz was in two pieces, and we only had access to one of them. *Treasure* was on the line.

We reasoned that there was at least a chance that the gem – and the unfortunate adventurer holding it – had moved sufficiently far in the remorhaz's digestive system so that it was in the lower segments, and thus still accessible. Never mind that we had absolutely no basis in either real-world or fantasy-world biology for thinking this. We just didn't want to lose the damn gem and were prepared to argue our point until we got our way or the DM lost his will to live, whichever came first.

Hours later...

"So, is the gem in the remorhaz's butt or not?" our barbarian demanded, diplomatically.

The DM gulped down his aspirin, fixed us with a dagger-like stare and growled, "Fine. You can roll for it. If you get a 20, the gem is still in your part of the remorhaz. Anything else and the guys on the other side get it."

Now, there were many ways we could have argued that this was unfair. Judging by the sheer tonnage of remorhaz on our side of the portal, we thought we should at least get a 50-50 shot at the gem, but the DM had spoken, and, judging by the sizable vein protruding from his forehead, we knew we weren't going to get a better offer.

Erdrin, our psionicist, grabbed a 20-sider and a plastic sugar bowl from one of those toy tea sets we had lying around the room. He plunked the dice inside it, slapped the lid on, shook it and then rolled it out of the bowl and across the table.

Jaleigh Johnson

# # #

When I joined my brother's gaming group my first year of high school, I didn't honestly think I'd be contemplating the intestinal tract of a remorhaz. Then again, there were many things about gaming that I didn't see coming. I didn't know that the little room in back of Dex's garage would become a sanctuary and a second home for me, or that gaming and the friendships I made from it would get me through high school, land me my first job and help me realize my dream of being a published author. Believe it or not, gaming did all of those things and more.

The first thought I had when my brother invited me to join his group: *finally*.

My brother is 11 years older, and I'd been watching him and his group play *D&D* on and off since I was six. I didn't get to play back then, of course, but I'd sit in the corner of the room and listen to them playing what sounded to me like make believe. Well, I could do that! At six, I specialized in make believe. But it still took almost a decade for me to get invited to play and for my parents to give the okay. Luckily, I was a patient kid.

The second thing I realized when I decided to join my brother's group was that I could *not* tell anyone at school. It wasn't just because I'd grown up in a small town where a certain segment of the population still equated *Dungeons & Dragons* with devil worship and virgin sacrifices. Mostly, I didn't want to give the bullies more excuses to mock and make fun. It was freshmen year and they already had a lot of good stuff on me: I was quiet, shy, loved to read more than talk and they knew I was afraid of them. But gaming – that would be my secret, something nobody would touch.

I didn't worry about anyone else in the group betraying my secret. They were my brother's friends, and most of them were just starting college. High school was over for them, and oh, how I envied that freedom. They no longer had to worry about things like sitting in science class trying to take notes while the boy behind me leaned over my shoulder and whispered things like "Are you a virgin?" and "Have you bled yet?" Looking back, I'm pretty sure those were the sorts of questions people should have been scrutinizing if they were worried about virgin sacrifices.

I mean, why didn't the guys ever ask me anything important, like

146

how to calculate THAC0[6] or what's involved with the digestive processes of a remorhaz? I may not have been an expert at socializing or dating, but my *Player's Handbook* fell open to the experience point table every time I cracked the cover. And damn it, I *did* know how to calculate THAC0 and was proud of it. But I knew I wouldn't get rewarded for that type of knowledge. Whenever I brought fantasy and science fiction novels to school to read in study hall, I covered up the title and artwork so people wouldn't catch me reading them and conclude that I was even weirder than they'd originally thought.

I loved gaming and everything about it, but it was still a secret, something I felt I needed to keep hidden.

Then, one day in the fall of 1993, a unique little collectible card game called *Magic: The Gathering* came into my life, and my perspective gradually started to shift.

Up until that point, our gaming group played roleplaying and miniature games, but we embraced *Magic* and played it feverishly as well. Once we understood what the game was all about, we couldn't get enough of it. We entered tournaments, stayed up until 3 a.m. playing afterwards, and spent most of our spare time designing decks. I bought starter decks and booster packs with any bit of money I could scrape together.

Fresh out of college, one of the guys in our group – character-name Drell – worked at a local card and collectibles shop that was just starting to sell online. They were selling *Magic* cards like crazy, but most of their staff knew very little about the game, so they needed people like Drell who knew how to talk to customers. Their over-the-counter traffic surged, and they wanted someone to help with all the *Magic* card questions, so they asked Drell if he knew anyone looking for a part-time job and who was familiar enough with the game? Drell recommended me, and, before I knew it, I was having my first job interview.

I'm pretty sure it wasn't a typical interview, as the main thrust of the questions was how well I knew the various *Magic* expansions. How well did I know *Magic*? How well?? I had a counter spell deck that made my opponents weep and shake their fists in fury. I could get an army of merfolk into play by turn three with a good draw from my underwater deck. I'd seen a channel/fireball combo used to end a game within the first two minutes – back when that sort of thing was allowed.

They hired me.

6 *To Hit Armor Class Zero (0)*, a calculation to see if an attack succeeds. In brief, you take the target's Armor Class number and subtract the attacker's THAC0, then roll. If you equal the THAC0 number or go higher, the attack works.

Jaleigh Johnson

It was a surreal moment. Someone actually wanted to pay me for my knowledge of a game – a game! – and one I was already obsessed with. Up until that point, my jobs had been things like babysitting and helping paint the house for pocket money. Suddenly, my secret hobby was about to become public knowledge. Kids from my high school regularly came into the shop, sometimes just to point and stare at the Chains of Mephistopheles card in the display case. I was excited about the job, but also a little afraid they were now going to be pointing and staring at me.

But the people I worked with didn't think me or my hobby strange. The employees and owners were all older, but they treated me like an adult. I started to feel less afraid of what people thought of me. *Magic* was a game, but it was also an important part of the shop's business, and they took it seriously. It was the first time I'd ever really recognized gaming as an industry, something that people made their living from. At the time, it seemed like a small thing, but it broadened my view of the world.

I was also interested in the internet, which was just starting to become a serious thing when I was in high school. My bosses were willing – more than willing – to teach me anything I wanted to learn about HTML and graphic design for their website, among other things. By the time I left the job years later, I knew almost every part of that business, from sales to shipping, and I draw on that experience to this day. All of that came from a card game, a hobby.

But in the meantime, there was still high school.

I hadn't managed to fit in there. Gaming and my job helped give me things to look forward to, but I still dreaded getting up in the morning and facing each school day not knowing whether I was going to come home crying or just generally feeling awful about myself. For a distraction, I used to scribble notes from our weekly gaming sessions while I sat in study hall. Sometimes those notes would lead to daydreaming, and I'd make up stories in my head based on whatever roleplaying game we were involved in at the time.

I don't remember at exactly what point those daydreams evolved into my own stories, but my scribbling got more intense and started to fill up notebooks. My gaming roots were always evident; I naturally gravitated to fantasy. There were monsters in my stories, of course, the kind that you could slay with a bit of luck and a sharp sword – and the kind that weren't so easily defeated, the invisible monsters like self-doubt, anger, fear and helplessness. Writing became an outlet for my imagination and a way to cope with those invisible and more insidious monsters. By the time I'd gone through my fourth or fifth notebook, I knew that writing would become a major part of my life. I just didn't know exactly how.

Years later, when Wizards of the Coast announced an open contest for writers for their Forgotten Realms novel line, I remembered those notebooks full of stories and all the fantasy novels I'd read and loved. I remembered what it felt like when we all gathered around the gaming table in Dex's garage, and the DM would start describing the scene for us. In that moment, our characters came alive. The world they inhabited lived and breathed. No matter how much we loved to argue with the DM, we were always mesmerized by the way he could tell a story and draw us into it so completely. I wanted to be able to tell stories like that.

I decided to enter the contest, but I never really expected anything to come of it. The prize at the end was a novel contract, and it seemed far out of my reach. Getting to write a novel in my all-time favorite fantasy setting wasn't even something I'd allowed myself to daydream about back in study hall. Up until that point, I'd only had a few short stories published and a couple of novels securely trunked and gathering dust. Too many people with more experience and talent were going to be competing for the same prize, so I didn't think I stood a chance.

Turns out, I was half-right. I didn't win the contest, but Wizards of the Coast liked enough things about my proposal to keep me in mind for novel auditions in the future. One of those auditions was for a book in *The Dungeons* series. I put together a proposal – there wasn't a remorhaz in it, but I had plenty of other dungeon-delving experiences to draw upon – and submitted. A few weeks later, I got an email that I will never forget. Wizards liked my proposal and offered me the chance to turn it into my first novel: *The Howling Delve*.

I was a long way from becoming a published author when I was scribbling those campaign notes in study hall, but that was the beginning of it. And those fantasy novels I kept under wraps, books such as *Spellfire*, *Elfshadow* and *The Dragonlance Chronicles*, were part of my inspiration. It's amazing, strange and wonderful to think about my name on the cover of one of those books, to imagine some other young girl reading them between classes – hopefully without having to cover them up the way I did.

Eventually, though, the habit of keeping my hobbies under wraps started to wear on me. As I inched closer and closer to my senior year, I got tired of the secrecy. Finally, one day, when one of my teachers asked me what I was reading, without thinking I peeled off the book cover and showed her the Forgotten Realms novel, acutely aware that a few of my classmates had turned to look. I held my breath while I waited for her reaction and had a brief internal panic attack, an *oh God what have I done?* moment.

"What's it about?" she asked.

The question caught me off guard. I had expected her to give the swordsman on the cover a funny look while the rest of the class erupted into laughter. But she seemed genuinely interested, so I explained a little about the adventurers and their quest.

"That sounds like a good book," she said when I finished.

And that was it. A couple of the other students sitting nearby murmured agreement, and the subject dropped. I let out the breath I'd been holding and just sat there, marveling at how I'd worried and worried about everyone's reaction, yet revealing my secret obsession hadn't been nearly as painful as I'd thought it would be. Or maybe I was just tired of hiding who I was, and it was a relief to finally share a part of myself after having kept it hidden so long.

I wish I could say that everything got easy once I started to accept myself and the things I enjoyed, that life became all unicorns and rainbows. But high school was still high school, and there were still completely awful days, though I eventually made it through my senior year and was on the cusp of graduating.

"You'll miss it when it's over," Drell remarked one Sunday while we all stood outside enjoying the spring weather in Dex's driveway.

"High school?" I said, incredulous. "You've got to be kidding."

He shrugged. "High school's usually the best time of your life; a lot of people say so, anyway."

I suddenly felt sick to my stomach. Images of the boy in science class asking me if I'm a virgin flew through my head, along with the echoing laughter of groups of girls pointing at me while I walked down the hall. "I really don't think I'm going to feel that way," I said.

Truthfully, I think I said something that included a string of profanity and involved my face turning different shades of purple, because Drell and the rest of the guys gave me a look like I was having a seizure.

But the funniest part about that conversation actually came about 15 years later, when I mentioned it to Drell. "Okay, I don't remember saying anything like that," he protested.

"You did, and now I get to hold it over you forever." I grinned. "You thought high school was going to be the best time? Not college, not travel, not getting published, not – oh, I don't know – *our wedding?*"

"We weren't even dating back then! We didn't get married for another ten years."

"Still, you have to admit you stepped in a pile of irony there."

"Well..."

"Totally going to hold this over you forever."

"Great."

My husband and I are still gamers, and we both remember the remorhaz story and that fateful roll. My husband was the DM for that campaign, and it was his vein bulging out of his forehead, so of course he remembers – fondly, I think.

#

Our psionicist heaved the 20-sided out of the little plastic sugar bowl, it rolled across that old bowed table – and of course, it came up a 20. Somehow, we all knew it would, and the room erupted. Probably took us an hour to calm down enough to continue the game – and another hour in game time to dig the gem out of the remorhaz. But it was one of those moments of pure, crazy fun and excitement we shared in that garage playing games together. Our private world that we treasured, where we could be ourselves and obsess over experience points and THAC0 tables and which *Magic* card was the best in a certain deck, and on and on. Some of the people that I gamed with back then are still a big part of my life. Their friendships make everything else I had to go through totally worth it.

The expression on our DM's face when we rolled that 20 and got to dig a priceless gem out of a remorhaz's butt was totally worth it too.

Chicks Dig Gaming

Let Us Play

Lene Taylor is a writer and co-host of the long running podcast *Look At His Butt!*, in which she and her best friend Kitty talk about *Star Trek*, science fiction and (mostly) William Shatner. In her spare time she watches too many videos. Her favorite games are *Q*bert* and *Evil Dead: Regeneration*.

Location: Sony Gaming Academy, Luna University
Year: 2250
Time: Early morning seminar (3 p.m.)
Class: Let's Plays – Interpretation of Gendered Historical Gaming Documents (Early 21st Century) 101

Thank you for arriving on time today, kits; there's so much to do on the first day of class. I'm your instructor, Doctor Professor Mak'tar. Now, just so that we're all clear, this is Gendered Gaming Documents 101, not Non-Corporeal Gaming 101 – that's down the hall in the invisible classroom about 30 feet above the ground, can't miss it – so please make sure you're in the right class. Ah, there's always one, isn't there?

Let's get started.

You will – and by *will* I mean *had better* – remember from your previous history classes that in the ancient days of gaming, games in all their forms were, for the most part, created and played by those who presented as human het males. Shocking, I know, but you must remember that this was before the Awakening, when the illusion of human het male superiority dissolved into foam, like an old-fashioned Sony mint candy dropped into Sony diet brown carbonated sugar water. In those Dim Times, there were even those who proclaimed that women were not only bad at games, but incompetent with technology, and also lacked a sense of humor.

Settle down! It may be amusing to you, cubs, but it's history, and you know the old saying, "Those who cannot remember the past are condemned to watch summer repeats of it." Now, we are fortunate that, even in those primitive times, there were enterprising women who managed to create mixed-media historical documents that conclusively refuted all three of these ridiculous claims.

Called "Let's Play" or simply LP, they were recorded video of game playthrough with the gamer's audio commentary – sometimes meant to be serious, sometimes done purely for entertainment value.

Sound familiar? It should. It's the same kind of guided game play you get from the personal avatars that were assigned to you on your first day at the Academy, but combined with the all the programming that is available on the Sony Gaming Comedy Network. Let's Plays were where this genre started, and, though women weren't the first to make them, they quickly caught up and surpassed the men, in quality and quantity.

Yes? Why weren't women first? Joeys, didn't they teach you any-thing? These were the Before Times, when women routinely received harassment, threats, mockery or were often simply ignored when they tried to participate in gamer culture. Of course, this was true of much of the women's participation in society in those centuries – it wasn't until women publicly seized control of the pre-Sony "interweebed" services known as Tumblr and Twitter that change began – but gaming culture was particularly male-oriented for a very long time.

This same "interweeb" – it's how the Sony neur-fi got started, which you really should have learned about in Dark Ages Tech 105 – allowed women some degree of anonymity, and therefore protection, as gamers. Believe it or not, kidlets, it was not unusual for women to present as men when playing, even going so far as to alter their voices if participat-ing in audio group play. Yet some women insisted on taking their rightful place in the gaming world, and played and won as themselves. And some of them made Let's Plays.

The advantages for women should be obvious. The barriers for entry were very low, even in those days of steam-powered or compressed-air or hamster-driven computers: the software for recording gameplay was free, or nearly so, and gamers already had the hardware for playing – and of course their vast collections of games (stored on physical media called "discuses," which conveniently doubled as drink coasters). There was no "men only" club or "my joystick is bigger than yours" competi-tion to keep them from putting their Let's Plays on the YouthTube net-work for all to enjoy.

And they didn't have to appear on screen if they didn't want to. Before the Awakening, much of the abuse aimed by men at women was based on their appearance. By using audio only, these intrepid LPers presented themselves – thoughts, personality, sense of humor, intelli-gence – with words and voice alone, neatly sidestepping all the issues that come with visual representations. Even now, watching these performances (and you will be watching many of them as part of the coursework), one is struck by the love of gaming that so clearly shines through, despite the many quaint (and sometimes puzzling) slang expressions such as "fucking hell" and "holy fucking shit" and "what the fuck is this"?

It is astonishing that, using equipment that was hardly very far ahead of stone knives and bearskins, these LPers crafted many thousands of hours of education and entertainment, playing through hundreds of games ranging from first-person gory Victorian horror to children's horse-based mystery stories – all for loyal audiences that reached many hundreds of thousands of people. Why were they so popular? Extensive scientifically conducted research with teenaged girl gamers of the era revealed remarkably consistent answers across geographies and social classes. I have provided verbatims to give you a flavor of the times:

- They were funny. "And no dick jokes every ten seconds."
- They provided non-condescending help on playing through hard games: "Totes better than written walkthroughs, and they don't yank the controller out of my hand if I'm not moving fast enough, like some people I could name!"
- LPs provided an opportunity to watch gameplay on games they would probably never buy, but were curious about: "Those *Silent Hill* games are way too creepy and bloody for me, but I love seeing someone else get the shit scared out of them." (Class, presumably this is not meant literally, but we can't be sure.)
- It helped gamers decide if a new game was worth buying: "Because I can't be blowing all my money at GameStop every week, especially when something like *Sonic 06* sucked big red rocks." (Again, probably not meant literally.)
- Simply because they were fans of a particular LPer: "She has real skills and she's so funny. All the lolz without the dick jokes."

By the way, if anyone has insight into what "lolz" are, please see me after class. Current thinking is that the term is related to sugar-based candy treats of the time.

Too, we must remember that before the Awakening, all Terrans believed in the Cult of Celebrity, and the gaming community was no exception. LPers were highly present, if not visible, to gamers, and developed their own followers and even fandoms (the most highly evolved form of appreciation). But, because LPers were not hydroponically cultured media stars, they were actually available to their audiences through such channels as virtual mail, or Tweeters, or the Book of Faces (which also came under the control of women shortly after it was founded, although this was unknown to the public for many years). Let's Plays became interactive, LPers often took the time to respond to questions and comments in subsequent videos. Fans sent them games to play, sometimes because the games were challenging and fun, but often simply for entertainment value (without the dick jokes).

Let's take a look at one of the well-known Let's Players, who we will be studying in much more depth over the course of the semester. She went by the name MangaMinx, and is remarkable in that, during her many years as an LPer, she never appeared in photos or video, although there are fanciful representations of her as a small girl smiling and holding a butcher's knife, and others of her as a purple-haired pirate complete with eyepatch. She specialized in horror games, playing them "blind"; that is, without having played them before; in this way, the viewer experienced the game simultaneously with the LPer, creating shared memories and emotions that approach a relationship. Many of Minx's LPs show her involvement in multiplayer games, which she played with friends on archaic shared wirefree data networks; these mostly involved avatars running through badly pixelated landscapes and shooting each other repeatedly. (Remember, foals, pre-Awakening.)

Minx's popularity had much to do with her fearless nature – playing the most terrifying and bloody games – and her habit of narrating each LP by directly addressing in-game characters, inanimate objects and even the game designers as she played. As you will hear, the word "fuck" figures heavily in her commentary, whether directed at a tree or a monster. Many of her fans particularly liked the fact that her narrative – usually calm, broken by the occasional scream or uncontrolled laughter – is delivered in an accent from what was then known as Britishland (one of the tiny tea-drinking, garden-obsessed superpowers of the twenty-first century, along with Jappan).

But many scholars of the form agree that the pinnacle of Minx's work is her playthrough of a disturbing yet whimsical game called *Surgeon Simulator 2013*, the goal of which is to complete a heart transplant using only one badly controlled hand and a few crude instruments on a rapidly bleeding-out human patient. Minx rips out both of the patient's lungs, dumps all the surgical instruments into the chest, breaks all the ribs, and somehow still manages to win the game, all while cursing like a drunken sailor and laughing hysterically. It is a magical piece of performance art.

Another important artist in the genre was Lucah Jin, who had hundreds of videos for games as diverse as *Legend of Zelda: Ocarina of Time*, *Leisure Suit Larry* (contrary to the title, not a fashion game), *Oregon Trail* and *Paper Mario*, all classics of their kind. Her LPs show striking diversity, both in game genre and in purpose: some are basic walkthroughs aimed at yearling players, while the sole purpose of others is to mock badly designed games. An excellent example of the latter is Lucah Jin's LP of the barely coherent *Barbie Horse Adventures* games, which seem to involve non-human female lifeforms (their proportions are certainly outside normal Terran boundaries) and robot horses. Her play of *Mystery Ride* involves a robo-horse named, mysteriously, "My Balls"; her co-host on this LP seems to find simple exclamations such as "Oh no! I lost My Balls!" alarmingly amusingly. Linguists are currently working to understand the context.

Women Let's Players were creating content from many locations, in the many languages spoken at that time. As you might expect, they were popular first with other women, but men too gradually became fans. They provided an important social aspect to gaming, especially to women who did not have gaming communities at hand. Let's Players functioned as virtual communities, providing guidance, education, a network of friends (through other fans and LPers), and many hours of free entertainment. In the language of the time, they evangelized for gaming.

The number of Let's Plays by women grew steadily in the twenty-first century. Given enough time, they would probably have achieved parity with men LPers, but the ingrained social imbalance at the time was so severe that it might have taken millennia before it was realized. It is hard for us now to imagine that time and how dramatic the change was, when the population was Awakened by the simple contact with the Other. Eyes were opened; points of view converged; language barriers erased. Who could have predicted that things would change so dramatically in such a short space of time?

I think the women of the Before Times would be proud to know that at Sony Gaming Academy, the most prestigious institution of its kind, the faculty and student population are almost entirely, and comfortably, female. It is wonderful when men decide to take up gaming! We encourage it, but, despite the scholarships and special hats, there just doesn't seem to be much interest. All the men on Terra seem to be working in nursing and cake design.

During this course, we will do close readings of these Let's Plays, and examine them within their historical, social and political contexts. By viewing them, you will learn much about the history of gaming, especially the worldview of the women who boldly played where few women had played before. And I hope that, as I did, you will become a fan of Let's Plays.

Now, pups, we can take a short break before the second half of the class, where we'll ingest many of the archival historical documents I've been speaking about. Take notes, because you *will* be tested on this. And I know it's early in the day, but no one had better fall asleep – and if you need something to keep you from getting bored, I've got a cupboard full of invisible textbooks that have to be inventoried.

NB: The Let's Play Wikia has a good (but by no means comprehensive) list of women LPers: http://letsplay.wikia.com/wiki/List_of_Female_Let%27s_Players

Chicks Dig Gaming

The Hero in My Story

Caitlin Sullivan is a QA Analyst for BioWare Austin and an aspiring environment artist. She is also a failed travel journalist and a sometimes actress. In addition to playing RPGs, shooters, puzzlers and MMOs, she plays the piano quite competently and the guitar quite clumsily. Caitlin enjoys movie theaters with full bars and waiters, making goofy 3D models, Netflix-binging with her boyfriend and dog, and any activity where she can exercise her right to be a layabout.

It's a strange feeling to not like yourself. And it's really not hard to come to that realization: you are the only person that you have to be around 24/7, you know yourself on a level that you'll never know another person, you can't hide your dark, dirty little secrets from yourself. But you don't have to be a terrible person to not like yourself.

When I discovered that I didn't like myself, I considered myself to be an average, regular person in every way. I was gainfully employed at an international insurance corporation. I made good money. I had three bachelor's degrees from the University of Texas, a circle of close-knit friends, a long-term relationship. I played the piano, did volunteer work, visited museums and went for hikes in my spare time. But most of those things I did to impress or please other people, not because I knew they would bring me happiness. I would only take an interest in something after considering how it would make me look to everyone else. I was not a proactive person – I didn't know the meaning of initiative – and the only time I took action was if it was a reaction to something that happened to me. For years, I had been building my life, but it was out of parts that other people were handing to me. I didn't throw myself into anything, and it felt like I had been hibernating for years.

But then I woke up. And when I did, I came to the agonizing conclusion that I had constructed a life where I didn't fit in.

When I was growing up, my dad was very flighty: intelligent, often described as a free spirit, but often absent. My mother practically raised and supported me by herself, and she was the responsible, disciplined, driven and ambitious one. She was a teacher and was involved in many functions in our small community, and her voice was often in the back of my mind, questioning whether what I was doing was appropriate for a young woman. So when I graduated from high school, I set out to make myself into something that would please my mother and make her proud, even though I felt more like my father. I wanted to do something creative – acting, writing, playing music – but none of those things were realistic, my mother's voice told me. So, I went through the motions of what I was "supposed" to do: apply for college, choose a major, attend classes, find a part-time job. As I made these choices, I only considered how it would look to my mother and other family members, to the people back in my hometown and to the friends I had had since childhood. I put no thought into whether or not I was starting down a path that would ultimately make me a happy and productive human being. I only thought about whether the image I was carefully crafting would be impressive enough.

Since I absolutely refused to venture outside my comfort zone in college, I had trouble making new friends. I had no idea how to bond with the new social circle I found myself hanging out with, a group of guys in my apartment building whose idea of a joke was to ask, "What's the capital of Thailand?" and then shout "Bangkok!" while hitting each other in the crotch. I got really good at *Call of Duty* and *Halo* and *Mortal Kombat* and *Street Fighter* and learned to trash talk while we played. Other than a few old-school console games, I didn't play many video games as a child, and I had no idea they could be as much fun as we were having.

After college, I got that insurance job because it was the "realistic" thing to do. I had never been more miserable in my life, and I'm glad that I got out before it became too difficult to leave. While I reveled in my newfound freedom and dreaded searching for another job, my boyfriend lent me his copy of *Dragon Age: Origins* to play in my spare time. I had no experience with any kind of role-playing game. I grew up a country bumpkin in a town full of country bumpkins; there were no nerds in my high school who could have introduced me to *Dungeons & Dragons*. I didn't know that these types of video games were unlike any book I had read, or movie I had seen, where you simply observe a hero and her struggles. In an RPG, *you* are the hero, and the success or failure of a quest or a mission depends on *you*. After a few hours of playing, I quickly learned that unlike the video games I was used to playing, I wouldn't win by sitting in one spot (with no goal, no objective) and shooting random players as they ran by. As the protagonist of the game, the Warden, I held the responsibility of saving the entire world from an invading force known as the Darkspawn, and I couldn't just sit around and wait for them to come to me, like I would probably do in real life. The Warden had to be take-charge, had to seek out allies, and had to make decisions that could forever alter the lives of everyone around her.

I really liked the Warden. I liked who she was and what she stood for, what she fought for. And then I eventually realized that the "Warden" was an empty shell built out of computer code, 3D models and painted-on textures. The Warden had no personality of her own. The reason I liked her was because I had poured bits and pieces of my own identity into her with every decision I made, with every encounter I faced as the game progressed. I liked the Warden, and, by extension, I liked myself, for the first time in years.

But there were still some qualities that I saw in the Warden that I lacked.

The Warden sought out allies from different walks of life, different races, even different species. I, on the other hand, struggled with making mundane conversation with people I saw in everyday places, like the grocery store or the bank. I couldn't even talk on the phone without having an anxiety attack. I couldn't keep friends outside of the few I had already been acquainted with for over 20 years. The Warden was a natural-born leader; people looked up to her and valued her judgment and guidance. I was a follower in every sense of the word, always kept my head down and was too afraid to speak up much for fear of having my thoughts and ideas ridiculed or mocked. I couldn't plan for or think about anything in my future because I was too caught up in the present, mostly obsessing over how my actions and choices would be perceived by other people. I was so afraid of making mistakes or somehow being seen as "less-than" that the only thing I cared about was what other people thought about me. I realized that this was what a lot of my issues with low self-esteem stemmed from. I valued everyone's opinion about myself except my own. I didn't care that I hated myself, so long as everyone else liked me.

Even as I write these words, I struggle with thoughts about how my friends and family will react if they read this, what they'll think of my issues with self-loathing after I've hidden them all this time.

Other people didn't talk to me much, so that must have meant that there was something off about me and my personality. No one ever really asked me to be involved with social plans, so that must have meant that I was boring. So it was easier to just be silent, stay at home, isolate myself; those were the only ways I could guarantee that I wouldn't feel like there was something wrong with me. It never occurred to me that if I could just say, "To hell with what everyone else thinks," and break out of my shell, if I could just be like the Warden and seek out the company and companionship from others instead of their validation, if *I* was the one who struck up the conversations and asked people if they wanted to hang out instead of hiding, then I could see that there really was nothing wrong with me after all. I still struggle with making myself do those things sometimes. But once I learned how to do them, I was happier and ready to face different challenges head-on without retreating to my safe place of avoidance.

In my entire life, I've only ever had one goal, and that was to leave my very small hometown: a place so small that diversity of viewpoints doesn't really exist, which makes it hard to find a niche to fit into. After I achieved that one goal, I had no clue where to go from there. For a few years, I got by. I was *existing*, but not really chasing or working toward anything.

Around the time I finished my first play-through of *Dragon Age: Origins* (and started playing my second-ever RPG, *Mass Effect*), I got a new job, then another, then another. The common denominator of each of these positions was a feeling that I had contributed nothing; no one asked for my opinions or ideas, no one expected anything from me, there were no chances for me to be visible, to be the hero in my story. I would come home every night struggling more and more with my self-esteem issues. Even though I still considered myself very much a follower, I suddenly was not content to work jobs that had no upward-mobility possibilities. I was no longer satisfied with the prospect of being a nobody with nowhere to go for the rest of my life. I wanted to try my hand at creating things, making things that didn't exist in the world before I made them, and to do that I couldn't continue my habits of sitting around and waiting for an opportunity to fall into my lap.

At my boyfriend's suggestion, I applied for a quality assurance position at a video game development studio here in Austin. He worked at a different studio, and he listed all of the things I stood to gain if I worked in the video game industry: relaxed environment, fun work, interesting people, getting to be a part of creating something that millions of people enjoy. Part of me screamed not to send in my application. It was uncharted territory for me, I had no experience, there was plenty of opportunity to be judged for my lack of ability and expertise, and I would have to endure physically painful panic attacks every day as I interacted with brand-new people. I drowned out the doubting voices in my head and clicked "send" on the email.

A few months later, I got a call from a recruiter letting me know that I had the job. My first day of work, I experienced everything that I had feared I would: the anxiety of the social interactions; the fear of making mistakes and being judged for them; I even felt some guilt at the thought of everyone who had helped me earn college degrees that were now being wasted. But I powered through all of it and tried to feel at least a little bit of excitement. After all, I hadn't just applied for a job where I would toil away for a steady paycheck, like I did after I graduated college. I was experiencing the start of what felt like an actual career, at a place that made *video games*, one of my favorite hobbies. And I'd be lying if I said that I didn't have fun those first few days; I never thought I'd have fun at my *job*.

And as time went on at the studio, I felt less and less affected by the problems that were contributing to my low self-esteem. I was working at a job that I had chosen for myself, that made me happy. I had a fresh, clean slate to work on my social anxiety with my new coworkers. With them, I experimented with something new: I stopped constructing a façade that I thought would appear the best and offered up only myself. The fact that we all had a common love of playing and working on video games (a subject that I really couldn't comfortably delve into with most of my friends) made it much easier to ditch the worries about what other people thought of me. I bonded more quickly with my fellow QA testers than I had with any other coworkers or new friends. I felt like my work (and I, as a person) was valuable to my team and to the developers that I spoke to on a regular basis. I felt like I was an important part of completing the game.

That spark of self-worth set off a flame of wanting more. I went back to school and learned how to write music and model art assets for video games, and I found out that I was really, really good at those things. I feel like I have a lot to offer, and the more I hone my different skills, the less I feel like I hate myself. I'm still working as a QA tester (at a different studio, but they develop my favorite MMO, so essentially a dream job), but, after a few years as both a consumer and producer of games, I have goals again, and I've laid out a road map for my future instead of idly wondering where in the world I could go next.

It's a good feeling to like yourself, not just who you are, but where you're headed. It took a lot of difficult decisions and pain and failure and doubt to get to this point, and I still have a long way to go before I'm the Warden. But for now I can say I was brave enough to battle the problems that contributed to my self-loathing. I can say I reached down and lifted myself up from a path that went nowhere. I saved myself. I was a hero.

When the Stars are Right

Wendy N. Wagner's short fiction has appeared in *Beneath Ceaseless Skies* and the anthologies *The Beast Within 3: Oceans Unleashed, Armored* and *The Way of the Wizard*. Her first novel, *Skinwalkers* (a Pathfinder Tales adventure), was published in 2014. She and her family make their home in Portland, Oregon, and you can keep up with her at http://winniewoohoo. com.

Every August, my husband and daughter and I drive up into the mountains to catch at least one night of the Perseid meteor shower. We pack thermoses of hot tea and load up the car with sleeping bags and pillows. At six thousand feet above sea level, it gets cold at night.

We lie together, sprawled across the glacier-scraped soil, trying to ignore the stones jabbing into our sides or our necks, and we watch the skies. The stars don't fall frequently. We might go ten or 15 minutes without seeing a single meteor, or we might see a cluster go off, one after another. We eat cookies and drink tea and talk and talk; it's a peaceful family time.

And yet, a part of me is never really comfortable watching the stars. They are ancient, after all. They belong to something huge and vast that we will never fully know.

I am not alone in my sense of unease, watching the stars. H.P. Lovecraft wrote reams about the feeling, calling it "cosmic terror." When I'm watching the glittering expanse moving over my head, I can't help but think of his poem "Nemesis":

I have seen the dark universe yawning
Where the black planets roll without aim,
Where they roll in their horror unheeded,
Without knowledge, or lustre, or name.

With so many fictional universes and games, the goal is to flesh out a world; much of the pleasure from *Harry Potter, Lord of the Rings, Game of Thrones* and more comes from the detail that's marbled into the story, from what *is* known about the realms in question. But the horror genre and the games spawned from it play by very different rules – it's more about what *isn't* known, the uncertainty of it all, that causes such delight. With horror games, the questions posed are frequently more intriguing, and far more terrifying, than any answers provided.

Arkham Horror: Where Death is Frequently the Preferred Option

When Lovecraft created what's retroactively named the Cthulhu Mythos, he crafted a fictional universe that would inspire artists across the globe to address their fear of what lay beyond their own corner of space. He reminded us that the universe is large, and we small beings have seen very little of it. The space beyond could be filled with beauty and wonder – but it's just as easy to think it filled with horrors outside our ken. And it's for that reason that one of my favorite games is *Arkham Horror*: a board game that's part of a larger series, including the RPG *Call of Cthulhu*.

In *Arkham Horror*, the vastly powerful ancient beings from Lovecraftian works are here on Earth but sleeping fitfully. They await the right moment to awaken: a time with the perfect planetary alignment for implementing their intergalactic plans.

The game board is a stylized map of Arkham, a New England town during Prohibition. Unfortunately for its inhabitants, the presence of a waking Ancient One creates portals to dangerous alternate worlds. Some characters in the game work to aid the Ancient Ones: cultists, priests, witches and maniacs are common threats. Other dangers are science-fictional monsters with wings and scales and horrible teeth. And there are some horror staples like zombies and vampires. The Cthulhu Mythos can incorporate all of these elements.

Coping with the Ancient Ones is no easy feat. Take, for example, the hulking, semi-humanoid Dimensional Shambler. The red border on its token indicates that it's a "fast" monster: it moves twice as far as an ordinary creature, so characters are more likely to run into it. It's also smart, so characters face a high handicap to sneak around the beast. If you choose to fight rather than elude the thing, you must first draw on your willpower – and if you don't roll well, you face losing one of your limited sanity points. If you lose entirely, the Dimensional Shambler will yank you out of reality and discard your character in time and space. You might die, or you might suffer damage and lose crucial clues and special items.

It's the potential loss of sanity points that troubles me the most, because...

Insanity: Not Comprehensible on So Many Levels

Mental trauma that results in insanity is one of the hallmarks of Lovecraft's writing and the Cthulhu Mythos. But, for so many modern readers, the very idea of an experience that breaks your mind is hard to fathom. Partly, it's because real-life psychology and therapy has advanced so much since Lovecraft's day, making us feel as though we understand the causes of mental instability better than we probably do. And partly, it's because our generation grew up watching hours of monster movies and disaster flicks. If a hideous monster showed up on our doorstep, most of us would be alarmed, yes, but we would quickly formulate a plan to cope with such a creature. We fool ourselves into thinking we could deal with such perils, even if that self-same confidence often makes us vulnerable. In some ways, our zombie survival manuals have acclimated us to horror too well.

Because the monsters on display in *Arkham Horror* have such an otherworldly quality, game play sometimes entails a "horror check" when facing a monster, or taking "sanity damage" when confronting new creatures. Lovecraft envisioned creatures so far outside the rules of our own world, they *cause the very order of reality* to break down in our own. Imagine functioning in a world where one plus one no longer made two. Really – lift up a pointer finger on each of your hands and set them beside each other. You have two fingers, side by side. There's no way to deny that, there's no other way to conceptualize that. That's just what two is. But in the realm of the Ancient Ones, that can't be taken for granted.

I lack the imagination to envision a universe where one and one together makes something that isn't two. I can't conceive of any way to make it work, and, even if I try, I don't truly believe in it. I have a hunch that if I was walking down the street and reality warped around me, creating a disturbance so powerful that the rules of basic mathematics failed, my mind would be dealt a harsh blow.

As Lovecraft understood, a person's psychology can be strained by many different kinds of information. Someone who is deeply religious can have their faith challenged, or new scientific theories can cause secular-minded people to re-envision their paradigms of thought. But there are limits to how much the mind can cope with. The books and games of the Cthulhu Mythos speak to the part of me *awed* by the real world and science. It doesn't take evil entities bent on the world's destruction to make my head spin; physics does the job just fine.

When I try to imagine the forces at work in the heart of a black hole,

I am astonished and amazed. When I try to envision the distance from Earth to just Proxima Centauri (the next closest star to our planet), my mind reels. Humanity's fastest-moving spacecraft, moving at 60,000 kilometers per hour would take *78,000 years* to reach it. That's longer than the expanse of recorded human history, and then some.

Space is huge. We see such a tiny amount of it through telescopes and space probes. And while we've done an admirable job creating a picture of the universe around us, it's far from complete. But if what we *do* know about space fills me with such astonishment and awe, how could I handle even *more* cosmic information? I'm not sure if I could. I don't mind being a tiny speck on a tiny mote of a planet in the back corner of a small galaxy. I know I'm a terribly unimportant conglomerate of carbon and water – but my world, like every human's, is framed by my own ego, by the sense that I matter. Every time a monster inflicts sanity damage in *Arkham Horror*, it's a reminder that the universe is more than happy to take our egos down a peg or two.

Strangely enough, playing games about cosmic terror comforts me as to how little I really know about the universe. I will never be an astronaut. I will never travel to another dimension. In real life, I am unlikely to face any creature more unusual than an opossum. But I can play *Arkham Horror* and *try* to imagine what I would do if a new kind of reality appeared in my hometown, and we confronted the unknown.

Bringing Science and the Esoteric Together

It's not like I'm unwilling to make the effort to understand new information, to re-examine my place in the universe. I try, I really do. It's just that I have a healthy respect for the difficulty involved in this.

For as long as I can remember, I have had an abiding interest in the esoteric *and* a fierce love of science. It's difficult to reconcile the two. I yearn to live in a haunted house, but scoff at pseudoscientific accounts of ghost activity. I collect books about witchcraft and alchemy, but firmly believe them nonsense. I'm a skeptic, but I'm also not sure if I'll ever give up the hope that, someday, I'll find a mystical tome with a kernel of truth hidden beneath the smoke and sulfur.

In the Cthulhu Mythos, the smoke and sulfur only serve to give validity to that kernel of truth. University professors find the secrets of ancient civilizations in ancient art. Mathematics students uncover the mysteries of interdimensional travel, only to realize witchcraft tapped into the same principles a hundred years earlier. In *Arkham Horror*, your character might go to Ye Old Magick Shoppe and buy a spell to fight monsters... or he/she might earn clues by presiding over a dissection at the Miskatonic University Science Building. Science and the esoteric are just different sides of the same coin, two expressions of a larger truth.

Since you need to fight monsters and close interdimensional portals using both science and mysticism, you collect a number of strange and wonderful items. Some are oddball mystical weapons such as enchanted daggers, or rings emblazoned with stones from other worlds. Others are imbued with more classic powers, such as ornate silver crosses and bottles of holy water. Magic books appear frequently, usually a nod to Lovecraft's many scholarly characters and his famous *Necronomicon*. Of course, these mysterious books and tools are used in conjunction with plenty of maps, historical documents, dark cloaks, axes and whips. Every character feels a bit safer with a weapon at hand. Maybe a knife or a sword? How about a Tommy gun? They're all available for you to collect. You can even buy a bottle of whiskey to help reduce the sanity damage taken when fighting a particularly hideous monster, or casting a very powerful spell.

Alcohol might not seem like such a valuable asset when you're faced with oncoming inter-dimensional terrors, but, in this game, you cope however you can, and hope it's enough.

The Wonder of the Unknown

When we go up to the mountains in August, I talk to my daughter about the development of astronomy and humanity's attempts to explain the space beyond our own solar system. While doing so, I try to keep my imagination and so much of what I have learned from Lovecraft tucked safely at home. The space between the stars is a dark void, a powerful gap that some look to fill with religion (the Perseid meteor showers, in fact, are sometimes called "the tears of St. Thomas," because they are most visible on or around August 10th, his feast day). Other people, like me, prefer to fill the gaps with science. We read about dark matter and the expanding universe. We cheer at the scaffolding of knowledge we are building, the tools we've developed and the information we've found.

On those warm August nights, I choose a sense of wonder over terror, and do my best to pass that on to my daughter. But when there is a roof over my head, and the stars are sealed safely out of sight, I pick up my dice and monster tokens and ask myself: "Is there something stirring out there tonight? Are the stars in an evil alignment?"

And I will let myself feel a delicious shiver of pure cosmic terror.

A Vicarious Tale of Getting into Video Games for the Plot

Hannah Rothman is a self-titled casual gamer. A veteran of the Pokémon generation, she likes to spend her travel time listening to audiobooks while playing about four or five iterations of *Angry Birds* (old habits of solving problems by throwing cartoon animals at each other). She has also been writing live-action role-play adventure games for her amazing camp, The Wayfinder Experience, since 2008. In print, Hannah has written on *Doctor Who* for *Outside In* vols. 1 and 2 and her own series, *Twitter Who*. She can be found at hannahjrothman.com.

My parents never let me have a mainstream gaming console as a kid. I had my GameBoy, the family desktop computer, and the TV, so they figured that was plenty of entertainment for me. Of course, growing up in the 90s meant that it was an optimal time for kids to hang out by going to each others' houses and playing video games. Except I grew up in New York City and my friends were spread across all five boroughs. So, for most of my childhood, my gaming was limited primarily to hours of *Pokémon* and trips to my grandparents' house where I could play *Mario Kart* on my cousin's N64. All of my video-game knowledge came from my friends, virtually all of whom had consoles at home and frequently regaled each other with tales of the antics of the cast of *Final Fantasy, Kingdom Hearts, Sonic the Hedgehog* and later *Halo* and *Grand Theft Auto*. I was frustrated at being so shut off from this world that seemed to engulf the rest of my generation, leaving me out in the cold with just a small handheld battery-powered campfire while everyone else was inside a nice hotel with central heating.

And then I discovered video-game television. 2003 to 2005 was the heyday of G4 TechTV, a channel I discovered while browsing the DVR one day and ran across an episode featuring a review of the latest Sonic game. The show in question was *X-Play*, an entertaining review program. I wound up tuning in a couple more times in the next few months when they reviewed a game I knew by reputation but never had a chance to play. A few episodes in, something rather non-sequitur came cartwheeling in at the very end. Something naked. It all happened in a matter of seconds: the female host cut to a five second game clip with the palest man I'd ever seen doing naked cartwheels through a level, the male host screamed in terror, and then it was over.

... what?

Looking ahead, I found an upcoming episode entitled "Naked Man Cartwheels," which I figured would help clear up whatever the fresh hell I'd just watched. Hoping I would at least learn the title of that game, I wound up getting more than I bargained for. The episode featured a segment called Uncomfortable Moments in Gaming, which explained everything surrounding the polygonal streaking. The game was *Metal Gear Solid 2: Sons of Liberty*, a PlayStation 2 release from 2001, and the pasty naked cartwheeler was named Raiden, an apparently unpopular character who stole most of the gameplay time from series protagonist Solid Snake. At that particular point in the game, Raiden had been captured by the bad guys and had all his equipment stolen, only to be freed by a double-agent in their ranks. The goal of the infamous Naked Raiden level was to find Snake and get Raiden's clothes back, all while avoiding getting shot by enemy soldiers and thus suffering a highly undignified death.

The clips they showed intrigued me even more. A protagonist duo of a chiseled agent with a mullet and an effeminate blond guy with a sword? Terrorist organizations that looked like a team of Bond villains? Why did that one guy have giant robot tentacle arms? Also, ninjas?

I wanted to know more. I wanted to learn these peoples' stories.

Since the release of *Metal Gear Solid 3* was imminent, G4 TechTV had plenty of programming in the coming months to help fill me on the world of *MGS* and the colorful cast of characters who inhabited it. This series went far beyond the "gotta catch 'em all" and "collect all these gems to save the world" game plots that I was used to. While on the surface each game had the conventional spy-movie premise of "sneak into the enemy base and take out their Ultimate Weapon," it boasted interesting, well-rounded characters and thematic depth. Solid Snake wasn't a fresh-faced sharpshooter with biting wit to match, he was a world-weary veteran approaching middle age and desperately trying to retire from a line of work that kept dragging him back into the hero role (with dry wit to match). Quirky scientist Hal "Otacon" Emmerich wasn't just the token nerd and part-time comedic foil for Snake, he had the pathos of a man who kept losing loved ones and went into robotics to fulfill a childhood dream, only to be taken advantage of for his talents and sensitive nature. *MGS 1*'s love interest, Meryl, wasn't a Damsel in Distress, but a wide-eyed rookie Action Girl who was just in over her head. Even poor Raiden wasn't just a naïve newbie who looked up to Snake as a living legend, but was a man trying to bury his horrific past as a child soldier under a new life in New York and a romance he didn't quite know how to handle.

Between the G4 TechTV shows and the aid of a fledgling Wikipedia, I was able to gradually piece together essential bits of the larger *Metal Gear* mythos: Solid Snake was a clone of a legendary soldier, Big Boss, and had an Evil Twin Brother named Liquid Snake who served as a major series antagonist; the titular Metal Gear was a walking tank that could fire nuclear missiles to and from anywhere on the globe; each game took place about seven years in the (respective) future; it was soft enough on Moh's Scale of Sci-Fi Hardness to allow for a small handful of characters to possess supernatural abilities (also for the existence of a cyborg ninja character in a couple games). Most importantly, the stealth aspect of the gameplay encouraged the player to avoid killing and added to one of the core themes of the series: it was an interactive action story that denounced war instead of glorifying it.

But I wasn't that interested in playing *Metal Gear Solid* for the actual gameplay. I wanted to play the movie. I wanted to get the full story of this wonderfully weird alternate Earth of clone agents shooting rockets at giant robots, severed arms that possessed people, cyborg ninjas, blond guys having swordfights on the roof of Federal Hall to avenge the murder of their parents, AI systems that went haywire and started demanding scissors, and psychics who mocked you by breaking the fourth wall.

Unfortunately, YouTube was still a couple years off, so I turned to the next best thing: sharing the madness with my friends in a desperate attempt to drag them down with me.

This tactic soon worked with my best friend, who wound up digging *MGS 1* out of her family's communal game pile and started falling in love with it just as hard as I had. The next couple of times I went over to her place, she'd saved the game at certain places so we could watch the cutscenes together with minimal interruption from the gameplay (although we did have some fun making Snake run around in a cardboard box during a brief elevator interlude). We played through both of the game's endings, starting with the one where Meryl dies so we could get the sad ending out of the way first. It was an emotional ride, and I felt ready to take the next step: actually owning one of the games. I only had one option, but it was a pretty good one. An expanded re-release of

Metal Gear Solid 2, called *Substance*, had a port for the PC. With some help from another tech-savvy friend in getting me set up with an Xbox controller adapter, I could finally enter this world for real. After spending a few days training with the VR Mission mode to get the hang of the actual game controls, I clicked New Game and sat back to drink in the rivetingly orchestrated title sequence and the sweeping opening shots of Snake striding slowly through the midnight rain before launching himself off the George Washington Bridge and bungee-jumping onto a tanker ship below. Time to learn firsthand what happened next.

Getting inside the game opened up all those hidden nooks and crannies of character and story that had eluded me in the G4 TechTV segments and the online synopses. I got to experience the little moments, like Otacon reciting Chinese proverbs and getting their meanings hilariously mangled, and Raiden's gentle flirting with his girlfriend Rosemary whenever I saved the game. I learned soon after that Raiden and Rose's relationship was, shall we say, not terribly well received by most fans. Of course, I was a 14-year-old girl and found it romantic and super adorable that they would take breaks from rescuing the President of the United States to reminiscence about watching classic monster movies on their first date. It gave them depth, a glimpse into what these characters were like as people and what they might be like in their off-hours when they weren't trying to avoid a global disaster.

I beat the game three times and breezed over to my best friend's house a couple times for some *Metal Gear Solid 3*, after which I turned to the next logical step: fanfiction. I was just a reader at first, being most interested in stories featuring Raiden. I'd officially adopted him as my favorite character at that point, taking pity on him as the series underdog and quite frankly finding him much more relatable than Snake. Unfortunately, there were a fair number of fanfics that liked to dump on him, or do something horrible to break him up with Rose (I know I made at least one, rather poor, attempt at fix-it fic for this). Then, one day, I saw a new slew of fics crop up by the same writer on fanfiction. net. They were remarkably well-written, most of them nailing a very Douglas Adams sense of humor, and all the author's notes referred to being originally posted on "LJ." What was this "LJ"?

Long story short, that's how I discovered LiveJournal and made my first foray into online fandom. The folks I met there were pretty cool people, with equal love for all the major characters and reams and reams of excellent fanart and fanfiction. They were into *Metal Gear Solid* for the same reason I was: the great characters and story. I think my time in that fandom helped change me for the better, and prepped me for the future. Through some embarrassing trial-and-error, I learned a thing or two about internet etiquette the hard way (restrained use of exclamation marks, learning the difference between hate and constructive criticism, etc).

I also spent a lot of time in the *MGS* slash community, which singledhandedly undid my subconscious homophobia. I'd spent most of my childhood assuming that being gay was a strictly "adult" thing that you weren't supposed to talk about, and no one had ever told me plainly that it was "good" or "bad." But reading through some of the community's best slashfic, I finally grasped this crazy idea that love was more than just "this man and this woman get together" and that it was really a question of "are these two *people* compatible with each other?"

After a good solid year or two, I drifted away from *Metal Gear Solid* for a bit. I cosplayed as Meryl and Otacon for my first two conventions and I kept up with the *Kojima Productions Report* podcast, but that was pretty much it. I hit a full-on anime phase in high school and later became wholly consumed by events at my theater camp. Plus, new content for *MGS* was relatively minimal. The LJ community puttered along at a slow pace and any key details about an upcoming *Metal Gear Solid 4* were kept close to the developers' chests. I was perfectly content to chug along with my Adult Swim anime block and writing stories for camp instead of fanfiction.

But of course, I wound up keeping an ear out anyway. *Metal Gear Solid 2* had ended on a cliffhanger and *Metal Gear Solid 3* was a prequel. *Metal Gear Solid 4* would finally tie up all the loose ends of the story. I had to know what happened next.

And then, one day, the trailer came out and everything came flooding back.

It happened one ordinary morning as I was checking my email and social networking sites before heading off to school. This was our first real glimpse at what the actual game was going to look like. Teasers before this had just been vague concept art and a trailer running on the *MGS 3* graphics and character models... but this was the real thing. The world that unfolded before me was bleak. *Metal Gear Solid*, which had always been about a near future not terribly unlike our own, had finally gone over the brink into a full-fledged war story. It was a picture of despair, in the middle of a war-torn city with haunting choral music in the background and the ominous tagline "war becomes routine." There was Snake, now an old man with grey hair who needed frequent injections to keep fighting. A full ten minutes of gameplay footage followed, a segment I tried to skip so I could see what I'd come for. Then, at the end of the trailer, came the flickers of hope. Virtually the entire supporting cast of the first two games, the characters I'd fallen in love with in the first place, were back. And they'd grown. The ending of *MGS 1* where Meryl survives turned out to be the canonical one, and she was now leading her own team of rebels. Otacon had come to terms with the true gravity of the situation and took things more seriously than ever.

And then there was Raiden.

Series creator Hideo Kojima had hinted in interviews that Raiden was going to be "cool" in *MGS 4*, but I hadn't fathomed *how* cool. I loved Raiden already just the way he was, but now there might finally be a chance for the naysayers in the fandom to get to like him, too. The trailer reached Raiden's name in striking brush-stroke font across the screen and my breath caught in my chest. A man in black and silver armor appeared, face covered by a darkened visor. The visor lifted with a slight hissing sound, and beneath it was the face of an old friend. An old friend who had taken up the mantle of the game's new cyborg ninja. He was hardened, battle-ready and looking straight at the camera with icy blue eyes that had obviously seen so many horrors since I last saw him.

"Snake," read the caption translating the Japanese dialogue, "It's my turn to protect you."

I stopped the video and gazed at him in awe. Not caring how silly it sounded, I whispered to myself, "Oh my god, you're all grown up!"

It wasn't until a year after *Metal Gear Solid 4* came out that I had a proper sit-down with a friend of mine who had prepared videos of the last few hours of the game. We could skip over the gameplay that much more easily, cutting right to the heart of the story. To see how it all ended. Oh, how I wish I could have shown 14-year-old me that last scene with Raiden, where he finally gets his happy ending with Rose after losing most of his natural body and spending the entire game thinking that Rose had miscarried and left him for an older man. The loose threads between the previous three games were tied up, the last of the major villains were probably dead for good, Meryl got married, Snake finally found closure with what he was and was allowed to walk off into the sunset at last, and poor Otacon was left to explain his departure to their adopted little girl.

This was what mattered to me in the end. I didn't need to pick up a controller, I just wanted to sit back and watch the story unfold.

We Play to Lose

Emily Care Boss of Black & Green Games is an independent roleplaying game designer from western Massachusetts. Known for her trio of romance-themed games: *Breaking the Ice, Shooting the Moon* and *Under my Skin*, Boss edited the *RPG = Role Playing Girl* zine (rpgirl-zine.blogspot.com). She is a contributor to two diversity in gaming blogs: *Imaginary Funerals* (imaginaryfunerals.com) and the ENnie-award winning *Gaming as Women* (gamingaswomen.com). You can find her games at blackgreengames.com.

I walked through the forest, lost in thought, thinking about loved ones and preparing myself for what lay ahead. A turn in the path brought a stone semi-circle into sight. Women sat on the stone benches, holding lit candles, listening quietly as the memorial service for those who were lost in the Event ended. My two chosen partners sat together on a bench, holding hands. One saw me and gave a welcoming wave. I sat behind them and tried to focus on the briefing being given. We were here to be screened and interviewed for our potential as a family. Were we going to be eligible for access to sperm, preserved and frozen? It was now the only source of reproduction, since everyone who carried Y-chromosomes in their bodies was dead. The women spoke their memories of fathers, brothers, husbands, and friends. A woman sitting next to me passed me a candle and helped me to light it.

And this was how I entered the Nordic LARP, *Mad About the Boy.*

Mad About the Boy was run in Connecticut in October, 2012. It's inspired by concepts in the comic series *Y, the Last Man* by Brian K. Vaughn and Pia Guerra. As in the comic, all humans with a Y chromosome have been killed by a mysterious plague and the plot explores the resultant geo-political concerns about the fate of humanity. Journalist and LARP researcher Lizzie Stark worked with First Person Entertainment (who produce the live action game *Doomsday*) to bring the LARP version, with its distinctly Nordic flavor, to the shores of the US.

It was a 31-person game, run by Stark; Jeramy Merritt from First Person Entertainment; US volunteers including A.A. George, George Locke, Sarah Miles, Avonelle Wing, and myself; as well as three organizers from Norway. The Norwegians – Margrete Raaum, Tor Kjetil Edland, and Trine Lise Lindahl – had written the game and had run it twice before in Europe. We staged the game in a campground in Orange, Connecticut, that had a good relationship with First Person Entertainment and that had been used for many LARPs in the past. The players were housed in fireplace-heated cabins, and play took place in the cabins and the main hall, where we met, ate, danced and learned.

The players ran the gamut from die-hard LARPers to people who had only played tabletop roleplaying games. In the European runs of *Mad About the Boy*, two games had been offered: one with an all-female cast, one with mixed gender participants. Since we were only able to offer one running in the US, we decided to go with the all-female cast, and hoped to offer a mixed gender run at a later date. Transgender women were welcomed and encouraged to take part. People of all genders were supportive of these choices, with many men referring women to information about the event, and a mixed-gender team adapting and putting on the LARP.

Nordic LARPs often have in-depth sets to provide a "360 degree" game world. A game based on the Battlestar Galactica television show, *Monitor Celestra*, was run in March 2013 on a rented Swedish battleship. One game, *Mellan Himmel Och Hav* (*Between Heaven and Sea*), as inspired by the science fiction of Ursula K. Le Guin, was run on theater soundstages, with lights, sound and surroundings crafted to resemble an alien planet with an 18-hour daily cycle. Another common theme in the games is tackling problematic or weighty topics, such as the construction of gender in the alien world of *Between Heaven and Sea*, or imprisonment and detention in such games as *Kapo* and *System Danmarc*. *Mad About the Boy* had the serious issues of these games, but was lighter on the world simulation.

A LARPing Family

As *Mad About the Boy* unfolded, our chosen families – formally recognized triads – were offered the possibility of bearing children via use of sperm banks controlled by our government. But the questions we had about ourselves and each other were many: would *we* be chosen? What was the committee's criteria? Would the others be chosen instead of us? What would it mean for them, or us, to have a child? How would these different communities raise their children and keep them safe? What were our real hopes of being able to continue the human species?

In the face of this, our answers were largely hopeful. The time waiting for our turn being screened for physical or psychological strengths and weaknesses was spent in the common area. We mingled with one another and shared what we had done since the disaster that killed all the men, how we were rebuilding, and what our hopes were for the future. Our triad made some lucrative deals to provide shipping for important resources. We needed each other. We made tentative connections to help face the chaos of our world.

We also had the opportunity to test questions asked by feminist critique: how had patriarchal oppression and biases affected the development of society? In the absence of our traditional gender differences, what choices would we make about how we ordered and structured our new world?

Mad About the Boy used techniques common to Nordic LARPs (workshopping and debriefing) and some more influenced by Nordic freeform. The workshopping was the first difference we encountered. This involved a series of exercises, some intended to help us learn about how we would play the game, some to help us learn about our characters. We worked with small groups, family units that would hopefully become parents and try to repopulate the world. We talked about our characters, and brainstormed about what our relationships were, as well as our dynamics and challenges. We took the information we had read before the game and "made it our own." This allowed us to enter the game with a feeling of familiarity.

Each triad had a different background and focus: mine ran a successful business and was trying to help build up infrastructure in Pennsylvania. Others were a group of Islamic women who had a faith-based community; artists who were documenting the events (with some very pessimistic and hidden agendas); and conservative women who ended up feeling very isolated due to assumptions made about them by the others. When discussing our plans, hopes and dreams, we could share not only what our character would want the others to hear, but also our inner thoughts. This allowed us to give our doubts and fears voice.

For me, a major part of the experience was the post-game debriefing. In Nordic LARP, that includes discussing the emotional impacts of the game... as well as thoughts and experiences that might affect one's life beyond the LARP. In the case of *Mad About the Boy*, there were so many aspects of the characters' experiences that could intersect with our own lives that post-game debriefing was extremely important.

The debriefing: It took place in stages. First, we mingled and the organizers would ask: "What was a high point of the game? What was something another player did that really made the game shine, or helped you play? What was a moment that resonated with your life or that you want to take home with you? What parts of the character you played are you glad to leave behind?"

Then we gathered in groups of five to eight and offered feedback on the LARP itself. Finally, we met in one big circle and had a wide ranging discussion about our impressions about the game. We learned about the other players' experiences.

End game: The game for me was powerful and moving. Of my triad, we were strangers at the onset, one never having played a LARP before. But we bonded as players and created a "family" that looked out for one another, even in moments when crisis hit and other groups were exploding along fault lines. We faced the insane opportunity (which also turned into a bit of a calamity) of a living man being found by reaching out and trying to keep each other safe and sane.

We "played to lose," meaning we embraced moments when things went wrong. Our "bad" decisions brought more interesting, dramatic outcomes into play. Being chosen as parents *wasn't* a goal traditionally found in a lot of LARPs. Instead, it was a (excuse me) pregnant situation, with potential for many things happening. My triad's dynamic was loving and supportive. Other triads made different choices. All of the players brought complexity to our characters and our play that gave us highs and lows. Highs and lows that let others interact with us, bounce off of our experiences and feed them into the complex system of strengths and weaknesses they were expressing.

We didn't use any "stats," like in many other games. If conflicts arose, it was up to us to use our judgment in resolving the issues.

Playing with a group of 30 other women was a wonderful experience. It was a rare opportunity, given that the typical gender ratio at gaming events is usually one-third women, two-thirds men. But there are more women in games all the time. We're simply becoming more connected and more aware of how many women already play, run, write, edit, illustrate, publish and do everything about games. But getting to be in the room with a couple dozen of them all at the same time, and affirm our experiences as women together, all of us, put it into a wonderful perspective. Transgender women participating spoke about it as a strong, positive experience, as was captured beautifully by Jo Kreil in her article "Mad About the Girl" in the *2013 Wyrd Con Companion Book*. Everyone brought so much emotion to their characters that I could have spent a week being with these women, and exploring the world we had to re-make together.

The situation facing us in the game was catastrophic, but it gave us windows and opportunities that we could explore if we worked together. The loss of every human on the planet with a Y chromosome was immediate and mysterious, owing to a disease or event of unknown origin. And, when a survivor was found, there was no explanation – only his story of being a fugitive, captured, escaped, and on the run.

The game was powerful. I walked home with new experiences, new thoughts, and challenges to assumptions I had made. Also, with a greater appreciation for how much goes into putting on an event like this. My responsibility of making sure that everyone had props and equipment was such a small part of the logistics of space, comforts, time and organization that went into making the game happen.

We learned lessons about the strength of the issues – and got feedback about what worked, what did not, and what players and organizers would need to see changed for future events. Major issues discussed included the difficulties of portraying sensitive roles and issues of gender, particularly around the inclusion of transgender women. Post-game discussion has been fruitful and helped us look forward to being able to offer games that strive for even greater inclusion.

The biggest inspiration for me from *Mad About the Boy* was that we were able to create an event that gave players a deep, thoughtful and emotionally complex experience, using techniques that LARPers in Sweden, Norway, Denmark and Finland have practiced. We have a rich and long history of LARP in the United States to draw on as well. The players of this game indicated they wanted to participate in more. We can work together to create strong, safe and illuminating play. I look forward to collaborating with this team, and many others, again.

Author's Note: For another look at this game, see Lizzie Stark's article "Mad about the Techniques" in the *Wyrd Con Companion Book 2012* and "Mad About the Girl" by Jo Kreil in *Wyrd Con Companion Book 2013* at www.wyrdcon.com/ 2014/ 05 / the-wyrd-con-companion-book

Other links of interest: lizziestark.com; lizziestark.com/ tag/ MAtB/ ; firstpersonentertainment.com; en.wikipedia.org/ wiki/ Knutepunkt; nordiclarp.wordpress.com/ ; www.celestra-larp.com/

Chicks Dig Gaming

It's Five O'Clock Somewhere

Delaware-based author and self-confessed book nut **Amy Hanson** has been publishing professionally since 1995. She covers myriad subjects ranging from multi-genre music journalism and literary biography to pop culture, health issues for the layman and an assortment of metaphysical oddities.

I stumbled into *Second Life* like Alice tumbling down her rabbit hole, following a friend who talked me into joining because she wanted a friendly face to keep her company (a perfectly formed and airbrushed face with nary a crow's foot, I might add) as she researched the world for her own purposes, while I swore left, right and center that I would only observe.

I created an avatar, chose her a name. I had my starter-kit clothing (I'd be buying more as soon as I learned how to make money in this place), and I lived in a park because I didn't know where else to go. Hours spent fumbling with my newbie skins and hair and painted-on panties, hiding behind a fountain that sprayed mist into a rabidly pink sunset, and I was terrified. What if someone talks to me? What if that weird guy standing next to that purple tree asks me if I want to go some place quiet and *do* things? How do you even do them to begin with? (It turns out there are ways, animations for *every* conceivable occasion.)

Wait. Stop. Hang on and re-hinge. This is make-believe. Not quite *Plants vs. Zombies* make-believe, but it's still only as real as the power you give it. It's like playing Barbies, only with a Skipper or Ken who talks back. Okay. Good. Back on track and time to make myself fabulous...

Some weeks later, I was behind my fountain, looking stunning with my brand new skin and shape, changing to go to a blues club, boobs bouncing in the wind as I layered on couture.

"Excuse me," a woman said.

"Yes?"

"You can't be naked here. This is a Christian Park and you have to leave. God doesn't like sinners. You're banned."

Shit.

Log off log off log off, why won't it log me off?

I was mortified. Mother would not have been pleased. But after those feelings of shame passed, I was furious. Who did she think she was, to speak to me like that? She didn't even know me; she only saw what she wanted to – and I am not really a sinning, naked, hide-behind-a-fountain-changing bitch, thank you very much.

But how was she, or anyone else, to know that? Confronted with two sets of reality that are separated only by keyboard strokes, the edges have no choice but to blur.

Second Life, then, is nominally a game where you can build, travel, quest and socialize until you can't type anymore. Deeper down, it is also a platform for Jungian projection, for pulling out the shadows, and giving them tangible form in a tactile world. The ramifications of which are exciting and horrifying in turn.

Those that are there only, for example, to build fabulous buildings, 3D dioramas of the world throughout history, alien planetscapes or cinematic überworlds would probably deny this. So would those who are there to perform music, concerts, poetry and literature. So, even, would those who are there because their real lives have been obliterated by whatever horrifying circumstance has befallen them.

But the shadow is there all the same; it's always there and, when you free your mind, even just a little, the walls come tumbling down.

The seeds for multi-user platforms, which is what *Second Life* is, have been around since the 1970s. *Habitat*, developed by LucasFilmGames for the Commodore 64 gaming system is widely given credit as the first "virtual" world to lure in the living with the promise of an alternative existence. But it was the debut of Linden Lab's *Second Life*, in 2003, that kickstarted a new revolution. By the end of the 2000s, the game was a worldwide powerhouse and people everywhere were hooked.

Getting on the grid and creating a new life in a brave new world was manna for millions in the wake of global economic instability. Real life felt tenuous and dangerous. Forget the chat rooms that had hitherto dominated cyber society. There you were just a voice and an icon. *Second Life* allowed you to become a person as well, and not just any old person. *Second Life* gave you the opportunity to rebuild yourself from scratch. And because it was a worldwide phenomenon, suddenly you could flirt and wile your way across five countries, five *continents*, in a single evening. Letting your own four walls fall away and being utterly outrageous in full view of the universe was sexy. Even better, you could wear your old yoga pants and have the television on in the background.

It was easy – too easy perhaps – to forget about the things that kept us grounded, feet firmly planted in the world of Wal-Mart and mortgages, real-life marriage and real-life children and real-life pain. Do you remember the couple in Korea who let their daughter starve to death while raising a baby in the *Second Life* knockoff, *Prius*[7]?

Sadly, yes, that happened, and it's all too simple to judge a scenario like that. Harder to place on the side of right and wrong is the woman who allows *Second Life* to supplant her first life because her real-life husband beats the crap out of her on a daily basis, whereas her *Second Life* spouse is perfection personified.

Morally, you can still take a stand. Is she *actually* cheating on her human spouse by living a cyber romance with an online husband who lives in Romania? Yes, she is. But does it give her a sense of worth that she lacks in her own world? Yes, it probably does. So is she right to seek happiness and self-validation wherever she can? It's not really your business to judge.

Part of the hook of *Second Life* is freeing your mind from the constraints of right and wrong. Hopefully, once ensconced in your new skin (and new face and new hair and a wardrobe that you couldn't afford in several thousand real lives), there isn't much difference in how you *ought* to behave world to world. Society is society, whether or not it is controlled by keystrokes. But there are those moments when you flip a zinger (or better yet, plant a nuke beneath a perfectly formed bottom) to the spiteful chick who just sassed you, and who you *know* is most likely a guy sitting in his mother's basement, probably wearing yoga pants with the television on in the background. It. Feels. So. Good.

Where do you draw the line between freeing your mind and ferreting out your shadow, and blatant lying, though? Some don't draw that line. This petri dish is a vast expanse of primordial psychic soup – it's a psychiatrist's wet dream, really. Everyone is in-world for their own reason. At the base, it's a game. Layer up, level up and it's a place to explore a sexual fantasy you won't admit, even to yourself; it's a place where you have complete freedom to try something new – building, singing, stripping, curating; it's a therapist's couch with a captive audience every night. It's a place to lie, cheat and steal, or worse, prey on the weak and vulnerable. Or it's a place to be the benevolent, charitable, *giving* human being that we all wish that reality would let us become.

I'm savvy in real life. I'm a good judge of character and a thoroughly upstanding member of society. Remember, I was only going to observe.

---

7 *The Guardian*, March 5, 2010.

So, did I get sucked into high drama and stalked by predatory slime-balls who thought I was as naive as my earliest avatar appeared? You bet I did. Did I think coma-girl really *had* been near-fatally injured in a head-on collision? Absolutely. Did I defend her bad behavior until her stories started to fall apart? Embarrassingly, yes. Was it after she developed terminal brain cancer when her accident scans revealed an underlying glioma that I secret-squirrel investigated until I found out the truth? Ohhh yes, my beauty.

But did I confront her? No, I did not. At the same time as my cats were wondering why my mouth was open to the floor, and were contemplating rolling a manky old toy into it, I was puzzling out why on earth someone would even think of fabricating something so horrendous, and then running all the way with it. What makes someone tick so wrong that they planted fantasy in real life, in order to feel validated, comforted and loved in *Second Life?* The more I looked, the more of it I saw, and it made me profoundly sad. Until the next drama came along. Then it was game on.

And that, I realized, is where my own shadow flickered. I was fascinated by the human condition sprawled out among the Slurls. Even better, I could observe *and* orchestrate situations amongst the group of people to whom I was attached, just to see what would happen. It was like high school all over again, but this time I was the mean girl, the puppet mistress in a world of my making, not the kid-all Stevie-Nicks-gypsy who spent her time in the art studio.

That, too, made me profoundly sad, and I flipped Jung the bird, dismantled my home and retrenched. I didn't give up the small circle of people who transcended the virtual world to become email pen pals, because that is one of the benefits of *Second Life*. Nor did I stop logging in. Your scope does widen. You do meet people who you'd sit down to coffee with. BDSM club owners by night and dorky friends swapping recipes by day. It happens.

On the flip side of chaos, thankfully, is the utterly normal and often banal side of the game. It is entirely possible to buy land, build a home, get married, have a child, go to bed and do it all again the next day. There is something eternally comforting about routine, even if it mimics first life in minute detail. It's relaxing to sit on a deck and look at the water and have non-conversations and to laugh so hard you lose your breath with a group of friends. There are those who would argue that energy in that pursuit should be expended in real life, but I'm not so sure. Those moments, those conversations, are as valid, as real and as important as any in daily life and they may even be more so, since you can choose to drop the baggage of your first world problems at the teleport.

There is value in the virtual world, more than I would have expected. Again, it's subjective. It doesn't matter, in the end, why you are there, or what your motives are, not really. All you need to do is own that reason. Don't even advertise it – that's boring – just look at yourself in the mirror and own it. At the end of the day, it's all just a game. Maybe.

Tomorrow, I'm think I'm going to rent some land and recreate Xanadu – from Coleridge's "Kubla Khan," not the movie. If you want to be naked in my pleasure-dome, it's fine by me. The milk of Paradise will be on the plinth to the left.

Saving Throws

Jody Lynn Nye lists her main career activity as "spoiling cats." When not engaged upon this worthy occupation, she writes fantasy and science fiction books and short stories. Before breaking away from gainful employment to write full-time, Jody worked as a file clerk, bookkeeper at a small publishing house, freelance journalist and photographer, accounting assistant and costume maker. For four years, she was on the technical operations staff of a local Chicago television station, ending as technical operations manager. Since 1987, she has published 43 books and well more than a hundred short stories. Although she is best known as a collaborator with other notable authors such as Anne McCaffrey (the Ship Who series, the Dinosaur Planet series), Robert Asprin (Dragons and Myth Adventures), John Ringo (*Clan of the Claw*) and Piers Anthony, Jody has numerous solo books to her credit, mostly fantasy and science fiction with a humorous bent. Her latest book is *View from the Imperium* (Baen Books), which she describes as "*Jeeves and Wooster* in space." During the past 25 years or so, Jody has taught numerous writing workshops. She also speaks at schools and libraries. When not writing, she enjoys baking, calligraphy, travel, photography and, of course, reading. Jody lives in the northwest suburbs of Illinois with her husband, Bill Fawcett, and Jeremy, their cat.

I started playing *Dungeons & Dragons* in 1976 – but let me backtrack a little. I got into roleplaying because I have a concerned uncle. He taught music at my college one day a week. Naturally, I took his course (he is a terrific teacher, and I love music), and we would chat afterward. He noticed that I was lonely. He introduced me to a former student of his who was then in law school. This nice young man took me to a party held by his sister, where I met:

- The sister and brother-in-law who would introduce me to the Society for Creative Anachronism.
- The man who was moving on from a job who recommended to his bosses that I take it, which led to my first (and last) job in television.
- The couple who ran the local *D&D* group. The nice young man and I didn't date for long, but the three connections I made on that night pretty much formed my future as it has since unfolded.

Apart from those people in Lake Geneva, Wisconsin, who played with Gary Gygax and his friends and those who subscribed to *Chainmail*, *Dungeons & Dragons* was not yet widely known. The rules, recently upgraded from what were known as "the purple sheets" (those of you too young to have experienced mimeograph printing, please check Wikipedia) consisted of three little manila soft-cover pamphlets and came with a small set of polyhedron dice in a white box with red and black print on the cover. I knew nothing about *D&D* when I arrived at my new Dungeon Master's apartment on the north side of Chicago. I pretty much jumped in at the deep end. I had to read from other people's copies of the rules, but I caught on to the basics right away. I rolled up a character, gave her a name and began to play.

I loved the idea of a game that needed so little equipment to play. Someone always had a copy of the rules. A map and playing pieces were optional. Use of an official module from the parent company was entirely up to your DM. All that you really needed was a pencil and paper – any paper – to keep track of your hit points, and a few weirdly shaped dice for rolling against random encounters and battle sequences. (The original four-sider could never pass safety inspections today: it was a yellow plastic pyramid with points so sharp, it would have made a great caltrop.)

The thing I loved about roleplaying from moment No. 1 is that *D&D* is simply pretending out loud in the company of other like-minded individuals. In a *D&D* game, you got to play "make-believe," and no one would make fun of you. You could be a brave fighter, or a dastardly villain, or a creepy monster, or, as I almost always was, a magic-user. Everyone concentrated on their own characters and what they needed to do to survive against what the DM had devised for the day's adventuring.

To me, it was as much fun as when I was very small and played Winnie the Pooh on the playground with my best friend. (I was Pooh and Piglet; she was Christopher Robin and everybody else.) *D&D* was an empowering game for all of us, in different ways. My dungeon group met once a month at the DM's apartment. Among the players, two of us were female and four were male. My best buddy in the group always liked to play a big, dumb fighter. His day job was as the manager of the computer department of a major department store chain. Not to have to be the smartest guy in the room was a respite for him. "Hit the door!", he would declare, as we reached yet another chamber in the underground dungeon. "It's already open," said the DM. "I don't care! Hit it again!" It was stupid, and he loved doing it. The rest of us thought it was hilarious. The other woman in the group liked playing thieves, sneaking around, opening locks, picking pockets and climbing walls, a departure from her normal, honest personality.

For me, an impecunious college student in a difficult family, my escape was to be a powerful magic-user, blasting my enemies with magic missiles and fireballs. Alas, my four hit points at level one usually meant I spent the later part of the game sitting on the sidelines, being dead. The rest of the party didn't last much longer, either. Our DM was impatient to get us playing the complex situations he had devised deeper in the dungeon, so he let us draw from a Deck of Many Things. I was boosted to Level Eight on the spot. From then on, I had plenty of hit points and I could zap things! It took a lot of the frustration out of my everyday life and helped save my sanity.

I started going to game conventions in 1977. As a female in the early years of gaming, I was an oddity at the tables. When I attended my first Gen Con that year, I was one of only six or so women present, and one of only three not named Gygax. Because it was 1977, and I was a brown-haired, brown-eyed girl who could sew, I attended the first day dressed as Princess Leia. (Yes, I have pictures.) I probably would not have attended on my own, but at the time I was dating one of the founders of TSR, Brian Blume. I played in a few of the tournaments, and enjoyed myself enormously.

At no time did the other gamers treat me as an intruder. If I could roll dice and help out the party, I could sit down among them and play. Being mostly adolescent and 20-something males, they might have felt awkward having a female at the table with them. I caught many a shy and admiring glance. It was great for my ego.

I do admit that I felt more uncomfortable trying to play more traditional wargames with the older male players. I put it down to the subject matter as much as anything. Men who are attracted to playing generals and admirals with thousands of miniature figurines on a gigantic field grid also thought that roleplaying games were frivolous. I found their games dry and uninteresting. There were too many other games that interested me to devote my time to theirs. To play D&D, you didn't need an encyclopedic knowledge of the troop movements in World War II.

I loved game conventions, especially the dealers' room. Game companies, large and small, premiered their new wares at Gen Con. I bought some games; some because I wanted to play them, others because they made me laugh, like *Woof Meow*. Lou Zocchi sold dice in a massive booth at the front of the room. The dice came in every size, from a quarter inch on a side to several inches across, all made of bright, clear acrylic in every possible jewel color that made all my elvish instincts go on overdrive. (Still have my bag o' dice.)

The miniature figurine booths, such as Ral Partha, were always thronged with gamers looking for the newest releases. In those days, Lou Zocchi usually did a minifig painting demo. Artists who illustrated the covers of *Dragon* magazine and TSR's modules, such as Larry Elmore and Clyde Caldwell, sold prints of their art from their own tables. I suppose I could have become upset over the fact that most of the art was of scantily clad women of pneumatic physiques, but there were also paintings of men with unlikely muscles wearing just as little. The objectification never bothered me, because it never applied personally. What mattered to me was that games and objects connected to gaming were for sale.

As each year went by, the number of women at the conventions increased. Many of them came for the first time as someone's girlfriend. Afterward, they showed up on their own, drawn by the fun and social interaction of the games. They enjoyed it, so they began to bring their own friends and, many years on, their children, too.

Roleplaying also helped me get my first job in publishing. As Brian's girlfriend, I was admitted within the inner circle of TSR. At that time, Gary Gygax was working on manuscripts for the new *Player's Guide*, *Dungeon Master's Guide* and *Monster Manual*. Because I could type well, the owners worked out a deal for me to type up Gary's handwritten pages (and fix typos and grammatical errors as well) for a dollar a page. I didn't get credit in print, but I did get copies of the oversized hardcover books.

Gaming helped me build confidence. I was a shy child. I found it very difficult to approach people one-on-one, but the one thing I have never experienced in my life was stage fright. Put me into a role, and I was Ethel Merman. With my character sheet and dice in front of me, I knew what I could do, and I did it. I learned to give and take with other players. I stuck up for myself and defended others who needed backup against bullies. We rubbed some of the unsocialized behavior off one another. My newfound backbone helped me cope in outside situations as well. I learned to manage better in speaking to potential bosses and other strangers.

D&D provided a forum to meet new friends. Sitting together over game tables, we found similar tastes in movies and books, as well as arguing happily over new supplementary modules published by TSR and its rival Mayfair Games (Role-Aids). We had wonderful conversations in restaurants that often resulted in other patrons fleeing in terror. ("So, when he jumped out from behind the door, swish! I chopped his head off with my +2 sword! The blood spurted about ten feet in the air!" "Did you get his treasure?" "Oh, yeah. He had a bag of silver, but I had to search the body to get it.") In the earliest days of D&D, we could clear a restaurant to a radius of three tables around us. I dated a couple of fellow gamers after breaking up with Brian, though the love of my life was almost within arm's reach all the time.

Gen Con is the best and the biggest of the games conventions, but there are many others, such as Origins Game Fair, Little Wars in Chicago, Winter Fantasy in Indiana and Gary Con, a small but growing convention in Lake Geneva held in Gary Gygax's memory. DragonCon in Atlanta hosts a gaming track that qualifies as one of the largest in the country. There have always been smaller ones as well. One very hot summer, three of the members of my dungeon group and I drove to Flint, Michigan, to a convention held in a high school that was closed for the summer. It was so miserable in the building that everyone was sweating and chugging endless bottles of pop. To keep cool, I wore a one-piece red bathing suit and a pair of blue jeans. (Gimme a break; I was 21.) I did notice that some of the judges in the tournaments I played often gave me an extra saving throw to keep me from being knocked out.

Fast-forward seven years, to a science-fiction convention in Chicago. A dear friend introduced me to Bill Fawcett, one of the owners of Mayfair Games. At that time she was working for TSR. The two of them had been sounding each other out, trying to glean trade secrets from one another without much success. When Bill found out that I was not only an SF fan and writer but a gamer, we started discussing past conventions to see if our paths had crossed before. They had. Not only had he seen me walking around Gen Con in my Princess Leia costume, but he had been sitting at the end of a table with me in Flint. He remembered my red bathing suit rather vividly. Small world, indeed. Within a week he and I were dating, and within four months were engaged. We've been married 25 years.

Roleplaying games provide a forum for creative minds to exercise their whimsy. My second gaming group consisted almost entirely of writers and artists, many of whom have since gone professional. It was also almost all women. Though fantasy books of the time were canted largely toward male adventurers, fantasy gaming had a much greater contingent of women.

It didn't matter what your mama gave you; you could play a different gender, a different race, a different age, a different alignment. At times, my DMs threw us into situations where we changed from our normal bodies and personalities. I enjoyed the challenge to think as a different character. It's similar to skills I use to build characters and situations in my novels.

D&D in particular among the roleplaying games was a collaborative exercise of imagination. Any scenario given to any one of a hundred groups would run in a hundred different ways. Although the players are bound to follow the map as envisaged by the DM, how they follow it is up to them, acts of DMW[8] aside. Is the group cooperative, or not? Cowardly or inclined to barge boldly through? Did somebody's cleric get his pout on and refuse to throw healing spells because he decided that the other members of his questing party were not sufficiently holy to merit intervention by his god(s)? The farther into one's role a player delved, the more fun the game became.

In the first dungeon I played in, we created non-player character assistants and apprentices to increase the size of our group. At one point, a female NPC, assistant to the aforementioned big, dumb fighter, absented herself from the game, to "go visit her aunt." Nine months later – yup, you guessed it – she returned with a baby. The rest of us who had not been in on the joke howled with laughter. Then we had a wedding, and threw dry Cream of Rice cereal at the mini-figs of the characters. I drew a cartoon of the proud parents standing beside the little one in his first suit of plate armor. "Go on, sweetheart, say 'surrender or die' for your daddy!"

In a way, the characters we played took on a measure of reality, with all the foibles and weaknesses of human nature. They were extensions of our psyche, male and female, evil, good, chaotic or neutral. We felt free to take those beings we had evolved and acted through them, exploring being other people, being powerful, bold and adventurous. The more we relaxed among trusted fellow players, the farther outside our comfort zone we could venture. Playing together at a table with paper and pencil is a terrific equalizer. You don't have to heft a sword to fight. You just have to roll the dice.

One of the worst things about growing up is that you can lose touch with the imagination you had as a child. Make-believe becomes a thing

---

8 DMW: Dungeon Master's Whim. Fear it.

of the past. It's why J.M. Barrie explained that adults could never enter Neverland – they had stopped believing in things they couldn't understand. The trouble is, for those who leave the bounds of imagination, they lose that spark of seeing wonder around them. To enter adulthood was to dry up and be serious.

I went to my first high school reunion five years after graduating and discovered that, in that very short time, many of my schoolmates had become middle-aged. They scorned what had been genuine fun in the past, for fear of looking frivolous. I had never deeply cared what others thought of the things I enjoyed. For me, *D&D* was an oasis peopled by likeminded individuals who wanted to keep their imaginations alive. A lot of people who felt they didn't fit in elsewhere ended up in one of three places: the Society for Creative Anachronism, SF fandom and gaming. There is enormous overlap among all of these, and, once you've found one, you've found them all.

I understand very well why certain groups fear roleplaying gamers. When you can reduce the most terrifying demons in the bestiary to a few unusual characteristics and a number of dice rolls, they stop being terrifying. Fear of the unknown is a great weapon used to keep the masses in line. Those who question are ostracized from polite society. Most of the friends I have kept from my youth are those for whom being ostracized was old hat. No one understood us in the first place. Roleplaying gave us a place we could be together. (Science-fiction fandom is another place for intelligent, creative and nerdy individuals, but that's a different anthology.) We opened our arms, and playing tables, to those who managed to find us.

I haven't been active in gaming for many years. With jobs and families, most of us have drifted away from our groups. Every time I hear of someone who has managed to keep their game group active, I feel envious. I don't deny my past; I revel in it. I can never forget the fun of being part of a questing group. Anyone who shared an intense experience with others has a sense of belonging that people outside don't understand. Those who have served in wartime form a lifelong bond with the others in the foxhole with them. While "old campaigners" don't merit the respect as those who literally were under fire, they can look back on the games they shared and the fun they had together, and enjoy that bond.

The part I think I miss most is the verbal collaboration on an act of fantasy. As a writer, I work alone most of the time. Bouncing ideas off others is stimulating to the imagination as well as wonderful social interaction. Discovering *Dungeons & Dragons* was a lifeline for me. It kept me sane at a difficult time of my life and opened up my world in so many positive ways. I made my saving throw, and then some, thanks to a well-meaning uncle and a bagful of colored dice.

Go For the Eyes, Gamer Girls, Go For the Eyes!

Sam Maggs is a writer, televisioner, and geek girl, currently hailing from the Kingdom of the North (Toronto). Holding an MA in Literature and named "Awesome Geek Feminist of 2013," Sam is an editor for geek girl culture site *The Mary Sue*; a games journalist for *The National Post*; an occasional pop culture commentator on the Space Channel and MTV Canada; and is one-half of the two-lady YouTube Let's Play duo "the c_ntrollers." Sam's debut book, *The Fangirl's Guide to the Galaxy* (a handbook for helping ladies live their nerdiest life) will be out with Quirk Books in Spring 2015. Right now, you can probably find Sam romancing Alistair (again), re-living the moment Troy Baker totally flirted with her during an interview or arguing on Twitter @SamMaggs.

I blame YA fantasy author Tamora Pierce for making me into a gamer.

Okay, that's not *entirely* fair. Let's hop through a Time Gate real quick, and I can give you the whole story.

I grew up in a family of folks who loved games, so I was pretty much doomed from the start. My grandparents would sometimes be late for work, caught up playing *just one more level, seriously* of *BurgerTime* on their Intellivision. When I was five years old, my dad would sit me on his lap in front of his Windows desktop in the basement, letting me "help" him with whatever game we were into at the moment. We played a lot of *Myst*, and those days – before you could just hop online to find the solution to whatever in-game mystery you were trying to solve – "playing a lot of *Myst*" meant dedicating basically your entire year to wandering around the island, finding pages and playing that awful rocketship piano. As an aside, *Myst* taught me that people in games are never to be trusted. I can also remember a lot of hours spent in the dark playing *DOOM*, shooting our way through cacodemons and bullpigs with our "Big *Fancy* Gun 9000."

Yeah, so, okay, *maybe* not the best parenting, but I think I still turned out okay.

In the years following, I still loved gaming, but I primarily enjoyed it as a way to spend time with my family. My parents and I poured *months* into *Mario 64* (I'm pretty sure that monkey still has my hat), and I could lay a wicked smack-down in *Super Smash Bros.* The thing about my personal experience with gaming up to that point, though, was that I was never particularly interested in dedicating my time to playing *alone.* I never felt invested in a story or a narrative in a game in the same way that I did when watching a TV show or reading a great book – which brings me back to Tamora Pierce.

In grade school, I was the founding (and often only) member of my school's Library Club. Yeah, I bet you're not surprised in the least. It meant I didn't have to go outside for recess in the dead of winter, *and* I got to read a ton of awesome books with that extra time while avoiding all social interaction, so *who is the real loser here, kids who made fun of me a lot?* That's what I thought.

Anyways, during one particularly snowy sixth-grade recess in Canada, I found a book on the fiction shelf that I'd never bothered to pick up before. I was into serious kid sci-fi at the time – you know, books about boys (and they were always boys) getting downloaded into computers, or becoming obsessed with some virtual reality, or transforming into aliens. *This* book, on the other hand, had a bright-pink spine, featured a horse on the cover, and was called *Alanna: The First Adventure.* It was completely unlike anything I'd ever bothered to pick up; but, honestly, I was running out of interesting things to read – two recesses and a lunch every day meant a *lot* of reading time – and in a pre-teen act of nerdy defiance, I decided to go for it.

Spoiler alert: this book by Tamora Pierce changed my life. It's set in a fantasy world, similar to Westeros (though Pierce's book was released 13 years before G.R.R.M. began killing your faves in *Game of Thrones*), and all the usual fantasy trappings are there; knights, mages, kings, romance and rogues, to name a few. This book, though – *this* book was different because of the *protagonist.* Alanna starts out as an 11-year-old girl who refuses to let her gender determine her fate, and decides to become a knight by disguising herself as a male until she becomes an adult. Alanna was a girl who became the hero of her own story, not because she was the prettiest or the funniest or the richest, but because she worked *really hard,* and didn't let anyone tell her "No, you can't do that, because you're a girl." When other characters inevitably tried to tell her *just that,* she took off into the world, and proved them all wrong. I'd never read anything like it, or seen anything like it on TV.

Above all else, I'd definitely never *played* anything like it. That was the problem, you see; Mario (though adorable) was a dude, rescuing his girlfriend. Link? Same story, different outfit. Samus just looked like a big, metal suit. *Myst's* Stranger is referred to during in-game dialogue as a "he." The *Doom* marine was called "Doom*guy*." The little pixilated sprite on my (atomic purple) Game Boy Color in *Pokémon Red*? Also a boy. So, while I enjoyed playing these games as a girl, I couldn't directly *identify* with any of the characters I was supposed to be inhabiting. Game narratives weren't for, or about, women. Sure, it was fun to game with my family, but I couldn't immerse myself in their fictions the same way I could imagine myself as Alanna, taking swings at squires and learning how to control my magic. Games were about boys, and they were *for* boys (as I was often reminded by kids at school). They were stories for someone else.

Until *Baldur's Gate*.

I honestly can't remember how I came across the game, or why I thought I'd enjoy a game so completely dissimilar to the other games I was playing as an 11-year-old with huge glasses, but it hardly matters. What I *do* recall is opening the BioWare game after loading it, and coming across the best thing I'd ever seen in a video game: *the character creation screen.*

Not only was I suddenly able to pick the color of my outfit, but I could also completely customize my character's alignment, race, abilities and skills. Most importantly – above all of those things, things that seriously affect your gameplay – the very first option I was presented with was the choice of my character's *gender*. I could decide to be a *girl*, and I could give her a cute outfit and a great, high-fantasy name, and pick a lovely painted portrait for her, and she could be *me*, and we could run around doing all the things Alanna got to do, and it would by *our* story. A story about a girl, for the girl playing. It was the first game that told me it was okay to spend an hour in what was essentially a high-end online doll-maker; that girls could also game; that I *probably wasn't the only girl playing*. I was enthralled.

Once I got past the character screen and was actually in the Forgotten Realms, I became completely absorbed in the world. Candlekeep became as real to me as the capitol city of Corus had in Pierce's books; my character (always artfully named something like "Raina" or "Kalendria" for that full fantasy feel) was the baddest chick around, and she could beat up any gibberling or ettercap you threw at her. For a while, I even stopped playing the main quest line, and just wandered around the Realms, talking with AIs, inventing stories in my head about the landscapes and the NPCs and my character. Some of the first short fiction I ever wrote was inspired by the craziness I dreamed up while playing as my lady-character in *Baldur's Gate*. When *Baldur's Gate II: Shadows of Amn* came out two years later, well... so much for learning how to socialize in high school, I guess. Between that and my endless obsession with *Stargate*, who had time for hanging out?

After I'd finished the second *BG*, I slipped back into casual gaming. I got so busy with school and dance and reading and TV that playing fell into the background for a while. I forgot about the Forgotten Realms. Games came and went, but nothing really appealed to me outside of a group setting; I mean, I was *awesome* as Daisy in *Mario Kart*, but I told myself that maybe I just wasn't meant for single-player gaming. It wasn't until 2009, just in time for my twenty-first birthday, that I suddenly, absolutely *had* to have a PS3. And why was that?

I'd heard about *Dragon Age: Origins*.

Made by BioWare as the spiritual successor to *Baldur's Gate*, DA:O suddenly brought back all those memories of playing as a kick-ass fantasy chick, and I just *needed it*. Winning Game of the Year and lauded across the board as one of the best games ever made, I suddenly became aware that *this* was the kind of game I liked to play alone – and I was now aware that it had a name: "third-person fantasy RPG." When *The Elder Scrolls V: Skyrim* came out two years after that, I'd had it pre-ordered for months in advance. In both games, I spent a whole day just creating the perfect lady character, my perfect in-game proxy, so that I could care about her enough to dedicate the next however-many-weeks of my life to her story. To *our* story.

And, yeah, I know there have since been a few other games made with female protagonists (and I say "few" because it's a true rarity – in 2012, only 4% of games were made with an exclusively female playable character, and those had only 40% of the marketing budget given to games with a male protagonist). *Mirror's Edge* and *Portal* are amazing, empowering, positive examples of games with female PCs, but those are only *two games*; far too many others (hi, *Tomb Raider* – new *and* old – and *Bayonetta*) present problematic representations of women who seem to be there solely to satisfy the male gaze. I mean, "jiggle physics," really? On the complete other end of the spectrum, Samus's gender is all but eradicated in most versions of *Metroid*. *Grand Theft Auto V*, the highest-selling *anything* of all-time, doesn't let you play as a female character at all. It's shameful.

And despite the fact that, as of 2012, up to 45% of games let you choose to be male or female when playing (almost half! Progress!), there are often still problems with this model. Even great games like *Borderlands*, which allow you to choose between male and female PCs, have a whole roster of differently-abled male characters to choose from – and then the token female, whose defining characteristic is basically "has boobs." We're still living in a world where female avatars weren't added to *Call of Duty* (and, even then, only in multiplayer) for ten whole years because "the game engine couldn't handle it," as if generating a slightly different character shape was much too difficult in a *first-person shooter where you can't even see your own character* for the majority of the game. In fantasy RPGs, this isn't an issue – there's usually no difference in stats between male or female characters, no stealth bonus for ladies or strength bonus for men. Your choice of gender – as it should be in all things, surprise! – is completely irrelevant to gameplay, outside of how it makes the player *feel*.

I also realize that not everyone needs to play as a person of their own gender in order to identify with the character – there are plenty of men out there who prefer to game with a female avatar, just like I'm sure there are women who aren't at all bothered by playing games with exclusively male protagonists, and that's totally fine. But for me, self-representation is an essential part of the gaming experience; without it, I feel unwelcome and disconnected – and I'm just talking about interacting with the game itself, to say nothing of the culture that has infested the gaming world, a culture in which women are so often ridiculed and rejected on principle. *That*, in case you were wondering, is why – despite my love for fantasy RPGs – I've stayed away from their Massive Multiplayer Online counterparts, like *World of Warcraft* or even *The Elder Scrolls Online*. Though I find myself feeling invited in by a game that treats me like a "normal" player and allows me to see a certain version of myself represented on-screen, the idea of interacting with other gamers online make me feel entirely *un*welcome, and so I reject it as part of my personal gaming experience. That online gaming is not always a safe space for women is a problem I hope is rectified in the near future – with harsher punishment from game companies and console manufacturers for online harassment, for a start. For now, I've accepted that I prefer to play online. It took me a long time to find the type of game that allowed me to enjoy single-player gaming, and I'm going to embrace it.

Every year, I go back and I re-read my Pierce books, because they get more and more relevant the older I get. There's no shortage of YA literature with leading ladies these days, but so often their stories tend to focus on a love triangle, and Pierce's books will never be about that. They were the first, for me, and they will always hold that nostalgic aura of perfection and brilliance that draws me to them endlessly. I feel the same way about *Baldur's Gate, Dragon Age* and *Skyrim* – even if gaming finally gets it together and includes interchangeable female protagonists in every game ever (one day!), fantasy RPGs will always have been the *first* to do it, and to not treat it like it was even a *thing*. It was just obvious. "Girls will want to play this game too." And to an 11-year-old girl, who feels weird and nerdy and solitary? That sense of inclusion, of "it's okay, you're not alone," of "girls can do this too" ("this" meaning either "play video games" or "wield a sword and chop down baddies in fantasy worlds," depending on your reading)? That will change your life.

Trust me. I know.

Looking for Group

G. Willow Wilson is the World Fantasy Award-winning author of the novel *Alif the Unseen*, as well as the writer of numerous comic books, including the all-new *Ms. Marvel* (Marvel Comics) and the Eisner Award-nominated series *Air* (DC/Vertigo) and *Mystic: The Tenth Apprentice* (Marvel Comics).

The guy who introduced me to *World of Warcraft* is the kind of ultra-bearded, kufi-wearing Pakistani who makes TSA agents get out their latex gloves. His name is Aziz. We met online ten years ago, when the blogosphere was just becoming a thing, and Aziz was webmaster of one of the very first online forums devoted to modern Islam. Unless you are telepathic, or at least fairly enlightened, if you were to see him walking down the street, "this man is a gamer" would not be your first thought. Nor your tenth thought. But as it happens, Aziz is an unrepentant, unreconstructed Massively Multiplayer Online Role Playing nerd. *World of Warcraft* was a regular topic of conversation in our online interactions, but when I first approached him about trying it out myself, it was for the purpose of mockery. At the time, I was writing a weekly column about comics and pop culture, and I had run out of stuff to talk about. Since a new *World of Warcraft* tie-in comic book series was in the works, I thought I would do a bit of investigative snark.

At Aziz's instruction, I downloaded the *Warcraft* game client (hours. gigabytes.) and logged on for my free ten-day trial. I chose a hobbitlike creature – in *Warcraft*, this species is known by the more generic moniker "gnome," so that nobody gets sued – and selected "mage" as a class. In minutes, I found myself running through a snowy landscape under a blue-white digital sunrise. Aziz, still sporting a beard – he is the kind of gamer who creates avatars more or less identical to himself – rode up on a grey horse, armor a-jingling, flavor text hanging in the air over his head. I laughed. He laughed. We killed a frost troll. All my sarcasm evaporated. I had discovered what was missing from my life.

An open-world, massively multiplayer online game essentially re-creates the interior landscapes of childhood. There are talking bears and elves and eternal winters. One's comrades do not die; they simply become invisible for a few seconds and reappear at convenient way-

G. Willow Wilson

points. There has been a lot of hand-wringing in the media in recent years over the sociological dangers of games that require you to run around killing things, but what actually makes these games so addictive, I think, is the absence of death. The world conforms to the cyclical thinking of the very young: nothing disappears without reappearing in some other form. You cannot actually hurt anything, including yourself. You are always the hero of the story, and you always win.

It is a seductive mindset. Prior to my *Warcraft* habit, I had operated under the elitist assumption that gamers fell into two categories: teenagers and socially diseased cat people. Aziz, who is a PhD and father of two in real life, must surely be an exception to the rule, or so my thinking went. But as I was sucked into the world of Azeroth, I discovered that the allure of digital escapism cut across every conceivable barrier. Grouping up with other players for dungeon runs – through underground caverns, celestial vaults, fetid caves and resplendent palaces, headphones pumping out a wall of noise as enemies toppled amid horn blasts and clashing steel and the tinny ding-a-ling of approximately a million different spell rotations all macro'd at once – I was as likely to meet shift workers and high school football players as the unwashed troglodytes I had imagined. After a wipe – for those of you in the real world, this is short for "wipe out," when all the players of a group die during an important fight – we would all stand around and chat, and the details of complex lives would filter through. One elf warrior was really a single mom blowing off steam in the precious hour between work and the end of her kids' school day. A hunter with a giant white lion at his side was an Iraq veteran on disability pay; one night there was a tank who gave instructions in verse, in all caps, using British spelling. (HEROES, ASSEMBLE! STAND YOU BENEATH THE GREEN-COLOURED TRIANGLE! He was from a role-playing server, and would also shout abuse at enemy NPCs. It got old fast, but he was a great tank.) Amid the traditional gamer epithets and insults to various female relatives, there was something astonishingly humane about the whole enterprise. Because, of course, we needed to help each other in order to win. We came from every conceivable background, yet here we were judged only by our skill at the game, and how well we cooperated with each other. We were all different, but we were all on the same side. How often in life does that happen?

It was a humbling experience. Offline, I might be a reasonably successful author, but in game, I sucked. I was slow. My character builds were inefficient. I was constantly having my ass handed to me by 15 year olds who had been playing video games since birth, and who now pos-sessed the reflexes of Adderall-popping fighter pilots. How do you tell the irate middle schooler – who has already gamed the system, who has damage-per-second down to an art form, who started custom-modding his user interface at 12 years old – that in the real world, you are some-body semi-famous? That you do not, in actual fact, suck as hard at life as you do at *Warcraft*?

You don't, because it would change nothing. Instead, I came to know my place in the pecking order. I needed the overpowered 15 year olds in order to survive. In dungeons, I meekly accepted the blame when, once again, my damage-per-second was only marginally higher than the peaceful healer's. I was profuse in thanking the paladin who resurrect-ed me when I got one-shotted during a boss fight. I said nothing when I saw a low-level character in a battleground whose name appeared to be a homage to one of my books – though I might be having a seizure of delight on the inside, there is something about a gnome avatar, in bad armor, shouting "That's ME! That's my book you're homage-ing!" that does not inspire confidence.

Why did I keep coming back? When you're used to thinking of your-self as a competent person, it's frustrating to be bad at something, espe-cially something fun. Yet I was never drawn to single-player games, in which I could wipe out to my heart's content without ever facing public humiliation. It was the group dynamic that kept me going, even though I was often the weakest link. I wanted what everyone else wanted: an excuse to rely on others. An excuse to contribute to something bigger than myself. Somehow, the community feeling that had been sucked out of our real life interactions by the brutality of work schedules and isolated living arrangements and giant box stores was present in-game. It was there in the barter economy, there in the spontaneous groups that would form, often wordlessly, to take down a particularly difficult mon-ster, there when the kindly high-level druid would come skipping up to heal you when you were down to your last health point, for no other reason than to be nice.

And so I went back, and back, and back. You can spend years in MMOs. I would fly over that snowy starting zone where I first met Aziz on his grey horse and feel actual nostalgia for this fictional, digital place, complete with the tingling Proustian sensation one gets in one's gut for things past. Eventually, Aziz and I met in real life, at a lecture I gave in his hometown, and we laughed at the realization that you can accumu-late so many shared experiences with someone you've never actually seen. Faced with this unique opportunity to discuss something other than computers, we talked – naturally – about the next *Warcraft* expansion pack.

As the months turned into years, I started to suck less and less, until finally I became, if not good, then at least competent. I have learned to accept that I will never be as masterful as the teenagers who've been playing since they were in diapers. I may never get to the top of the leader board, but these days I'm routinely in the top third. It doesn't matter. What I love is what I had been missing: that public trust exercise that is putting your life, even your fictional life, in a stranger's hands. When I see the abbreviation "LFG" in zone-chat now – Looking For Group – it takes on a kind of accidental profundity. Beyond the fantasy setting, the superhuman powers, and the flaming swords, it is why we are all here.

Refuge

Mary Anne Mohanraj is the author of *Bodies in Motion*, Sri Lankan-American linked stories (HarperCollins) and nine other titles. *Bodies in Motion* was a finalist for the Asian-American Book Awards and has been translated into six languages. She has also written *Silence and the Word*, *The Best of Strange Horizons* (ed.), *Aqua Erotica* (ed.) and *The Poet's Journey* (a children's fantasy picture book), among others. In 2006, Mohanraj received an Illinois Arts Council Fellowship in Prose. Mohanraj lives in Chicago, where she teaches creative writing and post-colonial literature at the University of Illinois; she also taught at the Clarion workshop in 2008. She is a graduate of the Clarion West workshop, and holds an MFA and a Ph.D. in creative writing. Mohanraj founded and served, from 2000-2003, as editor-in-chief of the Hugo-nominated speculative fiction magazine *Strange Horizons* (www.strangehorizons.com). She also founded and served as editor-in-chief from 1998-2000 for *Clean Sheets*, one of the foremost online erotica magazines (www.cleansheets.com). Mohanraj currently serves as Director of the Speculative Literature Foundation (www.speclit.org). Her newest book is *The Stars Change*, a Kickstarter-funded space opera from Circlet Press. She can be found talking about books, gardening and more at www.maryannemohanraj.com.

I am 12 years old in 1983, playing Wizardry obsessively on my first computer, a Mac IIe, I think. In my faded memory, there are minimal graphics; I think the game was in color, but I can't swear to it. I am alone in my room for hours, taking comfort in this game. Frustrated with my immigrant parents, whose priorities are so different from my own. I have read countless books, but sometimes those stories only arouse longings they cannot satisfy. Wizardry offers a dungeon to explore, gold and weapons to accumulate, monsters to slay. A sequence of small, measurable tasks that can be accomplished and celebrated. A refuge.

When my aunts and uncles visit, they sit with my parents around the kitchen table late into the night, playing three-nought-four. Three-nought-four is a bridge variant, one they learned in Sri Lanka as children, and they play it with glee. They curse in Tamil, throw their hands up in the air, frustrated and delighted. I watch, perched on a folding stool, at the periphery. I try to learn the game, but it eludes me, and the truth is, I don't even necessarily want to play. What I *want* is to be part of that bright, charmed circle; I want to belong. Eventually, my sister, five years younger and far more determined, learns to play the game and joins them. Now she is the one who keeps track of every cousin's birthday, who knows who is mad at whom and who has been forgiven.

A few years later, I am in the basement with three boys. Rob and Tommy are brothers who live a few streets down; I can't remember the name of the third. I like all of these boys, but I don't have any idea what to do about that, if anything. My parents do not allow me to date, and even if they did, no one has actually asked me out. But I am allowed to play games, which must seem harmless to them, even childish. I am not really ready to date, but games offer a framework for safe interaction with boys. In this game, I choose to play a sexy thief, and Tommy's character flirts with mine. I am flustered, and flirtatious, and secretly thrilled. Some months later, Tommy will kiss me under the basement stairs, and while our relationship, if you can call it that, will not last for long, I will remember that kiss until the day I die.

In college, I join Skiffy, the science-fiction club. I meet my second boyfriend there, over endless games of *Family Business, Illuminati, Cosmic Encounter* and *Talisman*. Paul talks very fast, in nested parentheses – one tangent leading to another – but then he comes back, wrapping up one point after another in triumphant declaration. I can't help but laugh, and be charmed. I sit beside him at the scarred wood table, lean close to move my pieces.

The University of Chicago has a 60:40 male:female ratio, which is a blessing to girls like me who arrive never having really dated. The board games offer a way to interact that is friendly, cheerful and competitive. We are not in classes, trying to impress the professor; we are not at frat parties, drinking terrible cheap alcohol. We are in our element, laughing over the roll of the dice, the uncovering of a particularly unfortunate card. While the game lasts, it is everything, our whole world.

One strange evening, a woman from the club buttonholes me in the hallway outside and asks, angrily, "Are you really this happy? Doesn't anything ever go wrong for you?" I have no answer for her then, but now I would say, "Oh, sweetheart, you should see me anywhere else. This is my safe space, my haven. This is where I come to laugh and forget."

Later, my roommate Kirsten introduces me to math grad students; I am charmed. They are intense, passionate, ridiculous. Jordan will flip onto his hands and walk down the hall for the sheer joy of it. Alex and

Jordan play speed *Monopoly* in the middle of the night, shuffling out the properties at the start of the game, finishing a game in half an hour, calculating which properties offer the best odds for eventual triumph. (Baltic Avenue is a bad bet. I will say no more.)

Jordan and Michael and Alex and Bryan all play bridge; as with its cousin, three-nought-four, the game makes little sense to me. It doesn't really matter; perhaps I will learn bridge when I'm 80. The games give me an excuse to spend time with the boys; I may not understand them when they're talking math, but when they're playing games, I can at least follow along. I will eventually date three of the foursome (the fourth is gay), all at the same time. That doesn't last for long.

The math grads play poker, at first for quarter-ante stakes. I play too, though I inevitably lose all my money. We sit in the Barn, a long, low room at the top of Eckart Hall, and I lose slowly but steadily, until at the end of the game, the wild card games come out, and I lose the rest of my $20 in a mad frenzy. The longer we play, that endless summer, the more seriously they take it. Eventually, some of them are playing for serious money, and a day will come when I stand in Las Vegas, silent and sweating, watching Alex start with a hundred dollars in a "super satellite" and play and play and play until he wins the entire pot of $10,000, enough to enter him in the World Championship of Poker. That moment, watching Alex play against the famous Amarillo Slim, is glorious.

Alex will also teach me to juggle, patiently retrieving my dropped balls and handing them back to me, one after another, until I can finally do a hundred tosses in a row. I never progress further, but Alex, Jordan, Michael and Bryan all juggle balls and clubs and flaming torches in intricate patterns on the university quadrangle. The green grass and trees arching above are graced by their flashing symmetry. They bring clubs and torches to Grant Park as well, to the Fourth of July festivities, and I stand between the flickering torches, trusting in their skill, certain of my safety. Afterwards, we eat Michael and Bryan's berry pies, and my roommate Elissa leans over to me and asks if I want to trade. She is leaning against Kevin's chest, and I against Bryan's. Soon, she and Bryan will be married, and Kevin and I will be... complicated.

I don't only play games with people I want to date, though I can see how it might seem that way.

A few years later, in 1995, I am on a mountaintop in Sri Lanka, teaching my cousins how to play *Magic: The Gathering*. I am 23 and they are all much younger, ages ten to 17; I have traveled with them for a few days, and I still don't know them that well. It has been a fraught trip in many ways – I am fighting with my parents, who do not approve of the people I date, or that I am dating at all. There is a war on, and we have kept strictly to the tourist venues in this trip. My father will briefly travel north, to visit relatives, but we are not allowed to join him. In the national museum, the guard tells me to put away my camera, or they will confiscate it; they are worried that the Tigers are sending people in to take photographs of places they plan to bomb.

Rather than visiting with relatives, we have been doing the tourist tour: elephant orphanage, spice gardens, train ride through the hill country. I sit in the open door of the train, letting my legs dangle out, holding onto the rail with one hand and watching the countryside fly past, until my father comes to tell me to come in. I am briefly tempted to argue – but I am trying hard to get along. To keep the peace. This is one moment of real peace, dealing out the cards, teaching them the rules of the game. I wonder if anyone has ever played *Magic* in Sri Lanka before, or on a mountaintop. For the space of the game, there are no fights with relatives, no arguments about unimportant things. There is no war. Just the shuffling of the cards, the excited chatter and confusion. For a moment, we are all in this together.

But games are not all sweetness and light. At WisCon, my favorite SF convention, *Mafia* becomes popular. In this game, you need no board, no pieces, no dice. A deck of cards is sufficient, and that is only to assign the roles – black for the villagers, red for the Mafia, the king of hearts for the Inspector. During the day, the villagers try to ferret out which of them belong to the Mafia. They choose, they vote, they condemn one to expulsion from the village. Night falls, and the Mafia kill a villager. The rules get more complicated from there, but what is important is that the entire game is talking. Talking, talking, talking – mostly persuading the rest to believe that you are good (whether you are or not). Persuading them to go after someone else. It helps if you are a good actor.

It helps if you can draw on outside knowledge; it can be dangerous to date someone who is also playing the game. They may be able to tell if you are lying. They may convince the village, whether it's true or not, that you are lying. We would play this game for hours, and we could be cutthroat about it. Sometimes people got hurt. I was dating Jed by now, and he eventually refused to play anymore; it became his least favorite game. That wasn't the best thing for our relationship, but, thankfully, we managed to survive it. Though for a moment, I did think it was a near thing.

I am 35 when my partner Kevin and I have a daughter; with the baby's birth, I return to video games. There is no time, no energy for board games anymore. I am too utterly exhausted to talk to another human being, much less play a game. But I can wear Kavya on my chest in the sling, wait for her to wake for the next terrible feeding (they did not go well), and play video games to kill the time. I can't remember if I actually enjoyed those games; I was playing *Civilization* then, *SimCity*, *Caesar III*. The games offer little worlds I can control; a refuge again, an escape from present misery. If I just have to endure the sleep-deprivation and unceasing labor, I feel that I might go mad. For a little while, the games let me shut off my brain. I disappear for a few precious hours, and, when I return, I can go on, a little longer.

When Kavya is one and a half, Kevin buys me *War of the Ring* for Christmas. She is finally sleeping through the night, and, once we put her to bed, we play. I make him play again and again, obsessively. Although he is a mathematician too, and I had dated him along with all the others 15 years before, he had rarely played games with us, and I think he is surprised by my passion. He buys me two more soon thereafter, *Agricola* and *Race for the Galaxy*. We play *Agricola* as well, several times. The games feel oddly romantic, a way of reconnecting. We have had a rough passage to this place – years of living apart, dating off and on, arguing about marriage and children. We are still not married, but we have a child, and we are tentatively happy about that. But her infancy has tested us – the exhausted resentments have piled up until we are biting our tongues to keep from lashing out at each other, simply because there is no one else to blame. It has been a long, hard stretch. A misery.

But when we play the games, we become engaged and focused. We talk about something other than babies and diapers and scheduling and sleep. We plan strategies for orc campaigns and peasant farms, and, most of all, we laugh together. It works so well that Kevin goes out and researches two-person games and buys more: *Dungeon Lords*, *Tigris and Euphrates*, *Civilization*, *Dominion*, *Pandemic*. They arrive in their cardboard boxes, full of mystery and promise. Then we decide to have another child, and as a result, most of the games sit in their plastic packaging, unopened for the next two years. But we will get to them someday. They sit on the shelf, waiting for the future – a promise, a present.

Now the children are three and five; Kavya is desperate to play games with us, and I have no patience for it. I do *want* to play games with my children. It was one of the reasons I had children, one of the things I was looking forward to, along with singing songs to them, reading stories to them, baking cookies. It turns out that I like only one of those three things; as for the games, I like them well enough – the first time. I can play a game of *Candyland* and be reasonably amused; ditto *Chutes and Ladders*. But my limit on each is about once a week. *Go Fish*, surprisingly, has a bit more staying power, but I cannot play nearly as many games as she wants to. Kevin is much better about it than I am, and he plays chess and *Go* with her as well – simpler versions, designed for teaching. When she brings out the games, I run away and feel like a bad mother.

But I don't beat myself up too much; I still have hope. The day will come when they can both play more interesting games. *Monopoly* can't be too far away, and we have a copy of *Catan Junior* ready, just waiting for her sixth birthday. I have faith that we will someday soon spend hours upon hours together, playing games. We will introduce them to all our old favorites, and they will bring us new ones to try. We will teach them the love of games and give them that gift: shared joy with like-minded souls, a way to bond with strangers, or loved ones who have become strangers. A refuge in times of trouble and grief, shelter from life's storms.

If we teach our children nothing else in this world, I hope we teach them this, at least. How to play. If they know how to play, somehow, someday, it will all be okay.

Leopards at the Wedding: Finding Love in a Glitchy Landscape

Miriam Oudin is a lapsed academic living in the non-Toronto part of Canada. Her publications include the dystopian novelette "2 + 1 = 2" and a bleak Hansard transcript in the anthology *Fractured: Tales of the Canadian Post-Apocalypse*. Miriam spends most of her time discovering creative ways to die in roguelikes, looking at kittens on the internet and writing double dactyls about TV shows.

> Emergence is also chaos, and its charm is the beauty of a universe that could have been nothing, but turned out to be something instead. That something is both revolting and divine.
> —Ian Bogost, "The Squalid Grace of Flappy Bird"

Let me tell you about the time that my fiancé abandoned me at the altar on the day of our wedding.

Everything about our courtship felt accidental. I had been wearing the amulet of the love-goddess Mara for a quest, but the burly werewolf serving as my bodyguard (and pack mule, but don't tell him that) took this to mean that I was interested in him. I hadn't been thinking about Farkas, the bodyguard, "in that way," but I was enjoying his company and didn't really want to carry 300 pounds of iron ingots and thistle branches by myself. So when he proposed, I accepted with a shrug, and we travelled to a nearby town where we would be wed under the serene gaze of the goddess.

The fact that one's betrothed might walk out of the temple during one's wedding ceremony is a well-known bug in the game *Skyrim*, though I didn't know that at the time. I had already sunk more than a hundred hours into the game by that point, and had developed a long list of complaints about it – the quests were simplistic and repetitive, the writing was weak, the voice-acting almost comically bad – but I had apparently become more invested in the story than I'd realized, because I took Farkas' abandonment strangely personally. I frantically texted a

friend ("How *could* he?"), who offered to look up the console commands that would resolve the problem and return my husband to me.
(The PC *con*sole is the secret panel that a player can access to alter the
game's code, but it so happened that my friend's texts served to con*sole*
me as I worked through my visceral reaction to my own inability to
maintain even an imaginary relationship.) Eventually the cheat codes
worked and I got Farkas back, though for some reason he spent our
wedding night invisible and his friendly dialogue boxes would appear
out of nowhere.

Thinking about this in the year or so since it happened, it occurred
to me that the most vivid memories I have of *Skyrim* all arose out of such
glitches and infelicities. The invisible horse that I rode for a while, squat-
ting uncomfortably in the air. The chicken that somehow received the
benefits of a Courage spell, fighting a dragon alongside me (and winning). The scripted assassination that got a dead NPC's friends stuck in
"mourning" mode, making it impossible for them to talk to me and
thereby trigger the quest to avenge his death like the hero I supposedly
was. The mammoth that simply fell out of a clear blue sky and crashed
in a field perhaps half a mile away.

I can scarcely remember the names of the primary NPCs in the game,
and the main plot arc can be summarized in a single sentence ("dragons
are attacking the country, and you are the only person who can stop
them"). I would never recommend *Skyrim* on the strength of its plot or
its characterization. What the game does have going for it, besides its
beautiful graphics, is its sheer immensity of scale, which brings with it
an increased chance to encounter the unique combination of coincidences and quirks that makes for great storytelling. The Surrealists identified the most beautiful experience in the world as the "chance
encounter of a sewing machine and an umbrella on a dissecting table,"
and the parade of glitchy Skyrim videos on YouTube demonstrates that
when things go unexpectedly, the game's many sewing machines,
umbrellas, and dissecting tables can combine in ways that create a truly
surreal beauty. *Skyrim* the game (and, by extension, Skyrim the country)
are so huge and so complex that exciting and hilarious things will happen that go well beyond even the developers' intentions. In fact, I would
argue that the *majority* of the exciting and hilarious things that happened to me in that game were independent of the developers' intentions.

Literary critics will be unsurprised by this. A writer's intention, post-
modernists say, doesn't matter and has never mattered, since the author

of a work does not have access to a privileged interpretation of it. In the 1960s, the French poststructuralists, following Roland Barthes, and the American "Yale School" of deconstructionists, following Paul de Man and others, argued that a text, once it has been released into the world, is divorced from its author and freshly re-interpreted by each reader who encounters it. In this view, the author's own opinions – about her work or about anything else (politics, religion, art) – only create one interpretation among many. Furthermore, like the athlete muddling through an interview after a winning game, the author may not even be able to provide a particularly insightful analysis of her own accomplishments.

This isn't the time or place to take on the postmodernist project, for which I simultaneously have some sympathy and many, many critiques. I am not selling deconstructionism or "New Criticism" here. I am only pointing out the fact that drawing inspiration from glitches and infelicities is not new. Literary critics have been engaging in "productive misreadings" and "willful misprisions" for decades now. They resist canonical or institutional interpretations of texts, they expand their definition of "texts" to include phenomena beyond the cultural canon (advertisements, instruction manuals, cartoons), and they playfully allow subtexts, inconsistencies, gaps and missteps to create seeds for fresh insights. It can be argued that computer games are even more fertile than traditional books in this regard, since the experience of playing through a game really *is* different for each player. Unlike a book – which, in the age of the printing press, is usually "objectively" identical from copy to copy even if each reader brings her own unique perspective to it – a game's "pages" are experienced out of order and at different speeds as each individual player chooses to grant different skills and abilities to the PC, pursue or reject particular quests, solve or ignore particular puzzles, engage different NPCs, seek out or avoid combat, and so on. *Skyrim* and the sandbox games like it create the most unpredictable narratives, but even linear games seem to be more open to these player/reader-led transformations than books or movies are.

To return, for a moment, to marriages. One common complaint about *Skyrim* is that marriage in the game is more or less meaningless. Choosing one NPC over another as a spouse doesn't have any real in-game effect. The NPCs have very little backstory and, once they are married, most of their dialogue is collapsed into a simple menu that is shared across all the characters in the dating pool. Thinking back on the computer RPGs I've played over the years, I am startled by how often dating is reduced to a *mechanic*, a thing you grind just like combat or wealth. In a game like *The Sims* or the *Fable* series, you are expected to accumulate jewellery and other treasures in your adventures, which you then dump on your partner to keep their "happiness meter" up. Even in *Dragon Age: Origins*, which made a special effort to supply each romanceable NPC with a unique personality and detailed backstory, the algorithm for wedded bliss depended on certain gifts and dialogue choices that were depressingly reverse-engineered on dozens of spoiler websites to maximize the positive effects of the relationship for the PC. What this implies about real human relationships is too awful to think upon.

But the one-dimensionality of these relationships is delightful in another sense. In a game like *Skyrim*, I don't have to put up with another writer's idea of my partner's personality, nor do I have to micromanage that partner's interaction with my heroic narrative. I can choose a lover based entirely on the backstory I personally write about them, or better yet, the backstory that seems to arise naturally out of the chance events that occur in that particular playthrough. For Farkas, the bugginess of the game actually made this creative process easier, since his glitching out seemed to give him a spontaneous personality that developed on the fly. To my mind, this bugginess is preferable to a scripted romance that decides *for* me what I consider attractive or appealing, especially since romance is so often atrociously written in computer games. Women and LGBTQ players are particularly ill-served in this regard: when romance options are even available to us, which happens less often than one might think, they have often been tossed in only as afterthoughts. Some older games are made up entirely of dialogue aimed at heterosexual cisgendered males even if the player rolled up a female PC (if, that is, she was permitted to roll up a female PC at all); in a recent, ill-conceived replay of *Baldur's Gate*, I was yanked out of the story over and over again as my dialogue menus recommended that I catcall female NPCs and sleazily hit on all the women in my party. Even the Farkas who abandoned me at the altar is more attractive than that.

Emergence has become the word of the day when discussing these kinds of happy accidents in game design. The phrase "emergent gameplay" used to be used to describe any complex situation that simple games can create – the few dozen rules of *Go* or chess create billions of possible boards, for example. But, lately, the term has come to refer to design that's open-ended enough that players, while exploring or experimenting, can cause things to happen that are unanticipated even by the designers. If a game hits that sweet spot where an event is *both* surprising *and* simultaneously natural and fitting for the world, then something truly astonishing happens. Ideally, the moment is not so jarring as to pull one out of the narrative (or crash the game), but it should be just jarring enough to create a moment of unanticipated delight.

This sense of emergence is what inspired Stewart Butterfield to call his late and much-lamented massively multiplayer game *Glitch*. Butterfield has said in interviews that it's not the content created by the developers, but rather the unexpected interaction between game and player, where the magic happens; indeed, the premise of the game itself was that the characters were moving through a hallucinatory dream-world where nothing behaved exactly as one might expect. Now I suspect that Butterfield's assertion that players create stories through glitches is somewhat disingenuous. No designer, including him, wants to release a buggy or unpolished game. Terrible games are not automatically made fun by brilliant players alone, and brilliant games have a habit of pushing players to the edge of their creative capabilities in a way that, say, *Tic-Tac-Toe* does not. Saying "the best game in the world is a blank piece of paper," as some role-players claim, is true so far as it goes, but it overlooks the fact that a) it's immoral to charge $60 for a blank piece of paper, b) it's exhausting for each player to have to make a game from scratch every time, and c) forcing rules and worldbuilding details to interact with one another is much more fun (and, ironically, much more creative) than using no rules or worldbuilding at all.

Designers need to meet us halfway; they need to create a space for productive glitches to happen while making actual showstoppers a rarity. They should provide us with enough raw material to make stories of our own, but also invite us to invest in characters and situations that we wouldn't have thought of ourselves. I suspect that this is what Butterfield really meant when he praised the glitch; after all, he still had coders on his team to eliminate "real" bugs, even as he gave his players the tools to create dreams within his dream.

I find it paradoxical that games that are more "literary" or technically accomplished are often less compulsively playable than more colorless, simplistic, or even downright poorly written games. I think *Dragon Age: Origins* was a better game than *Skyrim* by almost any metric one could name, but, according to Steam, I've logged less than a tenth of the time on it. "Sandbox" games – which is to say games that don't compel the player to follow a particular plot but encourage her to just mess around in a fantasy world – seem to lend themselves particularly well to the productive glitch. Witness the Tumblr called "Sims Gone Wrong," which tells a series of surreal little stories about Sims based on buggy screenshots: "Two funeral guests," reads one entry, "decided to stay behind and build a goddamn snowman in the middle of my Sim's bedroom as he slept." The changelog, too, alludes to past moments that seem to have taken place in a parallel world whose rules are not quite the same as our own: "Sims who are on fire," the developers assure us, "will no longer be forced to attend graduation before they can put themselves out."

Or consider the sprawling civilization-building game *Dwarf Fortress*, which has inspired countless fan-written epics and comic strips – this, despite the fact that the game has no graphics and no dialogue, relying on bare ASCII characters and a news crawl to track the player's progress through an imaginary industrial revolution. The *Dwarf Fortress* player is expected to create whirring machinery and urban development out of the raw materials that she digs out of a mountain with a single pickaxe; the game's lead designer, Tarn Adams, spends much of his spare time researching ancient smelting techniques, fluid mechanics and agriculture to add dizzyingly realistic detail to the crafting in the game. As a result of the game's complexity, its bugs are magnificent; skimming through the online bug tracker is enough to evoke a drunken deity's botched creations. "Alligators needlessly use specific toes." "Diplomat arrives, immediately dies of old age." "Got hit with a raindrop and started melting." "Dwarven baby cancels Clean Self: Too insane." I remember when I first discovered *Dwarf Fortress* and tried to teach myself to play it with some guidance from a discussion board in 2006. Posters would write extended commentary on screenshots that were completely incomprehensible to me at the time, and I marvelled that these abstract symbols could create such beautiful stories. ("Bronzemurder" is one of my favourite fan creations, if you'd like to check one out for yourself, but Googling "dwarf fortress epic" will lead you to many rich narratives.)

In games like these, coincidences and surprises – and yes, bugs – coolly write themselves into the story and *become* the story, like the famous leopards of Franz Kafka's *Parables and Paradoxes*:

> Leopards break into the temple and drink to the dregs what is in the sacrificial pitchers; this is repeated over and over again; finally it can be calculated in advance, and it becomes a part of the ceremony.

Some games, like *Dragon Age*, are well-written and competently designed, but do not include many such leopards, being too linear and tightly controlled for any one's player's journey to change much from game to game. Others, like *Skyrim*, are flawed but so thickly populated with leopards that the ceremonies (literally, in the case of my wedding to Farkas) reinvent themselves with every playthrough. Still others, like *Dwarf Fortress* or *The Sims*, do not really have a pre-written narrative at all; these games include enough markers of development and progress to invite the player to weave an imagined narrative around them, aided by odd combinations of player actions and open-ended code that lead to results that the developers could not have prepared for directly, though the game can recover or even thrive if its inner structure is robust enough.

I have yet to encounter a game that has the perfect combination of good writing *and* a suggestive blankness for the player's imagination to fill in, and I wonder if these qualities are in fact somewhat at cross-purposes. If a game is scripted by a particularly talented team of writers, it may leave less "room" for the leopards to write themselves into its story, since the story itself accounts for every possibility that the player might encounter. This is not a bad thing, of course; I *want* game designers to commit to writing good prose, developing inventive plots and shipping games without showstopping bugs. Still, I hold out hope that some day there could be a game that is vast, rich, beautifully-written and *just* glitchy and unpredictable enough to create fresh surprises every time I play. In other words, I do not want to pay $60 for a blank piece of paper. Instead, let's call it a bumpy, gessoed canvas.

I opened this essay with a story about my wedding day. Let me close by telling you about the time Farkas and I almost split up.

It all started when Farkas started disappearing for no reason while we were out adventuring. Sometimes he'd have lagged out due to bad pathfinding, and I'd be able to find him by backtracking or fast-travelling to where he was stuck on a mountainside or between two trees. But other times he'd vanish entirely.

After one days-long stretch of Farkaslessness, I resorted to using the console to teleport myself to him just to see where he was. It turns out he was hanging around at Jorrvaskr, which is to say the mead-hall where the PC first meets him. I indignantly noted that he hadn't even bothered to return to our lovely matrimonial home, which we picked and furnished together, and where the game granted me an XP-boosting buff for spending the night with him (the buff is called, and I am not making this up, "Lover's Comfort").

Though I'm not a jealous sort in real life, I soon found myself neurotically checking up on Farkas every time he disappeared. I memorized the sequence player.moveto 0001A693 and typed it instinctively whenever I found myself alone in a dungeon. Sure enough, he'd gone back to Jorrvaskr every single time, ostensibly justifying my ugly paranoia. I texted anyone who would listen: "He's gone to hang out with his idiot friends at the bar again! Clearly he doesn't respect me as the Dragonborn! What sort of sham marriage is this?" Something seemed deliberate, mocking, *targeted*, about this game bug.

But it all worked out in the end. Farkas' bland, content-free game dialogue made it easy to forgive him for his drunken excursions, since he was incapable of saying anything cruel or passive-aggressive, and he was always endearingly happy to see me. "Hello, dear," he would say, offering me a homemade pie that boosts health and stamina regeneration. Even if I tried to pick a fight with him, his dialogue options always remained affectionately clueless.

So it seems that Farkas and I are in it for the long haul. And, thanks to its bugs and eccentricities, I will remember that relationship long after *Skyrim*'s much more generic story about saving the world from dragons has been forgotten.

Blood on the Hull: Gender, Dominion and the Business of Betrayal in *Eve*

When not wandering the distant shores of apocalyptic wastelands, **Jen J. Dixon** is often found pondering the origins of consciousness over a glass of good whiskey. Her gaming "career" began some 20 years ago with table-top RPGs and computer FPSs, but these days mostly involves narrative-style tabletop games. She co-founded *The Walking Eye*, a long running, award-winning podcast on gaming that offers actual play episodes, interviews with game designers and discussion episodes covering gaming-related topics such as gender and culture. She is currently working at Iowa State University on a master's degree in evolutionary biology, focusing on botanical systematics and phylogeny with a specific interest in plant sex. In her spare time, she works as a science advocate, LGTBQ ally and secular activist.

It's when I hear the sobbing that I wonder if I've gone too far.

Actually, on some level, I *know* I've gone too far. I've lied to a *real* person with *real* emotions for personal gain, and they're sitting in front of a computer somewhere crying real tears. The lies you perpetrate in *Eve Online* are so much more manifest than in other games. When you're role-playing around a table, a social contract exists: everyone knows you're role-playing, everyone knows it's a fiction. In *Eve*, you're genuinely, seriously lying to people. I've needed notebooks to keep straight the lies I've told people while going undercover – that I was a student at UCLA, that I was a customer service agent, that I was single, married, young, old, had kids, was childless. In the here and now, I'm hearing sobbing because I led someone to think that I was their teammate and friend, that I had their back, and then helped to murder them.

I keep telling myself I'll get through this, this won't finish me. I'm a stronger person for playing *Eve*, but there are *reasons* why I don't recommend it to anyone else. It will ruin them. In some ways, it's ruined me.

Plus, I don't need the competition.

I Evolve from Care Bear to Grizzly Bear

I first joined *Eve* in 2004 – the gist of the game is that humanity colonized a far-away sector of space via a wormhole, then got cut off from Earth, and the people in that area now contest with one another for resources, money and power. Players in this MMORPG can act as independent agents, or pool their resources as corporations and alliances to wage war over sovereignty. Inevitably, this leads to spaceship battles. Extremely vivid, pulse-pounding spaceship battles.

After a couple of years, I was hooked. The game is *gorgeous*, full of galaxies, star systems and *beautiful* space flight. It scratched my itch for hardcore Sci-Fi – I can't imagine myself as a troll in a fantasy jungle, but I can totally imagine myself piloting a spaceship wrapped in the endless dark of space. Also, your actions in *Eve* matter: the world's terrain, economy and political power constantly change. If you want to play a static MMO that remains the same when you go away for days on end, I can only recommend that you play *World of Warcraft* or ~~something else lame~~ something that's more your cup of tea.

Newcomers to *Eve* often start out as "Care Bears" – a derogatory term, I know, but I use it because I *was* a hardcore Care Bear. It refers to people who undertake relatively harmless missions (usually asteroid mining), stick to high security space and avoid the big sovereignty battles. When I first committed to *Eve*, I couldn't figure out why anyone in this game would slaughter other characters for profit. "Where's the joy," I thought, "in killing miners? Why be such a dick?"

So I floated around passively at first – I became really good at scanning (being fascinated with chemistry, I'd build probe configurations based on the Platonic solids), hack into modules and sell their datacores and relics to interested parties. I made some terrible rookie mistakes: I forgot to save wormhole locations, preventing me from jumping to safety during a crisis; I failed to update my character, losing skill points and implants when I died; and I innocently strayed into the path of dangerous (read: *a Finger of God on your little spaceship dangerous*) NPCs.

As a naive Care Bear, I hated this game – what was the point of just floating around all the time, trying not to die? Then one day, I got lost and paid some people to give me a wormhole exit location. They deliberated on whether to take my money and blow me to pieces anyway (a tactic I've now done countless times, I must confess), but let me live and opened my eyes to why killing other players made sense.

In *Eve*, the economy matters, so if – for example – you claim a system and *don't* destroy someone who comes to take your resources, you're totally screwing yourself. So, absolutely you should kill miners, even the ones who don't know what they're doing!

I quickly realized another upshot to this: mining might not sound like the most exciting of game-activities, but it's the fire in the engine of the *Eve* economy. These minerals are a base component for ship and module production. Take out the miners, and you can, thrillingly, upend the economy.

Also – and I know this sounds horrible – I found that I really did like stalking people and destroying them.

I Become a Teacher to Those I Stalk and Destroy

That's how I became a "teacher" in *Eve*... my piloting and intelligence-gathering skills grew to the point that I could adeptly paralyze miners and their ships, but I always felt a deep-rooted need to tell them what they did wrong just before I blew them up, so they could do better in future.

Here's a recent example: My wormhole opened up in a low-security system, and I went hunting there (I prefer low-sec because if I attack someone there, CONCORD – *Eve*'s automated police force – isn't going to show up and obliterate me). I happened across some guy out mining; let's call him Mining Guy. I was in a T3 spaceship with modules specialized to meet my needs, I gave Mining Guy enough time to relax and get comfortable... then I dropped my scanner probes, warped to him, decloaked, webbed his ship and scrambled it so he can't warp away. He retaliated with hammerhead drones, which couldn't hurt me – they bounced off my ship like raindrops.

It took me five minutes to annihilate Mining Guy; he had a good tank, but he was relying on drones for his offense and he sacrificed defensive modules for mining upgrades, probably because he was selfish and wanted a ship that could fit more ore. That's a fine strategy in high-sec – but in low-sec, mining without a care in the world makes you easy pickings.

Because I consider myself a teacher, I tell Mining Guy – while I'm cleaning his clock – the mistakes that have resulted in his defeat. Call me condescending if you must, but if you can't learn from a brutal death, *your* brutal death, it didn't count for very much. And, how are they going to learn unless someone tells them? So, I suggest over the game's chat that his ship should be aligned to a safe point and fitted with a warp-core scrambler, and that he use directional scan (AKA "D-scan"), which gives warning if anyone is in range. I even advise Mining Guy that he should D-scan wormholes every six seconds. I live in wormholes. A lot of predators do.

The only snag is that, when Mining Guy's ship is lost, the pod bearing his character slips through my grasp and gets away. A pity, that. If your pod gets destroyed, any implants in the clone piloting it are wiped out. Your "consciousness" revives in a new clone in your home station, but you have to pay to recover your implants and insure your new clone. And yet, I'm kind of okay with this turn of events, because matters can escalate and become more interesting, if your opponent escapes. I've given Mining Guy motive to exact revenge – which is very exciting, because then I have a fight and a challenge.

By way of throwing down the gauntlet (or so I think at the time), Mining Guy rages at me in local chat. He's very upset and threatening to destroy my ship. "Perfect," I think. "I'll wait."

There's a broader lesson on display here: if you go into dangerous places prepared, you can survive. If you go into dangerous places *un*prepared, nature will fuck you up. It's the way of things. By tearing apart Mining Guy's ship, I'm just doing nature's job. But, I've given him some insight on how to do better (and the time to independently verify my suggestions).

I hang around for two hours, using the time to look into Mining Guy's corporation, employment history and kill log, trying to predict what he could bring to bear against me. This is the way of things in *Eve* – information is extremely valuable, there to help you survive. I've squandered opportunities because I didn't do my research – once, I got royally pissed at myself because I fitted a new ship, but didn't become fully comfortable with its capabilities. I missed out on a freighter kill because I got scared during a counter-attack, forgot that I had the machinery to tank the gate guns, and wound up giving them the time needed to warp away. It could have been a tasty, tasty kill. After that, I made a habit of reading my ship's instruction manual; it's really stupid not to do this, given that the damn thing is available. This is an empire I'm building after all, not a Bucky Bookshelf from IKEA.

Anyway, Mining Guy has been gone long enough that I'm getting bored. So, I pay a locator agent, and...

... oh my God, he's just sitting there in another low-security system, mining away as before. He hasn't come back with a fighting ship, and – despite his cries of vengeance – seems to be acting as if nothing happened. The thought crosses my mind: *is he just forgetful by nature?*

What's maddening is that I was foolish enough to assume he would take my critique to heart. At this point, I'm still a teacher, but the lesson isn't complete.

You can guess what comes next... I do exactly the same thing as before. I scan Mining Guy down, warp to his location, decloak, ignore his pointless hammerhead drones, lock his ship up. No deviations on my part; I'm providing optimal chances to see if he's learned anything. The only difference is that I've figured out the escape maneuver he pulled before, so I've got my web ready in advance. This time, I trap his pod...

... and then I stop to look around the system, worried that he was cunningly offering himself up as bait, and that friends of his are going to swoop in and eviscerate me any second now. But, nothing happens.

It's so sad. I mean, I think the best of people – I *assumed* he had some fiendish trap ready to blow me away. But, nothing. No surprise attack from the Bowels of Hell. So, here we are again, with him completely at my mercy.

Before long, he starts begging for me to kill him – it's not as if he can go anywhere or do anything while I've got him snared. I let him stew for about three minutes; surprisingly long in game time, but about the same duration that you'd put a sulky kid in a corner. Finally, I just kill him. I really have no choice. Two strikes and you're out, Buddy. And, because he let fly at me with hammerheads he should have known were useless, the contest is considered a mutual engagement, so he gets no kill right[9].

Here, too, there's a lesson to learn: *know* when you're vulnerable, embrace the weakness, use it as a tactic. In *Eve*, it's counter-productive to fight if know you're going to lose. If you do, you sacrifice all future advantage.

You might be sitting there reading this and thinking that I'm an asshole – which is kinda true, it's a big reason why I play this game. On the other hand, I can't help but take some satisfaction from a job well done – I put in the *work, effort and time* needed to evaluate my rival, to know his history and what capabilities he could threaten me with. Then I assessed how best to approach the situation. Mining Guy could have done the same, but he just couldn't be bothered, so he's dead.

It was never about killing him just for the sake of it – in itself, that's

---

9 Kill right: If you attack and slaughter someone in a low-security zone, they have 30 days to find you, activate their kill right and attempt to murder you, even if you're in the relative safety of high security space. If you don't have a kill right and attack in high-sec – and you're not targeting someone of the same corporation as you – it's considered an act of aggression, and CONCORD can come and destroy you. But if you have the kill right, the police don't get involved.

kinda boring. It was about getting to know someone using game-tools that most people don't bother with. In *Eve*, that sort of oversight is the difference between thriving and perishing.

I Become Oracle, Delilah and Shiva All Rolled Into One (But Only If You're a Douchebag)

For all of my success at bringing enlightenment to doomed miners, few players do what I spend *most* of my time doing in *Eve*: advanced information trafficking, which I combine with a flair for what's called "awoxing." The term (nobody seems to agree where it originated from) means going deep undercover within a corporation to rob it blind or destroy it utterly from within.

This started out in my Care Bear days, when I was a coward who would sell locations of strategic/monetary value to people who could secure the areas with their fleets. My analytical skills quickly advanced out of a pressing need – griefer corporations can wind up war-decking a lot of Care Bear corporations who lack the resources to fight back. Easy prey. A friend of mine ran such a Care Bear operation, and his usual response to being war-decked was to quit and go play another game. I wanted him to keep playing, and besides, who *were* these assholes giving my friend such hassle? So I compiled dossiers on his enemies – who belonged to which corporation, what ships they flew, what battles they'd won and lost, that sort of thing. I became so proficient at this, I was like Oracle from *Batman*: someone who provided intel to a number of people (but for a hefty fee).

Before long, my analytical skills made me really good at awoxing – aided in large part, I have to confess, because I'm a woman. Over the years, my skill combined with my feminine wiles have brought about some game-changing corporate destruction.

But, here's the thing: I only awox corporations full of douchebags. And *Eve*, let me tell you, is rife with them. It was recently disclosed[10] that *Eve* players are 96% male, 4% female, and so many of the former are such horrible representations of their gender.

You can identify the douchebags oh-so-quickly. Within 15 minutes of my being in their team speak, they will ask for pictures of my boobs, post links to porn, make rape jokes, assume that I'm only playing because my boyfriend plays, and so on. One corporation had a recruitment channel named – and I'm not making this up – "Huge Tits!"

---

10 By David Reid, the chief marketing officer for CCP Games (the company that makes *Eve*).

(which was doubly ridiculous, as they didn't have any women in their ranks). One group that I joined changed their slogan, on the very first day I signed up, to "Now Gaming With Real Boobs!" without first asking me if that was okay.

The douchebags almost always joke that women are the best spies/awoxers, but never seem to realize the truth of this. I even tell them things like: "I'm a spy, here for all your stuff. I totally want to steal from you. *Ha-ha-hahahahahaha,*" and they love me all the more and find me cute while I'm plotting their total destruction.

A lot of players avoid the douchebags entirely, but there's an underlying lesson to my method here. Namely, if you take everything away from douchebag, perhaps he'll be nicer, or at the very least stop playing and making everyone's lives a misery. And the only way to do *that* is to seize their money and break their toys – often by capitalizing on their idiot belief that because I'm a woman, I don't know how to fly a ship, or even fit one, or generally play the game well.

There are times when I worry that, by being the Delilah to the douchebags' Samson, I'm just reinforcing their negative feelings toward women and deepening their misogyny. But, I don't know how else to attack the problem, because God knows, *talking* to people this far gone doesn't help. The best I can hope for is that if I prove I'm dangerous, perhaps one out of ten of my victims will stop and go, "Huh, maybe I shouldn't fuck with women any more." So I just get on with stealing as much as I can from them, breaking their corporation asunder, taking all their money, destroying their ships and demoralizing them.

Let me walk you through a recent awox... I approached a corporation of douchebags with a fresh toon with a clean record, and got onto their team speak (once I accomplish that, by the way, it's usually Game Over for them). None of the douchebags trust me at first, but they spare me some time because they all want to fuck me (or so it appears). I start giggling and feeding their egos with lines like, "Oh, that's a great ship you have. You want to bump hulls?" (That's my favorite line, actually. The persona that I become when I'm awoxing makes me a little sick, but also a bit amused.) There are lines I won't cross, by the way. Some female players sell the douchebags pictures of their boobs on market contracts to get isk[11], which makes me want to throw up (even if pictures are probably fake anyway).

I feed the douchebags a sob story about how I've dealt with a lot of

---

11 The basic currency of *Eve*, so named because it's the currency of Iceland, and Icelanders invented the game.

jerks in *Eve*, and they warm to me. Before long, they're desperate to have me join. There's another guy who also wants to sign up, and he's got the same skill set as me, but the douchebags want everything from him by way of verification while accepting my bullshit excuses. At no point do they ask me for API: the *Eve* equivalent of a credit/security check, listing your employment history, financial transactions and so forth, which helps to determine who you're affiliated with. I would've been sunk if they'd asked for it, but they never bothered.

I spend the next few months deliberately making piloting errors, becoming the douchebags' adorable little princess and wrapping them around my finger. If I cry out in trouble, they send in the cavalry. Most importantly, they give me the privileges needed to add and remove corporate bookmarks – warp points that team members can jump to if they're in trouble. You might be thinking: How did I, the alleged female rube, get access to such an invaluable resource? I asked them. I batted my eyes and said, "Hey, I'd really like to learn how to add and delete corporate bookmarks, can you help me?" And they did, because I'm a woman (and, to be fair, a lot of *Eve* players don't realize the value of corporate bookmarks).

After two more days, the douchebags tell me that they're planning to get a fleet together. Perfect. I'm ready to burn them to ashes.

I recruit about 15 of my friends – more than enough, although I can call on as many as 60 players from countries across the globe – consolidate them into a fleet, direct them to jump to the best position for an ambush and have them log off, making them invisible. I venture out in my own ship with the douchebags, but they're mainly dicking around, bumping hulls and waiting for more of their friends to show up. They're sitting in what they think is a safe, random spot in the universe, but they're perfectly placed for my fleet to come at them. Time for the hammer.

I pretend to freak out because I'm "being attacked" by RATs (non-player character pirates), and start screaming in team speak, "I'm going to lose my ship! It's the only ship I have!" As expected, what do the douchebags *do*? Everyone within four fucking system jumps to save my shitty, shitty ship from RATs. They run in like ants to bread. My screams sow more discord as they abandon their gate, their chokepoint, their everything *to save me! The innocent waif! Because I'm crying for help!*

Then I have my invisible fleet log in and warp to my location. I've equipped my own ship with warp scramblers, and immediately lock up the seven most expensive ships on the douchebags' side. Seven good kills. I sow more confusion by bellowing, "Oh my God, what's going on?! There's ships coming in! I'm being targeted!!" My targets try to give directives, but fail because I'm talking over them. And with their corporate bookmarks gone, they can't retreat to safety. Everything becomes chaos.

It's a glorious, one-sided massacre. I have my own fleet blow up my ship, just in case anyone checks the kill logs. The longer it's kept secret that I was running a scam, the longer the confusion will persist. Also, I have things to do: I warp my pod back to the douchebags' POS, take command of the douchebags' Orca – a huge ship in *Eve* terms – fill it with everything valuable from the corporate hanger arrays, then jump the Orca into a wormhole I had saved in the system...

... and log off.

The douchebags deduce I've conned them within two hours. Some figured it out right away, others took convincing. By this point, they can't touch me. They even can't kick me out of their corporation until I get to a station (which is a bit hilarious), and they can't track me in wormhole space. Besides, I'm logged off, and can chill out while they fume.

Four days later, I log in and jump the Orca into a high-sec space. The douchebags can't attack me there without the authorities bearing down on them, and they can't issue a kill right on me because I was in their corporation when I destroyed them. My total haul: 12 billion isk, a stack of ships and a load of shiny modules.

Within one week, the greater alliance to which the douchebags belong judges them incompetent and disowns their corporation. I don't have a smidge of pity. They were all assholes. There was only one other woman in the group, and they treated her like shit too.

Also, once I'd decided to cross them, anything less than their total destruction would have been a mistake. My mentor in *Eve* taught me to not leave loose ends. If you tangle with someone, destroy them utterly yourself or get an awoxer to do it. Leave them with no capability to hurt you. And preferably, brand into their hearts and souls the price of being douchebags.

It All Goes Horribly, Horribly Wrong (But If Asked, I'd Do It Again)

There's only been one incident in *Eve* that I feel genuinely, heart-breakingly bad about. It happened three weeks ago, and made me question what the hell I was doing.

I'd forged a profitable partnership with a player I met while awoxing

– we were infiltrating the same corporation, and we soon sensed the truth about one another, because a liar knows a liar.

After that mission, we started working together elsewhere. He'd call on me when he needed a woman's touch to feel out a corporation or gather intel on them (the latter remains my specialty). I'd call on him when I needed a skill set beyond my own – say, someone to fly a carrier while taking down a wormhole corporation. I'd work with his people, but didn't formally join his group, because I can't function within a rigid structure. But, ours was (and is) a mutually beneficial relationship.

I cannot stress enough, though, that this guy is fucking dangerous in *Eve*. He awoxes much better than I do, and his goal – unlike me at my better moments – isn't about divine retribution or proving a point. He's what's called a "griefer," because he deploys power, money and corruption to give individuals grief *as real-life people*, not players (there's a huge difference). Ideally, he wants them so upset that they quit the game. Let's call my associate Evil Guy, because crying and rage are his meat and drink.

Where things got awkward for me (not that I ever told Evil Guy this) is that one of Evil Guy's team-members was a moron. Let's call him Idiot Boy. He would go on rants in team speak about politics and science – believing that dinosaurs and man roamed the earth at the same time, that kind of thing. He was the sort of person that was impossible to pin down, because his point would constantly morph, making him "never wrong."

Worse for Evil Guy's purposes, Idiot Boy wasn't moldable. He couldn't be given a task and relied upon to go do it. And, he knew Evil Guy's real persona. Knowing secrets in *Eve* can be a real benefit, but also put you in jeopardy. As *Eve* players like to say, "Loose lips pod ships." And Evil Guy started to worry that Idiot Boy had loose lips.

Did I agree that Idiot Boy was a threat? God, no, he was too dumb for that. But, if you're Evil Guy, you can't take that risk. With hindsight, I suspect that Idiot Boy invested so much in team speak because had no connection to people in real life. But he was also arrogant and stupid – so much so, he never saw it coming when Evil Guy decided that he had to go.

Evil Guy wanted me to collaborate with his people to terminate Idiot Boy. I had two options: tell Evil Guy that this was none of my concern, or say yes. I chose the latter, because – remember – Evil Guy is an extremely powerful godfather of *Eve*. He can either be a valued ally or a lethal enemy, and I know what happens to people who don't fall in line with him. I *never* want him to see me as a threat; I just can't afford to wake up one day with a horse head in my pod.

In saying yes, I lost a bit of my soul. I just didn't know it until later.

Evil Guy's plan was that four of us would put on the charade of embarking on a mission with Idiot Boy, after he had decked out his ship with shiny new toys – a task for which Idiot Boy bought plex (a pilot license extension), meaning the upgrades cost him real-life money. A smarter player than Idiot Boy would have sensed danger, that the expensive gadgets he'd added were totally wrong for running a Level 5 (the highest level) mission in low-sec, and that his teammates had four shitty ships alongside his decked-out one.

We arrived at the intended destination. Evil Guy called out false targets, spreading confusion in the chat channels. At his signal, we locked up Idiot Boy... and destroyed him. We did, we honestly did. His ship was so badly fitted, it burned in seconds. It was awful. He melted like butter in an Iowa summer.

I listened to Idiot Boy's team speak, expecting fury and anger but instead getting nothing but a long, horrifying silence. Nobody said anything, at all. The dead air of space went on for a seconds, feeling like an eternity.

Idiot Boy, sniffling and trying to choke back the tears, finally said: "I don't know what I did to deserve that, I just liked hanging out with you guys."

... and then Evil Guy kicked Idiot Boy out of the voice channel, we blocked his further communications and we plundered the expensive toys that he had fitted onto his ship. We split the booty between us, and return to our home systems. My standing with Evil Guy solidifies; he trusts me completely now. I never hear from Idiot Boy again.

I legitimately feel horrible about this. I'm aware that whatever Idiot Boy's faults, he's a real person. I have a thick skin I can handle just about anything – but in looking back on our conversations, I realize that I was the kid throwing rocks rather than the kid getting hit. Which is why I really, *really* try in *Eve* to stick to targeting people who deserve it.

The fucked up thing is, if Evil Guy asked, I'd do the same thing again, every single bit of it. He gives me invaluable connections, and it's vital that I foster the relationship. There's just no way around it. But in doing so, I (effectively) must sometimes bomb a village.

I Become Jen J. "Mother Fucking" Dixon

I know I've done horrible, horrible things in *Eve*, but, at its best, it's given me the personal satisfaction of fulfilling goals that I created for myself in a dynamic environment. I'm like a monkey who's succeeded at engineering the best way to get a banana out of a jar – once the monkey walks that route, it really fucking loves banana-filled jars.

These days, as a graduate student teaching undergrads, it's so much less terrifying to enter a classroom knowing that, with enough time, effort and *preparation*, I can get through whatever banana-filled jars come my way. If *Eve* has contributed anything to my personality, it's self-confidence.

That ego boost has been worth some blood on my hull. Given time, I know it'll wash.

Castling

Racheline Maltese is a performer and storyteller focused on themes of sex, gender, desire and mourning. Her training includes a journalism degree from The George Washington University, as well as acting and directing coursework at the Atlantic Theater Company Acting School (New York City) and the National Institute of Dramatic Art (Sydney, Australia). She wrote *The Book of Harry Potter Trifles, Trivias and Particularities* (Sterling and Ross, 2007) and also works as an independent scholar focused on pop culture topics through her affiliation with The Society of Friends of the Text. Maltese's fiction, non-fiction and poetry has appeared in numerous outlets, and she is a regular speaker on pop-culture topics at fan and academic conferences. She also voiced Desire *and* Delirium in a benefit performance of Neil Gaiman's *The Sandman* for the Comic Book Legal Defense Fund. Additionally, Maltese is the co-founder of Treble Entendre, a musical theater production company. She lives in New York City with her partner; sometimes she sleeps. You can find her on the internet at: www.LettersfromTitan.com.

I learned to play chess when I was eight, taught by the father of the only boy I knew. The boy, Arzhang, lived in the apartment across the hall. He was a year and some months younger than me, and we played after I came home each day from my girls' school. He would ring the doorbell, and we would scurry into his parents' far larger apartment to chase each other across furniture, dare each other to say curse words, and sing along with the radio. Michael Jackson was a particular favorite, and we were consistently loud and incredibly off-key.

While Arzhang's parents were seemingly uniquely tolerant of the noise, sometimes we were clearly too much for them. His mother would retreat across the hall with a plate of stuffed grape leaves, and sit with my mother as they talked, smoked and watched the news together.

Arzhang's father would summon us to the dining room table for a quieter game: chess. Arzhang already knew how to play, and would say that he thought I was quite stupid because I did not. His father would scold him in Farsi, and then tell me that I wasn't stupid. Americans, he said, just do not understand the importance of games.

Bold, I would tell Arzhang's father that he was wrong, that I owned many games, and was given them for each Christmas (my father's holiday) and Hannukah (my mother's). I told him about *Battling Tops*, liberated from my cousin's attic; *Life*, played with a friend from school; and *Hungry Hungry Hippos*, which I kept seeing commercials for.

"But do you play games at home?" he asked, and I told him no.

"I play pretend!" I bragged, trying to make up for my obvious deficiency, and he asked me what things I pretended. I spoke to him of *The Brady Bunch* and Alexander the Great, and he approved, until I told him I did those things alone.

Chess is a game for everyone, he told me before showing me the pieces. As he explained how rooks and knights moved, and all the ways the game was not like checkers, Arzhang would drift away to his bedroom. His father told me, as the strains of Arzhang's Michael Jackson sing-a-long echoed through the apartment, that my job was now to teach my father chess.

My father was fairly resistant to chess. He had no time. Checkers had been good enough for his father, he said, and games had never much interested him. He talked of old men and the boring hours they seemed to spend on the New Jersey boardwalk pouring over dominoes.

But I had a mission: to teach my father, so that Arzhang's father would keep teaching me. "This is a rook," I would say, petting the pieces of the set I had been loaned. "That's a type of bird. It's also a bishop. Maybe bishops look like birds?" My father would ask why the pieces moved the way they did. I did not know, and said I would find out. But, first, of course, Arzhang's father has to correct me, the rook is the castle, after all. It took me a while to keep everything straight.

In those weeks, Arzhang, already impatient with my stumbling chess playing, drifted away more often as his father explained the history of the game to me. As I listened, my friend would yowl along with music in his room and call out sometimes that I was too ugly to play with him.

"Ignore him, he knows women are better at chess," his father would say, before introducing me to the queen. Arzhang's mother continued to escape, taking the grape leaves, stuffed and soaked in oil, to my mother.

Each night, I would beg to stay up until my father came home from work at eight or nine p.m. so that I could teach him chess, and each following day, after school, I would tell Arzhang's father what I had taught my father, so that he would then teach me more.

As we began to play full games, Arzhang would return to us. Beating me handily as his father watched, and crowing about his victories in a way that made me sullen and that his father, as far as I could guess from the tone in a language I did not speak, did not approve of.

I began, too, to play full games with my own father. He was aggressive and had little strategy. His goal, over and over, was to take all the pieces, like in the games of checkers that he said he continued to prefer. Although we played without a clock, the games ran fast; my father choosing to capture, always, and me impatient with my own inability to see even one or two moves ahead.

I was not good at the game, but my parents said I would be smarter now, and that I should practice, so that I could be a chess master, and famous.

Arzhang's father sighed when I reported this to him. A game is for its own sake, he said. Also, chess is about how you plan for war. It was not good that my father could not plan for war, even if he so often won our games, he said. I wondered how often he heard the way my father yelled at me through our apartment walls; I wondered if he understood that my father played chess with the same frightened anger he did most everything else, but I didn't know how to ask.

Now that I could play full games of chess, no matter how badly, Arzhang and I were left to play on our own again for hours, but my little friend had soured on me, because I wanted to get better at chess and not join him jumping on furniture. Chess was now something I would only spend 20 minutes with his father on each day, before I was sent home to eat dinner with my own family, but it was my favorite part, always, of visiting with my neighbors.

When I asked Arzhang to play chess with me, he refused. I offered the board games I had so often played by myself instead, but he would tire of those quickly.

One day, we stood in his parents' living room, and he took a small ceramic shoe off a shelf and dropped it onto the thick pile of the white carpet that covered their home. It bounced, and we laughed. I praised the carpet, reached onto the shelf, and grabbed another slightly larger ceramic shoe, dropping that as well and producing another spectacular bounce.

Arzhang's face lit up, and then we were racing, frantically, to grab every miniature bit of ceramic we could reach and drop it onto the carpet, trying to impress each other with the height of the bounces. We had found a new game, and my friend, blessedly, liked me again.

Buoyed, I wanted to impress him with my cleverness, and I took one tiny ceramic shoe and fit it inside its larger ceramic companion before dropping them and expecting another spectacular bounce.

Of course, that's not what happened. The two pieces of ceramic hit against each other as they reached the carpet, and when the shoes bounced up, they did so in dozens of tiny pieces. It was all my fault, Arzhang started yelling, as his father swooped in and deposited me back across the hall at my own home.

That night, my parents made me go over and apologize and return the borrowed chessboard. I was then sent to my room, my parents angry at having to pay for the broken ceramic shoes. I took out *Monopoly* and played alone, as I had done before – and now after – chess.

My father, however, as much as he was often angry and always fickle, was also kind; two nights later, he labeled the checkers in my set with chess piece names taped on with paper and said we could play, if I wanted. A week later, Arzhang rang the bell again. Two weeks after that, his mother and her grape leaves returned to my mother's company. Within a month, Arzhang's father, quiet and withdrawn now, would say, "Let us see if you have gotten any better."

I never did, but he was always kind simply because I continued to play.

Eventually, Arzhang and his family moved away, returning to Iran.

From that time on, I asked everyone I knew if they played chess, and if they did not, I taught them. A friend at school, the girls at summer camp, a science teacher kindly willing to keep the strangest of his pupils company at lunch. My parents bought me computer programs for my Apple IIe so that I could practice, but they made little difference. Almost everyone I have ever taught the game could beat me handily almost immediately.

Yet, despite this, for my junior high graduation, my parents bought me a chess set at the Village Chess Shop, a legendary chess establishment in Greenwich Village. It was wood inlaid with mother of pearl and its cost in light of my consistently inadequate skill shamed me. But I put it on display in my bedroom, took it with me when I went to college, and have set it up on display in every home I have ever lived in, a symbol of statuses I will never achieve, a tribute to the importance of play even when it is about desperately trivial things, and a reminder of one of the great and ordinary kindnesses of my otherwise difficult childhood.

My father still asks after the set sometimes. I don't tell him about the chipped corner, a handful of missing inlays, or the way I had to replace the original pieces it had come with some years ago, when about half of them went missing after a move. In return, I ask him, as I always did, if he wishes to play. I could, after all, bring a board over to my parents' apartment and set it up at the same dining room table I taught him chess at more than 30 years ago, but he shakes his head. Like a lot of the things that have aroused my passion and my melancholy over the years, chess is not for him.

The not-so-hidden secret, of course, is that, in some ways, chess has also not been for me. I still can't anticipate moves and rely on my gut over any intellectual understanding of what will bring me victories that remain almost entirely elusive. I have apologized to more friends and lovers than I can count for the quality of the game they are likely to receive from me.

But chess has remained a gift for me, from the moment it allowed me into the world of adults through the generosity of Arzhang's family to all the times it allowed me access to my own father, who was often puzzled about what to do with me. Chess taught me to teach, and has marked many rites of passage for me, both public and private. The chess board I was gifted with at my eighth grade graduation was the same one I laughed naked over with a lover in my twenties as I discovered for the first time that my body was not a thing in any way at odds with my mind.

Without chess, I would not have discovered *Go*, a game I am considerably more skilled at, or come to understand just how much can go wrong when people don't understand the simple difference between strategy and tactics. Without it, I also do not know how long I would have languished without the explicit permission to play and realize I may never have been granted access to the powerful truth that games are both a worthy and serious business. Most importantly, however, I would never have discovered the laughing delight of other perfectly terrible chess players grateful to have a peer with which to play the game for its pure and elegant beauty, which remains, always, regardless of our unsteady execution.

Editors' Bios

Jennifer Brozek is a freelance author for numerous RPG companies. Winner of both the Origins and the ENnie award, her contributions to RPG sourcebooks include *Dragonlance, Colonial Gothic, Shadowrun, Serenity, Savage Worlds* and White Wolf. Jennifer is also the author of the YA *Battletech* novel *The Nellus Academy Incident*. When she is not writing her heart out, she gallivants around the Pacific Northwest in its wonderfully mercurial weather. Read more about Jennifer at www.jenniferbrozek.com or follow her on Twitter at @JenniferBrozek.

Lars Pearson has served as editor-in-chief and publisher of Mad Norwegian Press since 2001, overseeing such works as the Hugo Award-winning *Chicks Dig…* essay book series and the *About Time* series, a seminal work on *Doctor Who*. With Lance Parkin, he co-writes the definitive *Doctor Who* timeline *Ahistory* (now 30,000 words bigger than *War and Peace*). For three years, he was a staff editor at Wizard Entertainment, working on such magazines as *InQuest Gamer, ToyFare* and *Wizard: The Guide to Comics*. As he discovered one day while shuffling Scrabble tiles about for no particular reason, his name can be rearranged to spell "Slap No Rears."

Robert Smith? is a dyed-in-the-wool, third-wave feminist from way back, so it considers it a very humbling honor that he was drafted to edit this book. He's the author of *Who's 50: The 50 Doctor Who Stories to Watch Before You Die*, the IPPY Award-winning *Who is the Doctor* and *Modelling Disease Ecology with Mathematics* (see if you can spot the odd one out). He's also editor extraordinaire of *Outside In: 160 New Perspectives on 160 Classic Doctor Who Stories by 160 Writers, Braaaiiinnnsss!: From Academics to Zombies* and two volumes of *Time, Unincorporated*. He has an unhealthy obsession with punctuation.

Jean Rabe is a fantasy and science-fiction writer who sometimes dabbles in military fiction and mysteries. She is an avid reader, who has far too many books to fit on her shelves. Always working on a new project or three, Jean is currently working on an urban fantasy series with a couple of writing pals, as well as an urban fantasy novel set in NYC. Her thirtieth novel was released this year. Read more about Jean at www.jeanrabe.com or find her on Facebook at http://www.facebook.com/jean.rabe.1.

Out Now... In Whedonistas, a host of award-winning female writers and fans come together to celebrate the works of Joss Whedon (Buffy the Vampire Slayer, Angel, Firefly, Dollhouse, Doctor Horrible's Sing-Along Blog).

Contributors include Sharon Shinn ("Samaria" series), Emma Bull (Territory), Jeanne Stein (the Anna Strong Chronicles), Nancy Holder (October Rain), Elizabeth Bear (Chill), Seanan McGuire (October Daye series), Catherynne M. Valente (Palimpsest), Maria Lima (Blood Lines), Jackie Kessler (Black and White), Sarah Monette (Corambis), Mariah Huehner (IDW Comics) and Lyda Morehouse (AngeLINK Series). Also featured is an exclusive interview with television writer and producer Jane Espenson, and Juliet Landau ("Drusilla").

ISBN: 978-1935234104
MSRP: $14.95. Also available Kindle, Nook and iTunes.

WHEDONISTAS

WHEDON, J.
48 - 152342

A CELEBRATION OF THE WORLDS OF
JOSS WHEDON BY THE
WOMEN WHO LOVE THEM

mad
norwegian
press

Chicks Dig Time Lords

A Celebration of Doctor Who by the Women Who Love It

This book has three settings!

OUT NOW... In *Chicks Digs Time Lords*, a host of award-winning female novelists, academics and actresses come together to celebrate the phenomenon that is *Doctor Who*, discuss their inventive involvement with the show's fandom and examine why they adore the series.

These essays will delight male and female readers alike by delving into the extraordinary aspects of being a female *Doctor Who* enthusiast. Contributors include Carole Barrowman (*Anything Goes*), Elizabeth Bear (the Jenny Casey trilogy), Lisa Bowerman (Bernice Summerfield), Jackie Jenkins (*Doctor Who Magazine*), Mary Robinette Kowal (*Shades of Milk and Honey*), Jody Lynn Nye (Mythology series), Kate Orman (*Seeing I*), Lloyd Rose (*Camera Obscura*) and Catherynne M. Valente (*The Orphan's Tales*).

Also featured: a comic from the "Torchwood Babiez" creators, and interviews with *Doctor Who* companions India Fisher (Charley) and Sophie Aldred (Ace).

ISBN: 978-1935234043
MSRP: $14.95 (available in print only)

mad norwegian press

www.madnorwegian.com
1150 46th St, Des Moines, IA 50311 . madnorwegian@gmail.com

Credits

Publisher/Editor-in-Chief
Lars Pearson

Design Manager/Senior Editor
Christa Dickson

Associate Editor
Joshua Wilson

Designer (Gaming)
Adam Holt

The publisher wishes to thank...
Jennifer, for being such a Rock of Gibraltar when we were buffeted by gale-force winds; Robert, for riding in and saving our collective asses; Jean Rabe, for her editing assists; Lisa Stevens and Margaret Weis, for taking time out of their busy schedules to talk with us; Katy Shuttleworth, for her reliably vivid cover art; Adam Holt, for his superb design skills; Christa Dickson, for oh so many things; Jen J. Dixon, Kevin Weiser, Allegra Lynn and everyone else at The Walking Eye podcast; Jack Bruner; Lillian Cohen-Moore; Karen Conlin; Vanessa de Kauwe; Matt Dirkx; Linda Elliott; J.M. Frey; Jaym Gates; Sarah Hans; Jess Hartley; Carrie Herndon; Manisha Mungsinghe; Rhonda Oglesby; Alina Pete; Cat Rambo; Cole Rehbein; Elizabeth Sampat; Jennifer Steen; Christina Stiles; Abigail Tassin; Amanda Valentine; Jen Van Meter; Elizabeth A. Vaughan; Kyla Ward; Karen Weekes; Christina Weir; Penny Williams; Josh Wilson; and that nice lady who sends me newspaper articles.

1150 46th Street
Des Moines, Iowa 50311
madnorwegian@gmail.com
www.madnorwegian.com

And please join the Mad Norwegian Press group on Facebook!